THE MYTHS WE LIVE BY

Mary Midgley argues in her powerful new book that, far from being the opposite of science, myth is a central part of it. In brilliant prose, she claims that myths are neither lies nor mere stories but a network of powerful symbols that suggest particular ways of interpreting the world.

'. . . an elegant and sane little book. Unusually for a philosopher, Midgley has a superb ear for the use and misuse of language.'
Edward Skidelsky, New Statesman

'She has, perhaps, the sharpest perception of any living thinker of the dangerous extremism that lurks behind so much contemporary scientistic discourse . . . Merely as anthologies of contemporary folly, Midgley's books are essential reading . . . we have Mary Midgley among us. We should pay attention and be grateful.'
Brian Appleyard, The Sunday Times

'For those who haven't yet read Midgley, these essays are an excellent place to start.'
Jon Turney, University College London

'The Myths We Live By is a wonderful short introduction to her ideas on this subject.'
Andrew Brown, author of 'The Darwin Wars'

'As with her other books, this both stimulates and instructs with a facility envied by many other writers.'
Contemporary Review

'Mary Midgley . . . brings together several strands of contemporary thought like threads in a tapestry, weaving together a picture in a way that makes the book increasingly pleasurable to read.'
The Tablet

THE MYTHS
WE LIVE BY

Mary Midgley

Routledge
Taylor & Francis Group

LONDON AND NEW YORK

First published 2004
by Routledge
11 New Fetter Lane, London EC4P 4EE

Simultaneously published in the USA and Canada
by Routledge
29 West 35th Street, New York, NY 10001

Hardback published 2003

Reprinted 2003 (twice)

Routledge is an imprint of the Taylor & Francis Group

© 2004 Mary Midgley

Typeset in Galliard by
Florence Production Ltd, Stoodleigh, Devon
Printed and bound in Great Britain by
MPG Books Ltd, Bodmin

British Library Cataloguing in Publication Data
A catalogue record for this book is available from the British Library

Library of Congress Cataloging in Publication Data
A catalog record for this book has been requested

ISBN 0–415–30906–9 (hbk)
ISBN 0–415–34077–2 (pbk)

FOR EVA
IN RETURN FOR MANY
WONDERFUL MYTHS

CONTENTS

CONTENTS

ACKNOWLEDGEMENTS

The theme of this book is the crucial importance of symbolism in all our thought and the resulting need to take our imaginative life seriously, even when we are dealing with what seem to be prosaic subjects.

Because I wanted to concentrate on this issue of symbolism, I have brought together here a number of articles in which I have previously dealt with that topic, re-working them in a way that I hope will bring out its importance. Since the sources of these articles are rather widespread, I would like to thank a wide variety of people who have helped me in my efforts to understand it. I have had a great deal of help from many colleagues who attended the very interesting conferences out of which several of these papers grew. Many good suggestions have come from the staff of the Hastings Center, to which I have made a couple of visits, and especially from Strachan Donnelley. My son David and my colleagues at the now-defunct Philosophy Department of Newcastle University have always helped me greatly, and in recent times I have learnt a great deal from discussions with John Ziman, Steven and Hilary Rose, James Lovelock, Evelyn Fox-Keller, Anne Primavesi, Martin Lockley, Raymond Tallis and Andrew Brown. Finally I would like to thank the editors and publishers of the books and journals in which these papers first appeared – not just for giving me permission to reprint them, but for their help and support during the process of publication.

These sources are as follows:

The first four chapters are based on a lecture called 'The Myths We Live By', which I delivered as part of an Amnesty Series, 'The Values of Science', in 1997. It was published in a book with that name, edited by Wes Williams, in 1999 by the Westview Press, Colorado.

Chapters 5 to 7 on an article called 'Reductive Megalomania', which appeared in *Nature's Imagination: The Frontiers of Scientific Vision*, edited by John Cornwell and published by Oxford University Press, Oxford, 1995.

Chapter 8 on 'Do We Even Act?' which is forthcoming in a Symposium Volume, ed. D. A. Rees and S. P. R. Rose, to be published by Cambridge University Press, 2004.

Chapters 9 to 11 on 'Why Memes?', which appeared in *Alas, Poor Darwin: Arguments against Evolutionary Psychology*, edited by Hilary and Steven Rose and published by Jonathan Cape, London, 2000.

Chapters 12 and 13 on 'The Evolution of Cultural Entities', published in the *Proceedings of the British Academy*, no. 112, 2002, pp. 119–33, and in *The Evolution of Cultural Entities*, edited by M. Wheeler, J. Ziman and M. Boden and published by British Academy and Oxford University Press, London and Oxford, 2002, pp. 119–132.

Chapters 14 and 15 on 'The Soul's Successors: Philosophy and the "Body"', which appeared in *Religion and the Body*, edited by Sarah Coakley, Cambridge University Press, Cambridge, 1997.

Chapters 16 to 18 on 'Biotechnology and Monstrosity: Why We Should Pay Attention to the "Yuk" Factor', which appeared in the *Hastings Center Report* for September–October 2000, vol. 30, no. 5.

Chapters 19 and 20 on 'Heaven And Earth, an Awkward History', which appeared in *Philosophy Now*, December 2001–January 2002.

Chapters 21 to 23 on 'Are You an Animal?', which appeared in *Animal Experimentation: The Consensus Changes*, edited by Gill Langley and published by Macmillan, London, 1999.

Chapters 24 and 25 on 'Beasts versus the Biosphere?', which appeared in *Environmental Values*, vol. 1, no. 2, Summer 1992.

Chapters 26 and 27 on 'The Problem of Living with Wildness', which appeared in *Wolves and Human Communities: Biology, Politics and Ethics*, edited by Virginia A. Sharpe, Bryan Norton and Strachan Donnelley and published by the Island Press, Washington DC, 2001.

1

HOW MYTHS WORK

————•◆•————

SYMBOLISM AND SIGNIFICANCE

We are accustomed to think of myths as the opposite of science. But in fact they are a central part of it: the part that decides its significance in our lives. So we very much need to understand them.

Myths are not lies. Nor are they detached stories. They are imaginative patterns, networks of powerful symbols that suggest particular ways of interpreting the world. They shape its meaning. For instance, machine imagery, which began to pervade our thought in the seventeenth century, is still potent today. We still often tend to see ourselves, and the living things around us, as pieces of clockwork: items of a kind that we ourselves could make, and might decide to remake if it suits us better. Hence the confident language of 'genetic engineering' and 'the building-blocks of life'.

Again, the reductive, atomistic picture of explanation, which suggests that the right way to understand complex wholes is always to break them down into their smallest parts, leads us to think that truth is always revealed at the end of that other seventeenth-century invention, the microscope. Where microscopes dominate our imagination, we feel that the large wholes we deal with in everyday experience are mere appearances. Only the particles revealed at the bottom of the microscope are real. Thus, to an extent unknown in earlier times, our dominant technology shapes our symbolism and thereby our metaphysics, our view about what is real. The heathen in his blindness bows down to wood and stone – steel and glass, plastic and rubber and silicon – of his own devising and sees them as the final truth.

Of course this mechanistic imagery does not rule alone. Older myths survive and are still potent, but they are often given a reductive and technological form. Thus, for instance, we are still using the familiar social-contract image of citizens as essentially separate and autonomous individuals. But we are less likely now to defend it on humanistic or religious grounds than by appealing to a neo-Darwinist vision of universal competition between

1

separate entities in an atomised world, which are easily seen as machinery – distinct cogs or bytes put together within a larger mechanism. Social atomism strikes us as scientific.

This same reductive and atomistic picture now leads many enquirers to propose biochemical solutions to today's social and psychological problems, offering each citizen more and better Prozac rather than asking what made them unhappy in the first place. Society appears as split into organisms and organisms into their constituent cogs. The only wider context easily seen as containing all these parts is evolution, understood (in a way that would have surprised Darwin) as a cosmic projection of nineteenth-century economics, a competitive arena pervading the development, not just of life but of our thought and of the whole physical universe.

At present, when people become aware of this imagery, they tend to think of it as merely a surface dressing of isolated metaphors – as a kind of optional decorative paint that is sometimes added to ideas after they are formed, so as to make them clear to outsiders. But really such symbolism is an integral part of our thought-structure. It does crucial work on all topics, not just in a few supposedly marginal areas such as religion and emotion, where symbols are known to be at home, but throughout our thinking. The way in which we imagine the world determines what we think important in it, what we select for our attention among the welter of facts that constantly flood in upon us. Only after we have made that selection can we start to form our official, literal, thoughts and descriptions. That is why we need to become aware of these symbols.

HOW NEUTRAL IS SCIENCE?

What, then, is the right place of such imaginative visions in our serious thinking? In particular, how do they relate to science? This question occurred to me forcibly some six years back when Amnesty International asked me to contribute to their lecture series entitled 'The Values of Science'. It struck me as remarkable that people answer questions about the values of science in two quite opposite ways today.

On the one hand, they often praise science for being value-free: objective, unbiased, neutral, a pure source of facts. Just as often, however, they speak of it as being itself a source of values, perhaps indeed the only true source of them. For example, the great evolutionist Conrad Waddington wrote in 1941 that 'Science *by itself* is able to provide mankind with a way of life which is . . . self-consistent and harmonious. . . . So far as I can see, the scientific attitude of mind is *the only one* which is, at the present day, adequate to do this'.[1] As we shall see, too, many serious theorists have claimed that science is 'omnicompetent', that is, able to answer every kind of question. And that must naturally include questions about value.

The eminent molecular biologist Jacques Monod noticed this difficulty and suggested heroically that science should take over this apparently alien realm of thought altogether:

> Science attacks values. Not directly, since science is no judge of them and *must* ignore them; but it subverts every one of the mythical ontogenies upon which the animist tradition, from the Australian aborigines to the dialectical materialists, has based morality: values, duties, rights, prohibitions ... True knowledge is ignorant of values, but it has to be grounded on a value judgment, or rather on an *axiomatic* value ... In order to establish the *norm* for knowledge, the objectivity principle defines a *value*; that value is objective knowledge itself ... The ethic of knowledge that created the modern world is the only ethic compatible with it, the only one capable, once understood and accepted, of guiding its evolution.[2]

Not surprisingly, Monod was for a time the favourite author of many scientists. Since what he meant by 'knowledge' was exclusively scientific knowledge, his ruling implied that the only value judgements that remained would be ones about whether a proposition in science was true or not.

This, however, would not have been a very convenient arrangement for the rest of life. The clash remained, and, as usual, the truth about it was more complicated than it looked. The word 'science' surely has a different meaning in these two claims. We do indeed sometimes think of science just as an immense store-cupboard of objective facts, unquestionable data about such things as measurements, temperatures and chemical composition. But a store-cupboard is not, in itself, very exciting.

What makes science into something much grander and more interesting than this is the huge, ever-changing imaginative structure of ideas by which scientists contrive to connect, understand and interpret these facts. The general concepts, metaphors and images that make up this structure cannot possibly be objective and antiseptic in this same way. They grow out of images drawn from everyday experience, because that is the only place to get them. They relate theory to everyday life and are meant to influence it. These concepts and images change constantly as the way of life around them changes. And after they have been used in science they are often reflected back into everyday life in altered forms, seemingly charged with a new scientific authority.

In this book we will consider several very potent ideas that have moved in this way from ordinary thought to affect the course of science and have then returned to outside usage reshaped by scientific use. Right away, one might name the concept of a *machine*, of a *self-interested individual*, and of *competition* between such individuals. Metaphorical concepts like these are quite properly used by scientists, but they are not just passive pieces of apparatus like thermostats. They have their own influence. They are living parts of powerful myths – imaginative patterns that we all take for granted – ongoing dramas inside which we live our lives. These patterns shape the mental maps that we refer to when we want to place something. Such ideas are not just a distraction from real thought, as positivists have suggested. Nor are they a disease. They are the matrix of thought, the background that shapes our mental habits. They decide what we think important and what we ignore. They provide the tools with which we organise the mass of incoming data. When they are bad they can do a great deal of harm by distorting our selection and slanting our thinking. That is why we need to watch them so carefully.

HOW DO IDEAS CHANGE?

This question is specially urgent in times of rapid change, because patterns of thought that are really useful in one age can make serious trouble in the next one. They don't then necessarily have to be dropped. But they do often have to be reshaped or balanced by other thought-patterns in order to correct their faults.

In this process, myths do not alter in the rather brisk, wholesale way that much contemporary imagery suggests. The belief in instant ideological change is itself a favourite myth of the recent epoch that we are now beginning to abuse as 'modern'. Descartes may have started it when he launched his still-popular town-planning metaphor, comparing the whole of current thought to an unsatisfactory city which should be knocked down and replaced by a better one:

> Those ancient cities which were originally mere boroughs, and have become large towns in process of time, are as a rule badly laid out, as compared with those towns of regular pattern that are laid out by a designer on an open plain to suit his fancy . . . one would say that it was chance that placed them so, not the will of men who had the use of reason.[3]

Today, too, another influential image, drawn from Nietzsche, works on the model of the *Deaths* column in a newspaper. Here you just report the death of something: Art, or Poetry, or History, or the Author, or God, or Nature, or Metaphysics or whatever, publish its obituary and then forget about it.

The trouble about this is that such large-scale items don't suddenly vanish. Prominent ideas cannot die until the problems that arise within them have been resolved. They are not just a kind of external parasite. They are not alien organisms, viruses: 'memes' that happen to have infested us and can be cleared away with the right insecticide (a suggestion that we will discuss in Chapter 9). They are organic parts of our lives, cognitive and emotional habits, structures that shape our thinking. So they follow conservation laws within it. Instead of dying, they transform themselves gradually into something different, something that is often hard to recognise and to understand. The Marxist pattern of complete final revolution is not at all appropriate here. We do better to talk organically of our thought as an ecosystem trying painfully to adapt itself to changes in the world around it.

THE DOWNSIDE OF DRAMA

In this book, I shall start by concentrating on certain particular myths which have come down to us from the Enlightenment and are now giving trouble, though I shall move on from them to mention a number of others that we need to attend to. Enlightenment concepts need our attention because they tend to be particularly simple and sweeping. Dramatic simplicity has been one of their chief attractions and is also their chronic weakness, a serious one when they need to be applied in detail. For instance, the Enlightenment's overriding emphasis on freedom often conflicts with other equally important ideals such as justice or compassion. Complete commercial freedom, for example, or complete freedom to carry weapons, can lead to serious harm and injustice. We need, then, to supplement the original dazzling insight about freedom with a more discriminating priority system. And again, the insistence on individuality that has so enriched our lives degenerates, if we don't watch it critically, into the kind of mindless competitiveness that is so destructive today. It impoverishes lives by locking people up in meaningless solitude.

In the case of the physical sciences, we already know that Enlightenment ideas have been much too naive and dramatic. They suggested that physics could expect to reveal a far simpler kind of order in the world than has turned out to be available. Of course this simplification played a great part in making possible the astonishing success of the physical sciences. It gave western civilisation an understanding of natural 'mechanisms' (as we still call them) far beyond that of any other culture, and a wealth of technology that other cultures have never dreamed of. And it is right to celebrate this tremendous achievement. But we, the heirs of this great intellectual empire, don't actually need to come together simply to praise it.

We don't now need to tell each other that science is good any more than we need to say that freedom is good or democracy is good. As ideals, these things are established in our society. But when particular ideals are established and are supposed to be working, we have to deal with the institutions that are invented to express them. Today, some people plainly do *not* think that science is altogether good. At times there are similar doubts about democracy and freedom. In such cases, those of us who care about the ideals need to ask what is going wrong with the way they are being incorporated in the world. We have to consider how best to understand the present condition of science, how best to live with its difficulties and responsibilities, and how to shape its further development so as to avoid these distortions.

In trying to do this, I shall start by discussing three current myths: the social-contract myth, the progress myth and the myth of omnicompetent science. These three myths are connected, not just because they are all over-dramatic and need rethinking, but because the last of them impedes our efforts to deal with the first two, and with many other problems as well.

Exaggerated and distorted ideas about what physical science can do for us led, during the nineteenth and twentieth centuries, to the rise of powerful, supposedly scientific ideologies such as Marxism and behaviourism. These systems are obviously not actually part of physical science but, by claiming its authority, they have injured its image. People who want to defend science today need to take outgrowths of this kind seriously and go to some trouble to understand its relation to them. It is equally urgent to get rid of the absurd and embarrassing claim to 'omnicompetence'. Science, which has its own magnificent work to do, does not need to rush in and take over extraneous kinds of question (historical, logical, ethical, linguistic or the like) as well. Lovers of physical science can be happy to see it as it is, as one great department of human thought among others which all cooperate in our efforts at understanding the world. This is a far more honourable status than that of a nineteenth-century political power trying to enlarge its empire by universal conquest.

2

OUR PLACE IN THE WORLD

—— ·•· ——

THE EXPANDING HORIZON

The three myths that I have mentioned still shape our intellectual and moral thinking, although the world has changed radically in the three or four centuries since they were coined. Most notably, our drama – the play in which we are all acting – has shifted to an enormously larger stage. We live now in a bigger world. It is bigger because the sheer number of humans has tripled in the last century and because we are now better informed about them, but also, even more crucially, because of the way in which our own power has increased. We urban humans have now become capable of doing serious harm all over the world, both to its human and its non-human inhabitants. This is something really new in human history. In fact it is possibly the biggest change our species has ever experienced, certainly the biggest since the invention of agriculture. No wonder if it throws us into culture-shock and makes us alter our concepts.

At present, the problems that arise here about our duty to distant humans are often discussed separately from those about our misuse of other animals and both are usually segregated from the environmental problems. Different academic departments and different political bodies commonly deal with these three matters. Feuds often arise between them. The division between the natural sciences and the humanities widens the split, but the link between them is crucial. (We will discuss it in Chapters 19 and 24.) The sudden enlargement of our power has transformed all these issues equally. In all these directions, technology has hugely multiplied both the range of matters that concern us and our ability to affect them. And though that ability often seems to be out of our hands as individuals, our civilisation as a whole clearly does bear some responsibility for producing this whole situation. Our trade, our investment and our expressions of public opinion do indeed affect all sorts of distant events.

We find it hard to believe in this whole expansion. Can it really be true that we bear responsibility for things that happen to people and countries so far away from us? Can we, still more oddly, have responsibilities towards the non-human realm? Our current moral tradition makes it hard for us to grasp these things. It doesn't leave room for them. Yet the changes are real. They do demand some kind of adaptation from us, adaptation of a morality that was formed for a quite different, more manageable kind of world. We can't go on acting as if we were still in that world. On that path, there is no way through.

HUMAN RIGHTS AND THE
SOCIAL CONTRACT

This difficulty comes up strongly at present over the concept of universal human rights. That notion clashes with the Enlightenment idea that morality is essentially just a contract, freely made between fellow citizens for civic purposes and ultimately for individual self-interest. Some political theorists, who are rather oddly known as realists,[1] claim that we cannot have duties to people outside our own nation-state because they are not contractors in our society and *rights* (they say) arise only from contract. This is the idea that politicians are expressing when they reassure us that British interests must, of course, always come first.

The social-contract myth is a typical piece of Enlightenment simplification. It was developed (quite properly) as an answer to the doctrine of the divine right of kings, a defence against the religious wars and oppressions that monarchs set going in the sixteenth and seventeenth centuries. It rested political authority on the consent of the governed, which is fine. But its limitation is that it leaves no room for duties to outsiders. This brings it into conflict with another equally central Enlightenment idea, namely, the unity of all humanity. *That* idea says that, if oppression is wrong, it is wrong everywhere and that, therefore, anyone who can do something about it ought to do so. Quite early on, this wider concept was expressed by bold, non-contractual talk about the Rights of Man, which made possible widespread and effectual campaigns against things like slavery.

The clash between these two ideas is not one between different cultures. It arises between two closely related ideas within the same culture. It is still with us because both these ideas are still crucial to us. Both of them have been parts of the same bold attempt to make human society more just and less brutal. They were both originally somewhat crude and have needed repeated adjustment. The idea of contract was the formal, legalistic, reductive side of this humanitarian campaign. The notion of universal rights expressed the outgoing, generous, sympathetic feeling that powered the campaign in the first place. The difficulty of reconciling these two elements has led to a lot of trouble. It has often been dramatised into a supposedly irresolvable conflict between reason and feeling.

This is always a confused idea because all reasoning is powered by feeling and all serious feeling has some reasoning as its skeleton. Thought and feeling are not opponents, any more than shape and size. They are complementary aspects which appear on both sides of any argument, a point that we will discuss further in Chapter 16. Polarising these two as opposites is, however, always tempting. On the issue of human rights it has been quite important that the reductive, contractual pattern was seen as the rational one and as being supported by physical science. The idea that people are solitary, self-contained, indeed selfish individuals, who wouldn't be connected to their neighbours at all if they didn't happen to have made a contract, looked rational because it reflected the atomic theory of the day, a theory that similarly reduced matter to hard, impenetrable, disconnected atoms like billiard balls. The two patterns, of political and scientific atomism, seemed to strengthen each other, and, for some time, each appeared as the only truly rational and scientific pattern of understanding in its own sphere. Social atomism, expressed as political and moral individualism, got quite undeserved support from the imagery used in science.

Today, of course, physics deals in particles of a very different kind, particles that are essentially fields, that is, patterns of connection. But on the human scene, and in biology, a quite unrealistic social atomism is still alive and kicking and still thinks of itself as scientific. The kind of individualism that treats people, and indeed other organisms, as essentially separate, competitive entities, ignoring the fact that competition can't get going at all without an enormous amount of cooperation to make it possible, has been the dominant ideology of the last few decades. Today it is under attack, which results in a lot of controversy.

This debate has not been just a futile zero-sum game. On its good days it has been a creative tension, a fertile dialectic in which each element has helped the other to become more adequate and workable. Talk of human rights is designed to express our current compromise between these two complementary insights. Most concerned people do now seem willing to use the words 'human rights'. In spite of the huge differences between various cultures, we do believe that there are indeed some things which ought not to be done to anybody, anywhere. Whatever the doubts about rights, we can all recognise human wrongs.[2] So, anyone who can protest effectively against these things is in a position to do so, whatever culture they belong to. This kind of belief is not, I think, confined to the West. Oppressed people in all kinds of countries now appeal to it. And in general they don't seem to be using it merely as a foreign language, but as a kind of intercultural dialect that everybody understands. It helps us to pick out the distant matters that really do call for our intervention, despite the gulfs that divide our societies.[3]

9

In this way we can try to bring the outgoing, generous element in Enlightenment thinking together with the narrowing, formal, legalistic side. In principle, and to some extent even in practice, we can combine the imperative force of the civic word 'rights' with the universal scope of species-wide sympathy. The work of reconciling these ideas still needs hard ethical thinking (which is different from scientific thinking though just as necessary) but for practical purposes the concept is usable. Bodies such as Amnesty International do make a difference to the world. Of course that difference is miserably small, but our official morality does have room for this extension. It does not force us to be fatalistic chauvinists, as it would if our ethics were really limited to contract thinking. We are not burdened, as we might have been, with the kind of moral ideas that would completely paralyse our efforts to help.

GOING BEYOND HUMANITY

So much, then, for distant humans. What about the claims of the rest of nature? It ought to be clear that, even if we don't care personally about the wilderness itself, all humans share a common interest in preserving the biosphere they depend on. But our culture has found it surprisingly hard to grasp this.

The chief reason for this is, of course, that the environmental alarm is much more recent than the social one. The bad news, that the house is on fire, only arrived during the last half-century, and many people still hope that, if they don't encourage it by attending to it, it will go away. More deeply, however, there is a difficulty because this matter is much harder to bring within the framework of contract.

The idea of universal *human* fellow citizens is slightly more familiar. Various images of a worldwide super-state or super-city already exist to relate it to civic thinking. The Stoics talked of the World City, Cosmopolis, and St Augustine talked of the City of God. But nobody has yet made coral reefs or the Siberian tundra our fellow citizens, and it is not easy to see how they could do so. These are not the kind of beings that live in cities or plead in law courts. They don't make contracts. So, on the familiar model, it was hard to see how they can have *rights*. And this does, apparently, make it hard for some people to take our duties to them seriously.

This is surely a point where the perspective of the natural sciences can really help us. For many scientists, love and reverence for the natural world that they study has been a powerful motive, whereas this love and reverence has been less central to the humanistic parts of western culture. Indeed, some kinds of humanism have deliberately excluded it. Enlightenment thinking has often neglected non-human nature, especially since the Industrial Revolution, though Rousseau did not and poets, such as Blake

10

and Wordsworth, did what they could to protest against the bias. That concentration on our own species is what makes it so hard for us now to take in the facts of environmental destruction or react to them effectively. Traditionally, we have taken the natural support system for granted.

Scientists who concern themselves with ecological matters can help us greatly here. They do so even though, at present, they themselves actually have a difficulty about acknowledging this outgoing, reverent attitude to nature because it became for a time rather unfashionable within science itself. It was associated with 'natural historians' – that is, with patient, wide-ranging observers like Darwin – rather than with the laboratory-based experts in microbiology who were for a time viewed as the only possible model of 'the scientific'. But this narrow, reductive perspective does seem to be shifting. The sociobiologist Edward Wilson has celebrated *Biophilia* – the love of all living things – as something absolutely central for science.[4] And again, James Lovelock's concept of 'Gaia', which expresses our proper reverence for our planet at the same time as suggesting scientific tools for diagnosing its troubles, is no longer viewed as something wild.[5] It is begin-ning to get the kind of serious attention that it deserves within science. In fact, the two aspects of science are beginning to come together again, a process that very much needs to be encouraged.

Should we say, then, that this love and reverence for nature is one of the 'values of science'? If we are to talk about such values at all it surely is. Perhaps indeed it is the only value that is in some sense special to the natural sciences. The other values that we think of as scientific are intel-lectual virtues such as honesty, disinterestedness, thoroughness, imaginative enterprise, a devotion to truth. Those virtues are indeed scientific, but they are so in the older and wider sense of that word which is not restricted to physical science. They belong to every kind of disciplined and method-ical thought, to history and logic, to ethics and mathematics and linguistics and law, just as much as they do to the natural sciences. But those enquiries don't deal so directly with the non-human world around us, with the plants and animals and stars that we should surely honour and revere, as the natural sciences do. The love of these things, and in particular the love of living things – 'biophilia' as Wilson calls it – has played a special part in the thought of most great scientists, and it is a vital element which their successors can bring to stir us up against our present dangers.

If we do manage to take up this wider perspective, it will, of course, make our moral position more complicated, not simpler. But that is bound to happen anyway. Already we have to arbitrate many conflicts between the interests of humans and non-humans such as elephants or trees. People who do this on a contractual basis rule out the non-human party in advance. But that simple principle no longer convinces us and we can't seriously go on using it. These clashes demand some sort of a compromise. Even in the short term the interests of the two parties do not always conflict and in the long term they often converge strongly. If the local people are forced to destroy the habitat, then they too will soon be destroyed, along with the trees and the elephants. This convergence is of course particularly plain over indigenous peoples, who accordingly have often campaigned heroically to defend it.

3

PROGRESS, SCIENCE
AND MODERNITY

——— .•. ———

THE PLEASURES OF OMNICOMPETENCE

So far I have been discussing the first myth that I mentioned, that of the social contract. I have been suggesting that this sweeping, monolithic thought-pattern, used for quite good reasons by earlier thinkers in the Enlightenment, now hampers our thought. The narrow civic stereotype makes it hard for us to adapt to a changed world in which our increased power makes traditional social-contract thinking disastrously parochial.

This is just one case, however, among many where Enlightenment thinking, after its initial successes, becomes oversimple and Procrustean. Often it seizes on a particular pattern of thought as the only one that can properly be called rational and extends it to quite unsuitable topics. This intellectual imperialism constantly favours the form over the substance of what is being said, the method over the aim of an activity, and precision of detail over completeness of cover. That formal bias is not in fact at all particularly rational, though it is often thought of as being so.

I have suggested that this simplistic habit is what people are usually complaining of today when they stigmatise recent thinking as 'modern'. The actual word 'modern' is quite unsuitable here. It can certainly not go on much longer being used forever in this way to describe what is manifestly out of date. Besides, it is too vague. We need clearer, more specific words for this range of faults. For present purposes I suggest that the terms needed are often ones such as 'dogmatic', 'one-sided', 'simplistic' and 'monolithic'.

The same kind of trouble arises about our next two examples, the linked ideas of inevitable progress and the omnicompetence of science. Here certain ways of thinking that proved immensely successful in the early development of the physical sciences have been idealised, stereotyped and treated as the only possible forms for rational thought across the whole range of our knowledge. As with the social contract, the trouble is not in the

13

methods themselves, which are excellent in their own sphere. It lies in the sweepingness, the dramatic zing, the naive academic imperialism that insists on exporting them to all sorts of other topics.

The myth of inevitable progress is one that has been around in a general form since the late eighteenth century. It arose then to express a new kind of confidence in Man and the works of Man, replacing the earlier Christian reliance on God and the afterlife in Heaven. Today it is often linked with the idea of evolution, though this link belongs to Lamarck rather than to Darwin and is rooted in wish-fulfilment or in religion, not in biology. That association has, however, probably helped to give the idea of progress a quite undeserved aura of scientific respectability. And it has also probably strengthened the idea that belief in progress required faith in the omnicompetence of science.

Since H. G. Wells's day, the future has been seen as a special kind of imaginary country, the country that we see on television programmes such as *Tomorrow's World*, a country dripping with all the latest science and technology. At first, this future land was approached with euphoric confidence, which was shown by odious talk about the need to 'drag people kicking and screaming into the twentieth century'. (Fortunately, we do not seem now to be talking in this way about the new millennium.) Later, of course, there was disillusion, which we will consider presently. But before disillusion set in, scientistic prophets proclaimed their total confidence in the omnicompetence of science.

That phrase is not just a satirical parody of their faith. It has been used, quite literally, by a number of influential theorists to claim that something called 'science' could indeed encompass the whole range of human thought on all subjects. Auguste Comte, the founder of positivism, originally sketched out this claim and the philosophers of the Vienna Circle crystallised it soon after the First World War. Thus Rudolf Carnap ruled, 'When we say that scientific knowledge in unlimited, we mean that *there is no question whose answer is in principle unattainable by science*'.[1] This extraordinary claim is still supported by some contemporary writers such as Peter Atkins,[2] though of course many scientists today have no wish to make it.

More importantly, the claim has been very influential in the outside world – so much so that it is not surprising if people now react against it. Many lay people, including some in high places, have declared a comprehensive, all-purpose faith in science. Thus Pandit Nehru, addressing the National Institute of Science of India in 1960, observed

> It is science *alone* that can solve the problems of hunger and poverty, of insanitation and illiteracy, of superstition and deadening custom and tradition, of vast resources running to waste, of a rich country inhabited by starving people ... The future belongs to science and to those who make friends with science.[3]

14

The interesting thing here is not just Nehru's confidence but what he meant by science, a point that I mentioned at the outset and that now becomes central. He clearly did *not* mean just a memory-bank, a store-cupboard of neutral information. He meant a whole new ideology, a moral approach that would justify using those facts to change society in a quite particular way. And during much of the twentieth century the word 'scientific' has constantly been used in this value-laden sense. It often has not stood for any particular form of scientific knowledge but for a new scale of values, a new priority system, leading to particular political projects. People such as B. F. Skinner, who claimed that 'we live in a scientific age', did not just mean an age that used science. They meant an age that is *guided* by science, an age that, in some way, chooses its ideals as well as its medicines and its breakfast foods on grounds provided by scientific research. This new system was certainly not seen as value-free but as a moral signpost that could take the place of religion.

SCIENCE ALONE?

Nehru and Waddington and Carnap spoke here for a whole mass of their contemporaries for whom science meant a great deal more than simply correct information. No doubt information in itself can be said to be 'value-free' but this is because information on its own has no value. It only begins to have a value when it supplies a need, when it is brought into contact with some existing system of aims and purposes and fills a gap in that system, when it becomes relevant to people's beliefs and attitudes. 'Pure curiosity' is a wish for understanding, not a wish for mere information. When we think of knowledge as valuable in itself we are always assuming something about the kind of understanding that underlies and connects the various pieces of information to form a coherent world view. That view cannot come from science alone because it involves a wider context in the life around the knower.

Thus the great scientists who have done so much to shape our present way of thinking have done it by expressing such a comprehensive vision, one that they did not draw only from the sciences. They knew that they vitally needed to consider other ideas in their culture and they often discussed those sources eagerly. Galileo and Huxley, Einstein and Bohr, Schrödinger and Heisenberg and J. B. S. Haldane all consciously and deliberately philosophised, skilfully using profound ideas drawn from those who had thought about their large problems before them. None of these people would have accepted for a moment the idea of science as an isolated imperial power, at war with other intellectual disciplines and anxious only to subdue them.

How, then, do the imperialistic writers we have been considering fit into this tradition? They are certainly within it in so far as they, too, aim to

15

promote a particular world view rather than merely furnishing neutral facts. All these writers have explicitly meant by 'science' a particular kind of spirit or attitude that includes far more than a mere set of facts or a curiosity about facts. Nehru saw this wider attitude, not as neutral but as the bearer of new values, as a moral force which *alone* could solve all his problems. He personified it, speaking of 'those who make friends with science' rather than just of those who use it. He saw it, not as a mere tool but as a powerful ally of secularism in the battle against 'superstition and deadening custom and tradition'.

Supposing we were to ask Nehru: can you really rely on science *alone*? Aren't you also going to need good laws, effective administrators, honest and intelligent politicians, good new customs to replace the old ones, perhaps even a sensitive understanding of the traditions that you mean to sweep away? Might you not even need to know a good deal of history and anthropology before you start on your destructive cleansing of tradition? Now Nehru knows, of course, that he is going to need all these things. But he is assuming that they are all included in what he means by science. He includes in 'science' the whole world-view which he takes to lie behind it, namely, the decent, humane, liberal attitude out of which it has actually grown. In fact he expects to buy the whole Enlightenment as part of the package. He has faith in the Enlightenment's humanistic ethics as well as in its chemical discoveries. He expects that the scientific spirit will include within it wise and benevolent use of those discoveries. He is certainly not thinking of science as something likely to produce industrial pollution, or the invention of refined methods of torture, or opportunities for profiteering, or a concentration on weaponry, or overuse of chemicals on farms, or computer-viruses, or irresponsible currency speculation made possible by the latest computers, or the wholesale waste of resources on gadgetry.

The prophets of this scientistic movement expected from the thing they called 'science' nothing less than a new and better ethic, a direct basis for morals, a distinctive set of secular values which would replace the earlier ones supplied by religion. They hoped that it would supersede and replace the corruption and confusion of traditional moral thinking. They did not – and their successors still do not – notice that the ethical component of this package is something much wider and actually quite independent of the science. At first they identified their new scientific values very simply (as Nehru did) with those that the Enlightenment had brought in as a reaction against Christianity, values which were already an accepted part of western culture. But as time went on they became bolder and really did try to produce something new. In these more confident moods they thought – and their successors still think – of the new scientific values, not as a contribution to an existing ethical culture, not as an outgrowth of it, not even as something harmonious with it, but as a conquering invader that must replace it.

That faith powered the huge exaltation of science that has gripped so many would-be reformers from the mid-nineteenth to the late twentieth century. It promised a new wisdom, a decisive spiritual and moral advance. Our disillusionment with this approach surely centres even more on the failure of this spiritual and moral project than on the mixed results of actual scientific practice. Certainly new technologies have often done harm as well as good. But the harm has been largely due to the lack of the promised new wisdom.

We must surely wonder now why so many people expected this wisdom to appear. That expectation set up a kind of cargo-cult which is only now giving way to blank disappointment. From Hobbes and Bacon to Auguste Comte and Marvin Minsky, scientistic prophets have regularly made Nehru's mistake of expecting the wrong kind of thing from science. They have been unconscious flatterers who got it the wrong kind of reputation. What they promoted as scientific thinking was actually a series of uncriticised ideologies, which gradually diverged from mainstream Enlightenment thinking in various alarming directions.

The first ideology that claimed to be specially scientific in this way was Marxism. But Marxism did at least appear explicitly as a thought-system. Being defended by arguments, it was clearly open to philosophic attack. Its successors, however, tended to bypass this dangerous stage, claiming rather to be parts of science itself and to share its absolute authority. That is why, when disappointment followed, it was science itself that became discredited. And this disappointment was bound to follow, partly because the good things that these prophets offered could not be supplied, partly because some of the things they offered were not good anyway.

OBJECTIVITY AS TURNING PEOPLE INTO THINGS

So what was this new ideology? The most obvious point about it – its hostility to religion – is actually a superficial one. It is true that, from the eighteenth century on, scientistic prophets have tended to be anti-Christian, holding that Christianity had failed to purify society and ought somehow to be replaced by science. The Russian Revolution eagerly pursued this project, but the results were disappointing. State atheism turned out to be every bit as convenient an excuse for crime and folly as state religion had been, and it is not at all clear that atheism itself – which is a metaphysical position – has anything to do with physical science. In any case, whatever the faults of religion, science cannot sensibly be put in its place. Attempts to expand it into a religion reverse the excellent move that Galileo and his colleagues made when they narrowed the province of physics, excluding from it all questions about purpose and meaning.

The functions of science and religion within a society are too different for this idea of a competition between them to make much sense once one begins to consider it seriously. Rivalry here only looks plausible when both elements are stated in crude forms (as of course they often are), or when the power-groups that run them conflict at the political level. Political entanglement with power-groups has had a bad effect on religion and does so equally for science, which today is increasingly sucked into the power-struggles of the market.

However, throughout the twentieth century, scientistic prophets repeatedly told a bewildered public that policies that in fact had little to do with science must be accepted because experts had shown that they were scientific and objective. A central case of this is the behaviourist doctrine that psychology, in order to be scientific, must deal only with people's outward behaviour, ignoring motives and emotions and regarding them, not just as unknowable but as trivial and causally ineffective. This led to many bizarre practical policies, such as the advice that J. B. Watson and B. F. Skinner gave to parents that they should not hug or kiss their children but should treat them in a detached and distant manner 'like young adults'. This treatment (they said) was necessary because it was scientific and objective.[4]

It is interesting to notice that what made this approach seem scientific was certainly not that it rested on research showing the success of these child-rearing methods. (If there had been any such research, it would have produced the opposite result.) Instead, the behaviourists' attitude seems surely to have been itself an emotional one, a fear of affectionate behaviour as something dangerously human, something beneath the dignity of scientists. It flowed from a more general fear of the conflicts and complications that attend ordinary human feeling. In order to escape these problems, psychologists stereotyped feeling in general as something 'soft', something that was the business of the humanities, not the sciences. The same kind of prejudice has also operated in medicine, especially in psychiatry, where a similar retreat from attending to the feelings of patients has also often been recommended as 'objective' and 'scientific'. In such cases, the mere fact of reversing a tradition and attacking ordinary feeling has often been enough to suggest that the claim was scientific, as Nehru's language shows.

Perhaps the most striking case of this distorted approach, however, is industrial Taylorism, which was commonly known quite simply as scientific management. This is the philosophy of the conveyor-belt, the view that workers ought to be treated like any other physical component on the production-line. Any reference to their own point of view was seen as subjective and thus an illicit, unscientific distraction. The economists who devised this approach, and Henry Ford who accepted it, did not think of it merely as a quick way of making money. They saw it as something much grander, as scientific progress, a laudable extension of physical science into realms formerly ruled by sentiment and superstition. It seemed obvious to them that it is 'subjective' to pay any attention to subjectivity.[5]

Another favoured way of appearing scientific is, of course, simply to mention quantities rather than qualities. Thus policies can be called scientific if they involve counting or measuring something, never mind whether that particular thing needs to be counted or not, and never mind what use is being made of the resulting data. Anybody who is using some statistics can make this claim. Reliance on the citation index, on exams, and on the league-tables that compare exam results, are examples of this habit. Similarly, the American spin-doctor Dick Morris claimed scientific status, saying that all he does is to 'reduce the mysterious ways of politics to scientific testing and evaluation'.

It is also often seen as scientific to talk as if people were actually and literally machines. This machine imagery has been so useful in many scientific contexts that many people no longer think of it as a metaphor but as a scientific fact. Thus, much as they might say 'soot is just carbon' or 'penguins are just birds', they remark in passing that the human brain is just a computer made of meat. They don't think of this as a metaphor at all.

This machine imagery became entrenched at the dawn of modern science because in the seventeenth century scientists were fascinated, as well they might be, by the ingenious clockwork automata of the day. They naturally hoped to extend this clockwork model, which – for a time – worked well for the solar system, to cover the whole of knowledge, and, as the Industrial Revolution went on, that hope seemed more and more natural. But physics, the original source of this dream, has now largely abandoned it. The clockwork model proved unsuitable for many central purposes, along with the simple atomic theory that fitted it. Indeed, physics has dropped the whole idea that the basic structure of matter is bound to prove perfectly simple, an idea that seemed obvious to seventeenth-century thinkers and one that made the abstractions of the machine model look plausible. Today, with talk of eleven-dimensional space-time, non-locality and multiple universes, that hope of simplicity has vanished. For inorganic matter as well as for organisms, complexity is now the name of the game. The idea that physicists will some day find a single all-embracing 'theory of everything' is just a speculation. Some distinguished cosmologists embrace it, others reject it entirely. But even if such a theory were found, it could not possibly be simple. It would clearly be hugely complex. And it would not be a theory of everything – only of certain abstractions that are discussed in theoretical physics.

UNIVERSAL?

In a very interesting survey of current views on this problem, Paul Davies states the difficulties. As he says, the current demand for a 'theory of everything' is in fact largely just an effort to bring together two distinct and apparently warring thought systems within physics itself, systems that now rule in different areas of the study. Their disconnectedness still blocks contemporary efforts to resolve the central question that he poses, namely; What makes the universe tick?

> Physics in the twentieth century was built on the twin revolutions of quantum mechanics (a theory of matter) and Einstein's theory of space. But it's extremely unsatisfying to find two ultimate descriptions of reality when you're looking for just one.[6]

After discussing various current suggestions for unifying them and ending up with a raft of unanswered questions, he rather suddenly introduces a quite different angle:

> Where does consciousness come from? Why do some swirling electrical patterns, such as those in a brain, have thoughts and sensations attached, whereas others, such as those in the national grid, presumably do not? . . . Are these even questions for physicists to answer?
> Some think they are for physicists to answer – myself among them. Relating the mental and physical world is something most physicists avoid, but *if physics claims to be a universal discipline* then it must eventually incorporate a description of consciousness.[7]

In what sense does physics claim to be a universal discipline? As he says, most of his colleagues answer this question with their feet by simply not visiting topics outside what is now recognised as the physical or material aspect of things. They do not share Carnap's ambition to wield a science that can answer every kind of question. Though they deal with large questions about issues such as time and the nature of matter, they are happy if they can end their discussions about these things with a coherent set of equations and if somebody managed to reconcile the two jarring physical languages in those terms, they would be content. They would not ask for a connection between them and other aspects of the world.

Davies, however, has always taken an interest in the spiritual aspect of things. He wants to relate the mental and physical world. He minds about mind. This is surely admirable. And obviously he, as a physicist, is quite entitled to follow out this interest. It is an interest that he shares with most of the great physicists of the past, from Archimedes to Einstein. But in doing so he, like them, will not be trying to discover further physical facts. He will be trying to fit together different thought-systems that deal with different aspects of the world. The connection of physics with other studies is not itself a part of physics. It is a piece of philosophical plumbing. Since most physicists now are narrowly educated, it is badly needed and we should wish Davies all success in his efforts.

4

THOUGHT HAS MANY FORMS

————— •◆• —————

COMPLEXITY IS NOT A SCANDAL

We need not, probably, go over any more of the cases we have been discussing where words like 'scientific', 'objective' and 'machine' are used with an equivocal and biased sense. We meet them all the time. And I hope it is clear by now that, in exposing these rhetorical attempts to turn science into a comprehensive ideology, I am not attacking science but defending it against dangerous misconstructions.

These doctrines are not parts of scientific work but half-conscious attitudes that have underlain it, producing outgrowths that have distorted its image. It is no wonder that they provoke 'anti-science' feeling. People who fear science today are chiefly disturbed by the way in which these imperialistic ideologies import irrelevant, inhuman standards into non-scientific aspects of life and lead people to neglect the relevant ones. Throughout the social sciences and often in the humanities too, distorted ideas of what it means to be 'scientific' and 'objective' still direct a great deal of life and a great deal of research. The crude dualism that treats mind and body as separate, disconnected things still leads people to take sides between them and to suppose that, having opted for body, they must simplify the scene by ignoring mind. The trouble lies in the exclusiveness, the either/or approach, the conviction that only one very simple way of thought is rational.

Even within science itself, this simplistic approach is beginning to make trouble. Our familiar stereotype of scientific rationality is still one modelled on the methods of seventeenth-century physics. As I have mentioned, for many purposes modern physics has moved away from those methods. But not everybody in biology has heard the news of this change. Many biologists still tend to see mechanism as the only truly scientific thought-pattern because they still think it is central to physics. And for some time this belief has concentrated their attention strongly on microbiological questions, leading them to neglect larger-scale matters such as the behaviour of whole organisms.

Today, a number of biologists are suggesting that this neglect is gravely unbalancing biology.[1] If Darwin had applied today for a grant for his research-project, which dealt entirely with the behaviour of whole organisms and with species, he would have been most unlikely to be successful. His advisers would have had to urge him to move away into something molecular. Since this does not seem to be a sensible situation, efforts are being made to bring these larger units into focus once more, thus 'putting the life back into biology' as Lynn Margulis and Dorion Sagan put it.[2] Even the largest unit of all – Gaia, the biosphere within which we all live – is no longer outlawed as unscientific but is beginning to serve as a useful focus of ecological enquiry.

In psychology (to end this rather crude lightning tour) the taboo that the behaviourists imposed on the study of consciousness has lately been lifted. That astonishing Berlin Wall has finally come down. Consciousness is at last admitted to be significant and is being studied, with results which are confusing but will surely be fertile. So this is one more area where narrow, distorted rulings on *what it is to be scientific* are crumbling fast.

WILD HOPES

As we have seen, the trouble with Enlightenment myths when they get out of hand is that they tend to exalt the form over the substance of what is being said, the method over the aim of an activity, and precision of detail over completeness of cover. In all the areas of science just mentioned the pseudo-scientific ideology that we have been considering has done this. In all of them, it is now being questioned and we surely need to intensify this process.

We need to stop treating 'science' as if it were a single monolithic entity, a solid kingdom embattled against rival kingdoms. On the one hand, the various sciences differ hugely. Ecology and anthropology are not at all like physics, nor indeed is biology, and this is not disastrous because they don't have to be like it. And on the other hand we need to stop treating this entity called 'science' as an expanding empire, destined one day to take over the whole intellectual world. Our current difficulties about the environment and about human rights are large problems that need cooperative work from every kind of intellectual discipline from ethics to computing, from anthropology to law and from soil science to Russian history. The intense academic specialisation that prevails today makes this cooperation hard enough already without adding the extra obstacles imposed by tribal warfare.

Scientistic imperialism has been closely connected with the attempt to reduce all the various sciences to a single model, as is clear from the way in which the Unity of Science Movement in the United States has devoted itself to asserting omnicompetence. Both errors, in fact, spring equally from an unduly narrow, monopolistic concept of rationality, a concept which we still draw essentially from seventeenth-century philosophers such as Descartes. (This is just one more case where people who refuse to have anything to do with philosophy have become enslaved to outdated forms of it.)

When Descartes started on his famous quest for absolute certainty, he did not, as his writings suggest, set out with a quite open mind about where he might find it. He already had his eye on Galileo. Already, he had decided that the kind of logical clarity found in this new mathematical physics could make it proof against error. He therefore thought it the only light which the human intellect could safely follow. This meant that the methods characteristic of that science must somehow be extended to cover all other subject-matters as well as physics. Eventually, it would unite the whole of knowledge in a Theory of Everything, a unified rational system balanced securely on a single foundation.

Thus the Enlightenment notion of physical science was imperialistic from the outset. From its birth, the idea of this science was associated with two strangely ambitious claims, infallibility and the formal unity of the whole of thought. We know now that these two soaring ambitions can't be achieved and that they don't need to be. Rationality does not require us to be infallible, nor to have all our knowledge tightly organised on the model of mathematics. But we are still haunted by the idea that these things are necessary.

In spite of his own interest in consciousness, Descartes put physics in a position where it was more or less forced to claim an intellectual monopoly over the whole of knowledge. This arrangement demanded a kind of materialism that, in the end, was bound to leave mind with no apparent standing-room in the universe. Later philosophers saw this clearly enough. But most of them were just as convinced as he was that they needed a comprehensive, unified system. So, instead of trying to bridge the strange gap he had placed between mind and matter, idealists and materialists responded by fighting wars to decide which of these two superpowers should control the whole system.

That conflict is still with us today. On the one side idealism, though it is not now much mentioned, still functions as a shadowy background to many sceptical 'postmodern' doctrines such as extreme constructivism. On the other, dogmatic materialists still see this metaphysical feud as a living issue, a battle that must be won. We need to step back and ask what the disagreement is actually about. The really surprising thing about the contestants is surely what they have in common. They are both still convinced that such a comprehensive thought-system is necessary and possible. They do not think we can be rational without it.

OBJECTIVITY HAS DEGREES

Our next question then is, how would we manage without such a system? Granted that a great deal of our perfectly legitimate and necessary thought – indeed, most of it – stands outside physical science, what is the relation between these different provinces? How (in particular) can we bring subjectivity and objectivity together in our thinking? What should we substitute for the current pattern which shows matter, described by a single objective system called 'science', on one side of the gap, confronting a mass of indescribable subjective experience on the other?

Here we need to see what an extraordinary myth the notion of this gap always was. In reality, our experience is not sharply divided into ghost and machine, mind and matter, into subjective and objective points of view. It spreads across a continuous plain. Virtually all our thought integrates material taken from both the objective and the subjective angles. And we have, by now, formed very useful concepts for doing this. Thus, dentists are not baffled when they have to bring together the objective facts that make up their professional knowledge with the subjective reports that patients give of their various pains. Indeed, dentists may in turn be patients themselves. When these dentists think or talk about their own toothache, they can use a whole familiar toolkit of conceptual schemes which connect the inside with the outside position intelligibly.

Objectivity, in fact, is not just a single standpoint. It is one of two directions in which thought can move. As Thomas Nagel puts it, when we want to acquire a more objective understanding of some aspect of life in the world,

> we step back from our initial view of it and form a new conception which has that view and its relation to the world as its object. ... The process can be repeated, yielding a still more objective conception. ... The distinction between more subjective and more objective views is really a matter of degree. ... *The standpoint of morality is more objective than that of private life, but less objective than the standpoint of physics.*[3]

Thus we compare elements derived from two or more angles in various ways that suit the different matters we are discussing, ways that differ widely according to the purpose of our thought at the time. Perhaps we do this much as we combine the very different data from sight and touch in our sense-perception. As Nagel points out, increased objectivity is not always a virtue, nor is it always useful for explanation. A dentist or psychiatrist who decides to become more objective by ignoring the pain of his patients will not thereby become more skilled or more successful in his profession.

How, then, do we actually manage to relate these various ways of thinking, and their various degrees of objectivity, when we use them together in our lives? The fashionable reductive pattern tells us that, in order to connect different families of concepts, we should arrange them in a linear sequence running from the superficial to the fundamental and ending with the most fundamental group of all, namely, physics.[4] This hierarchy fills the whole space available for explanation. The more fundamental thought patterns are then called 'hard' and the upper ones 'soft'. That rather mysterious tactile metaphor means that the upper or softer layers are only provisional. They are more superficial, amateurish, non-serious, because they fall short of the ultimate explanation. Classed as folk-psychology, these layers must only be tolerated as makeshifts to be used until the real scientific account is available, or when it is too cumbersome for convenience. They are just stages on the way down to the only fully mature science, which is physics.

The metaphor of *levels*, which is so often used to describe the relation between these various ways of thinking, unfortunately endorses this linear pattern. As Descartes originally conceived it, talk of a fundamental level simply invoked the image of a building's need for foundations. ('My whole aim was to reach security, and cast aside loose earth and sand so as to reach rock or clay.') But he coupled this modest comparison with one that is far more ambitious. He writes, 'Archimedes asked only for one fixed and immovable point so as to move the whole earth from its place; so I may have great hopes if I find even the least thing that is unshakably certain.'[5] Thus his aim was to find a single firm truth from which all others could be seen to follow, as the propositions of geometry follow from their axioms. The search for a 'foundation' thus became a search for this ultimate support, this outside reason from which the whole system would follow. Without this chain, all knowledge was insecure and suspect.

Descartes's use of this gravitational imagery as a defence against the scepticism of his day, and his confident casting of physics as the saving ground-floor, has had a lasting influence on our imaginations. Yet we know that gravitation does not work like this. Its force is not linear but convergent. What we need is not an ultimate floor at the bottom of the universe but simply a planet with a good strong reassuring pull that will keep us together and stop us falling off it. We exist, in fact, as interdependent parts of a complex network, not as isolated items that must be supported in a void.

As for our knowledge, it too is a network involving all kinds of lateral links, a system in which the most varied kinds of connection may be relevant for helping us to meet various kinds of question. The idea of piling it all up in a single tower was never very plausible and the enormous proliferation of different intellectual methods that has developed since Descartes's day makes it even wilder. We would have to envisage it as an ever-expanding skyscraper – a skyscraper from whose bulging sides balcony on balcony is continually being built out . . . This is hardly an encouraging picture of the security that was aimed at.

Nor is it clear how this pattern of a one-dimensional hierarchy could ever have been applied. It could only work if the relation between physics and chemistry (which is its original model) could be repeated again and again, not only for biology but beyond that to colonise other branches of thought such as history, logic, law, linguistics, ethics, musicology and mathematics, and to translate them all eventually into physical terms. It is not clear how anybody could even start to do this. History alone is an impossible case, because historical methods are complex and are quite unlike those usually quoted as being essential to physical science. And since historical methods are needed within science itself wherever a unique process is described – for instance in cosmology and in the study of evolution – that failure should finish the matter.

MANY MAPS, MANY WINDOWS

Why, then, is the fascination of this reductive linear pattern still so strong? What is the special value of the gravitational metaphor? Why, in particular, should we choose to represent the development of our knowledge always in terms of *building,* rather than, for instance, of an interaction with the world around us, leading to growth?

Gravitational imagery does, of course, make an important point when we want to test the detailed working of some particular piece of reasoning to check that it is secure. And this is where it has chiefly proved useful. But a great deal of our thinking does not involve such testing. Much of the time, we are exploring unknown or partially known matters, and we use whatever forms of thought turn out to be needed for them. Often it is our powers of perception that are central to the work, rather than the consecutive reasoning that can easily be tested. And in any human situation we must call on special powers of social perception and imagination that are not really formulable at all. (This is particularly important when we are assessing the force of human testimony, on which, of course, the answers to other kinds of questions often depend.) We cannot test everything and we do not need to start testing at all unless something goes wrong. Connected systems of thought – which allow of testing – come later.

For this general, initial understanding, the image of exploration seems to me much more suitable than that of gravitation. Explorers do not prepare for their trips simply by making sure that their ropes and ice-axes will never fail, testing them all to destruction. Infallible equipment would be little use to them if they did not know where they were going. They concentrate first on finding out all they can about the country they are exploring. Their first need therefore is a map. And this is at first a loose, provisional mental map that they themselves must frame out of whatever materials they can find, materials which they cannot always test in advance. The main need is that this initial map should be comprehensive – should say something about all the main factors that may be encountered.

It often happens that several of the existing maps or informants that they use will seem to contradict one another. When this happens, our heroes do not need to choose one of them in advance as infallible. Instead, they had better bear them all in mind, looking out for whatever may be useful in all of them. In the field, they can eventually test one suggestion against another, but it need not always turn out that either suggestion is wrong. The river that different earlier maps show in different places may actually be several different rivers. Reality is always turning out to be a great deal more complex than people expect.

This analogy between different maps and different sources of knowledge seems to me very useful. I have developed it more fully elsewhere in order to make the point that we need *scientific pluralism* – the recognition that there are many independent forms and sources of knowledge – rather than reductivism, the conviction that one fundamental form underlies them all and settles everything.[6] The central and most helpful case for the map analogy is perhaps that of the many maps of the world that are found in the first pages of atlases. We do not make the mistake of thinking that these maps conflict. We know that the political world is not a different world from the climatological one, that it is the same world seen from a different angle. Different questions are asked, so naturally there are different answers.

Just so, the different branches of our thought – history, geology, literature, philosophy, anthropology, physics and the rest, as well as our many less formal modes of experience – home in on our single world from different angles, led by different interests. In the long run they ought to agree. But it is not surprising that initially they often seem to clash, because the world simply is not simple. Different specialists may be talking about quite different rivers. These clashes are often worth investigating and they can lead to important illuminations. But they never mean that one of these specialities is always right and the rest are superficial or mistaken.

Besides the many-maps model, another image that I have found helpful on this point is that of the world as a huge aquarium. We cannot see it as a whole from above, so we peer in at it through a number of small windows. Inside, the lighting is not always good and there are rocks and weeds for the inhabitants to hide in. Is that the same fish coming out that we saw just now over there? And are those things stones or starfish? We can eventually make quite a lot of sense of this habitat if we patiently put together the data from different angles. But if we insist that our own window is the only one worth looking through, we shall not get very far.

It will be noticed that, in using both these images, I am taking it for granted that there actually is an external world out there, that we do not, in some sense, 'construct' the whole thing. The idea of ourselves as uncaused causes of everything – spontaneous universal world-creators – which is suggested by some extreme constructionists, does not seem to me to make much sense. Once again, the technological metaphor of *construction* – of building – is unsuitable. It is one of those exaggerations of human power that we shall meet again and again in this book.

Of course our own individual point of view makes a great difference to how we see things. But that difference is much better described as selection than as construction. It is quite true that, when we look at the Himalayas, every one of us sees them differently. But none of us can think them away, nor put them there in the first place.

All perception takes in only a fraction of what is given to it, and all thought narrows that fraction still further in trying to make sense of it. This means that what we see is real enough, but it is always partial. And a good deal of the narrowing is within our own control.

The real world that exists independently of us is not, then, a strange metaphysical spook, a mysterious entity eternally hidden from us behind a screen of delusive appearances. It is simply the whole of what is out there. We glimpse only that small part of its riches that is within our reach, and within that range we must continually choose the still smaller parts on which we will concentrate. The idea of it is what Kant called a *regulative idea*: a necessary part of our apparatus for thinking, not the name of something we shall eventually meet.

5

THE AIMS OF REDUCTION

——·◆·——

REDUCING WHAT TO WHAT?

Why, then, is reductivism still so often taken for granted as a necessary part of rationality? What gives it this status? It is worth while to look at the reductive approach as a general attitude, rather than just at the forms of actual reductions.

These forms vary. Reductivism comes in two phases. First, there is the monistic move by which we explain a great range of things as only aspects of a single stuff. Thus, Thales says that all the four elements are really just water and Nietzsche says that all motives are really just forms of the will to power. Second, there sometimes follows the separate atomistic move, made by Democritus and the seventeenth-century physicists, in which we explain this basic stuff itself as really just an assemblage of ultimate particles. The wholes that are formed out of these particles are then secondary and relatively unreal.

Both these drastic moves can be useful when they are made as the first stage towards a fuller analysis. But both, if made on their own, can have very strange consequences. Fairly obviously, Nietzsche's psychology was oversimple. And, if we want to see the limitations of atomism, we need only consider a botanist who is asked (perhaps by an explorer or an archaeologist) to identify a leaf. This botanist does not simply mince up the leaf, put it in the centrifuge and list the resulting molecules. Still less, of course, does he list their constituent atoms, protons and electrons. Instead, he looks first at its structure and considers the possible wider background, asking what kind of tree it came from, in what ecosystem, growing on what soil, in what climate, and what has happened to the leaf since it left its tree? This 'holistic' approach is not folklore but as central and necessary a part of science as the atomistic quest. So it is strange that, at present, many people seem to believe that science is essentially and merely reductive in a sense that includes both the stages just mentioned.

PARSIMONY, AUSTERITY AND
VALUE-NEUTRALITY

Why is reductiveness seen as necessary? The forms of reduction are many. But the use of the special word 'reductive' points to something they are thought to have in common. This element does not seem to be only a formal one. The point is not just that these are all ways of simplifying the conceptual scene. It concerns the intention that underlies that simplification.

Examining this intention is not an irrelevant piece of psychoanalysis. Formal reductions don't spring up on their own, like weeds in a garden. They are not value-free. They are always parts of some larger enterprise, some project for reshaping the whole intellectual landscape, and often our general attitude to life as well. When we get seriously involved in reductive business, either as supporters or resisters, we are normally responding to these wider projects.

It is not hard to see the general imaginative appeal of ideological reductivism. In our increasingly confusing world, the picture of knowledge as modelled on a simple, despotic system of government is attractive. It is surely no accident that the reductive method had its first triumphs in the seventeenth century, at the time when wars of religion filled Europe with terrifying confusion. The monolithic pattern of knowledge seemed able then to impose order on intellectual chaos, just as Louis Quatorze and the other despotic rulers of his day did on civil war. This was a style that accorded with the political and religious notions of the time. The unbounded confidence that Thomas Hobbes showed in both these applications was typical of his age.

In politics, that simple vision of unity no longer commands much respect today. But in the intellectual world it has not yet been fully discredited. There, monoculture still seems to offer order and simplicity – which are, of course, entirely proper aims for science – cheaply, skipping the complications that so often block these ideals. Oversimple intellectual systems are welcome because they contrast with the practical chaos around us, and we do not criticise them sharply when the particular short-cut that they offer suggests a world view that we like. They extend patterns that already suit us over areas we would otherwise find awkward. They express visions that attract us, and they obscure alternative possibilities.

The first point that matters here is that, in general, we need to be aware of these underlying dramas and to discuss them openly, even when they lead us far outside our specialities. We cannot settle the vast, looming, vulgar background questions indirectly by fixing the small logical issues. You can't shift a muck-heap with a teaspoon. The second point – about reductivism in particular – is that the large background projects involved are never just destructive. They always aim at something positive as well.

In our time, reduction overwhelmingly presents itself as purely negative, a mere exercise in logical hygiene, something as obviously necessary as throwing out the rubbish. But this presupposes that we have already made sure what we want to throw away and what we want to make room for. Parsimony is a respectable ideal, but it does not make much sense on its own. In thought as in life, there can be false economy. We cannot tell what we should save until we have decided what we want to buy with our savings. Of course there do exist straightforward misers, savers led by pure parsimony. And there are intellectual misers too, sceptics who pride themselves on being too clever to believe anything or anybody. But most of us are not like that. We think of saving as a means to an end.

Rationality does not actually demand the most economical account conceivable. It demands the most economical one *that will give us the explanation we need*. To get this, we need to consider carefully which lines to pursue: how wide our explanation needs to be, how large our question is and what other questions are bound up with it. Mapping these surrounding areas is an essential function of a good explanation.

Reducers, then, are quite entitled to make savings and to spend what they have saved on building explanatory structures elsewhere in order to balance those that they destroy. Things only go wrong when they do not notice that they are doing this and accordingly fail to criticize their own constructions. They think their work is much easier than it actually is because they feel sure in advance what they want to abolish. They often do not notice how much they are adding.

WHAT KIND OF AUSTERITY?

Confidence of this kind on the part of reductionists can make for a strange complacency. In his preparatory notes for a conference on this topic, John Cornwell wrote of 'reductionism's austere outlook'. And pride in that austerity is obviously very widely felt by reducers. But there is no reason to think of reduction as necessarily austere. Intellectual puritans, like other kinds of puritan, usually want a pay-off, an imaginative indulgence to compensate for their surface austerities. This pay-off may be something quite respectable and necessary, but we need to know what it is.

In extreme cases, reductivism finds its pay-off in quite undisciplined imaginative visions which may be called pieces of reductive megalomania. I shall say a little more about these later, but in case anyone doesn't know what I mean, it may be worthwhile just to give a few specimens here.

1   From Nietzsche:

> This world is the will to power and nothing beside . . .
>   Life itself is *essentially* appropriation, injury, subjugation of the strange and the weaker, suppression, severity, imposition of its own forms, incorporation and, at the least and mildest exploitation.[1]

2   From Richard Dawkins:

> The argument of this book is that we, and all other animals, are machines created by our genes ... Like successful Chicago gangsters, our genes have survived, in some cases for millions of years, in a highly competitive world. This entitles us to expect certain qualities in our genes. I shall argue that a predominant quality to be expected in a successful gene is ruthless selfishness ... If you wish ... to build a society in which individuals cooperate generously and unselfishly towards a common good, you can expect little help from biological nature. Let us try to teach generosity and altruism, because we are born selfish.[2]

3   From J. D. Bernal:

> Once acclimatized to space-living, it is unlikely that man will stop until he has roamed over and colonized most of the sidereal universe, or that even this will be the end. Man will not ultimately be content to be parasitic on the stars, but will invade them and organize them for his own purposes ... The stars cannot be allowed to continue in their old way, but will be turned into efficient heat-engines ... By intelligent organization, the life of the universe could probably be prolonged to many millions of millions of times what it would be without organization.[3]

VALUE-FREE?

In passages such as those quoted, though the tone is sternly reductive, the positive proposals made are certainly not economical. They are lush speculative outgrowths, designed to stimulate the imagination of readers to move in unexpected directions rather than to discipline it. Of course not all reductions carry such surprising cargo, and you may well wonder whether I am justified in saying – as I do want to say – that reduction is never value-neutral, never just aimed at simplicity, that it is always part of some positive propaganda campaign. You may ask: does reduction always aim in some way to debunk or downgrade the more complex thought that it simplifies away in order to exalt something else?

Now certainly the kinds of downgrading involved are very various, and some of them are so mild that they are scarcely noticed. Perhaps the mildest possible kind is the relation between chemistry and physics. Is this perhaps just a formal connection, just a matter of establishing inter-translatability? Does it mark no difference in value between physics and chemistry?

It is quite true that people who point out this relation are not attacking chemistry, nor campaigning to get rid of it. But there *is* still a value-judgement involved here, one of a subtler and more interesting kind. It concerns what is seen as more 'real', more 'fundamental'. Physics wins here because it stands nearest to the end of the quest that dominated science from the time of Galileo until quite lately: the atomistic project of explaining the behaviour of matter completely by analysing it into solid ultimate particles moved by definite forces, 'ultimate building-blocks', as people still revealingly say. Given that quest, and given the faith that it would finally provide the only proper explanation of everything, chemistry inevitably emerged as the subordinate partner, and all other studies as more subordinate still.

Modern chemistry has grown up with that status, and chemists probably don't usually resent it. Some of them have, however, said that this exclusive orientation to physics distorts chemistry. Similar complaints have often been made about distortion of biology, and it is interesting that Francis Crick, himself often a keen reducer, is among those complaining. As he points out, the accumulated effects of evolution give biology a kind of complexity all its own:

> All this may make it very difficult for physicists to adapt to most biological research. Physicists are all too apt to look for the wrong sorts of generalizations, to concoct theoretical models that are too neat, too powerful and too clean. Not surprisingly, these seldom fit well with the data. To produce a really good biological theory one must try to see through the clutter produced by evolution to the basic mechanisms lying beneath them . . . What seems to physicists to be a hopelessly complicated process may have been what nature found simplest, because nature could only build on what was already there.[4]

We need to ask, then, just what the assumed primacy of physics means. It does not concern only a hierarchy internal to the sciences. Right from the start, physical explanations have been expected to extend very widely, far beyond the boundaries of chemistry. Descartes established the assumption that, since physical particles moved on the model of machines, the things made out of them, including human bodies, must do that too. This assumption took the empire of physics right into the realm of human affairs, and, as long as the simple mechanical model held sway, it provided a kind of explanation there that seemed entitled to supersede all other ways of thinking.

Though Descartes himself exempted the mind from this machine, others quickly saw that it too could be reduced to fit the picture. Thomas Hobbes (always a most determined reducer) did this with great zest right across the psychological scene:

When the action of the same object is continued from the Eyes, Ears and other organs to the Heart, *the real effect there is nothing but motion or endeavour*, which consisteth in Appetite or Aversion to or from the object moving. But the appearance, or sense of that motion, is that we either call DELIGHT OR TROUBLE OF MIND.
  – Life itself is but motion.[5]

Physical explanations had primacy because – quite simply – they revealed reality, whereas subjective experience was 'only an appearance'. Reductive psychologisers like Hobbes did not see that there could be objective facts about subjective experience, that an appearance is itself a fact, and that some appearances – for instance the experience of pain or grief, delight or trouble of mind – can be centrally important parts of the facts that affect us. These things do not just appear to matter; they do matter. So we vitally need appropriate conceptual schemes for discussing them.

Hobbes's simple contrast between reality and appearance is easily read as the familiar one between reality and illusion. Ordinary, everyday life is then thought of, in an extraordinarily incoherent way, as some kind of dream or mistake. Thus, Einstein was convinced that ordinary, irreversible time is an illusion, since it had no place in his theory of physics. His close friend Michèle Besso long tried to convince him that this could not be right, but Einstein remained adamant and when Besso died he wrote, in a letter of condolence to Besso's family, 'Michèle has left this strange world just before me. This is of no importance. For us convinced physicists *the distinction between past, present and future is an illusion, though a persistent one.*'[6] But to say that something is not important does not justify calling it an illusion. Similarly Stephen Hawking (though of course his view of time is different) is happy to say that, 'so-called imaginary time is real time and . . . what we call real time is just a figment of our imaginations'.[7] The phrase 'imaginary time' is of course a technical term used by physicists with a meaning quite different from its normal one. But Hawking shows, by using the ordinary phrase 'a figment of our imaginations' in parallel with it, that he has slipped into using the term in both senses at once.

When people who talk like this are pressed to explain themselves, and are asked whether they really think that the part of our knowledge that falls outside physics – which is almost all our knowledge – is pure illusion, they tend to dither and retreat somewhat. 'No,' they say, 'it isn't exactly false or illusory, but it is somehow superficial and provisional. It is a kind of amateur guesswork because it has not yet been properly checked by scientists.' Thus, in a *New Scientist* article, Peter Atkins kindly makes room for other studies, conceding that:

there will always be room for constructing questions that package groups of deeper questions into units appropriate to the level of discourse . . . *It will never be appropriate to exterminate history, law and so on*, any more than it would be appropriate to insist that all discourse in biology should be expressed in terms of particle physics. Concepts must be allowed to operate at a pragmatic level.[8]

But this, he says, is merely because the deeper scientific account is unfortunately 'too cumbersome for daily use', not because any other enquiry could actually add anything useful to it. Science – meaning essentially just physics and chemistry, since Atkins names biology among the surface layers – remains 'omnicompetent'. It is, he says, able to answer, at the deepest level, all questions that could arise in any enquiry.

TRANSLATION PROSPECTS

Anyone who feels a longing to complete our knowledge in this way should try translating some simple historical statement into the deeper, physical truths that are held to underlie it. What, for instance, about a factual sentence like 'George was allowed home from prison at last on Sunday'? How will the language of physics convey the meaning of 'Sunday'? or 'home' or 'allowed' or 'prison'? or 'at last'? or indeed 'George'? (There are no individuals in physics.) The meaning of all these terms concerns very complex, far-ranging systems of social relation, not the physical details of a particular case.

For a translation, all these social concepts would have to vanish and be represented by terms describing the interactions of groups of particles moved by various forces. The trouble with this new version is *not*, as Atkins says, that it is 'too cumbersome for everyday use', but that it does not begin to convey the meaning of what is said at all. The sentence as it stands does not refer only to the physical items involved. Indeed, most of the physical details are irrelevant to it. (It does not matter, for instance, where the prison is or by what transport or what route George came home.) What the sentence describes is a symbolic transaction between an individual and a huge social background of penal justice, power structures, legislation and human decisions. The words it uses are suited to fill in that historical and social background. Without such concepts, the whole meaning of the sentence would vanish.

This piece of history – this little narrative sentence – is not something sketchy or provisional. It is not a blueprint that needs scientific validation. It is not just an emotive expression or amateur 'folk-psychology'. It is solid information of exactly the kind that is needed. It is precise in the way that it needs to be, and if more precision is needed – such as why he is let out – that too can be supplied through concepts of the same kind. And if anyone cares to try the same experiment with a sentence from the law, they will find themselves still more totally baffled.

6

DUALISTIC DILEMMAS

———·◆·———

COUNTER-SCEPTICISM:
THE IDEALIST REDUCTION

Reducers feel that there is still something unofficial about everyday language, because it speaks of entities such as human beings and homes and prisons that are not in the repertoire of physics, entities that cannot, therefore, be quite real. But to question their reality is to invoke not physics but metaphysics. What does 'real' mean here? What deeper reality are we talking about? Why (first) is there this profound faith in extending the mechanical explanatory system indefinitely, and why (next) is that faith expressed in this violently ontological language of appearance, or illusion, and reality?

Plainly, the atomistic pattern of explanation in terms of movements of ultimate, unsplittable particles still has a strong grip on our imaginations. Though physicists no longer believe in those ultimate particles, the kind of simplification promised by this pattern is extremely attractive, and of course it has often worked very well. Besides, from the debunking point of view, reducing wholes to parts is always a good way to downgrade their value. As people say, 'After all, when you get right down to it, a human body is just £5-worth of chemicals . . .'

There is also, however, a much more serious and reputable wish to bring explanations of mind and matter together in some sort of intelligible relation. Descartes's division of the world between these two superpowers, mind and body, that were scarcely on speaking terms, is most unsatisfactory. Once the pattern of unification by conquest had been proposed as a way of helping thought to cross such gulfs between enquiries, it seemed natural to carry it further. Materialists who reduced mind to matter certainly did think they were simply following the example of physics. But that example cannot decide *which* of the superpowers is to prevail.

Formally, it is just as easy to absorb matter into mind by being sceptical about the existence of outside objects as it is to absorb mind into matter.

Phenomenalism works quite as well as materialism. David Hume devised a sceptical, idealist reduction which cut out physical matter as an unnecessary entity just as sternly as it cut out God and the continuing soul. This triumph of general parsimony left Hume with a most obscure world consisting only of particular perceptions, atoms of mind without any real owner. But Hume still thought his economy was based on the example of modern science. In justifying his reduction of all motives to the search for utility, he cited Newton's example, writing hopefully:

> It is entirely agreeable to the rules of philosophy, and even of common reason, where any principle has been found to have a great force and energy in one instance, to ascribe to it a like energy in all similar instances. This indeed is Newton's chief rule in philosophizing.[1]

This shows most revealingly how tempting it is to see cases as 'similar' once you have got a formula that you hope might fit them all. In defending this fatal tendency, Hume writes, somewhat naively, as if simplicity were always just a matter of the actual number of principles invoked:

> Thus we have established two truths without any obstacle or difficulty, that it is from natural principles this variety of causes excite pride and humility, and that it is not by a different principle each cause is adapted to its passion. We shall now proceed to enquire how we may *reduce these principles to a lesser number*, and find among the causes something common on which their influence depends.[2]

This hasty habit has been responsible for a whole raft of grossly oversimple reductive theories of motivation. But it did not, of course, settle the question of whether mind should be reduced to matter or matter to mind. Formally, these projects look very similar. Both spring from the strong demand for unity, from the conviction that reality simply cannot be arbitrarily split in two down the middle. But this formal demand for unity cannot help us to pick sides. Nor does it have the sort of force that would be needed to make people go on, as they have, accepting the strange paradoxes that emerge later, when they try to carry through either monolithic materialism or monolithic idealism consistently. At that point, all simplicity is lost. So, if the search for simplicity were the real aim, people would naturally give up the reductive project.

GUIDING IDEALS

What makes thinkers carry reduction further must then surely be, not a formal search for order, but the pursuit of an ideal. Though theorists often claim that their metaphysical views involve no moral bias, metaphysics usually does express some kind of moral attitude to life, and there is no reason on earth why it should not do so. There is nothing disreputable about having ideals. What is needed is that they should be conscious and openly expressed for discussion. Bias must not be smuggled in as if it were a technical matter only accessible to experts.

In the case of mind and matter, the clash of ideals involved is often obvious at an everyday level. For instance, in medicine, and especially in psychiatry, there is often a choice between viewing patients primarily as physical organisms or as conscious agents. As current experience shows, choice can have strong practical consequences for treatment; indeed it can decide the whole fate of the patient. Yet it is often seen as determined abstractly in advance by conceptions of what is scientific.[3]

The metaphysical idea that only the physical body is actually *real*, while talk of the mind or soul is mere superstition, can have a startling influence on conduct here. The opposite folly – of ignoring the body and treating only the mind – of course also has its own metaphysical backing. But that backing tends to be more explicit, and it is not usually a reductive one. Freudian and existential psychiatrists don't suppose that bodies are actually unreal. They are not Christian Scientists. They don't support their methods by an idealist metaphysic. Hume's path of reductive idealism is in fact too obscure to influence conduct in the way that reductive materialism has.

THOUGHTS AS WHISTLES

It is this asymmetry between our attitudes to mind and body that makes our current idea of 'reduction' so confusing. It is not, of course, confined to psychiatry. The idea that mind and matter are competitors, that only one of them can determine conduct, has long had a wide influence. Its preferred form today is the 'epiphenomenalist' one devised by T. H. Huxley. This says that consciousness is not exactly unreal, but it is merely surface froth, an ineffectual extra. Our thinking (said Huxley) is like the steam-whistle that is let off when the engine starts, it makes a lot of noise and may seem to drive the train, but the real cause of locomotion lies in the boiler (here again, technological imagery makes its special contribution). The body does what it was going to do anyway, and the mind merely paints the scenery for this process, scenery which somehow persuades the owner that he is in charge. Or, as B. F. Skinner put it,

> The punishment of sexual behaviour changes sexual *behaviour*, and any feelings which may arise are at best by-products ... We do feel certain states of our bodies associated with behaviour, but ... they are by-products and not to be mistaken for causes ... [4]

I can't here go into the fascinating confusions embodied in epiphenome-nalism. (I have discussed them in Chapter 10 of my book *Science and Poetry*.) One interesting question is, of course, how bodies such as Huxley's or Skinner's managed to be so clever as to do all that theorizing if their minds really did not give them any help? Another – which has been recently stressed – is how consciousness could have evolved at all if it really had no kind of effect in the world. Indeed, the idea of anything occurring without having effects is an extremely strange one. Epiphenomenalism is, in fact, one more rather desperate distortion produced by Descartes's violent separation of mind from body. Once these two are seen as totally distinct kinds of item, unable to affect each other, it is simply not possible to connect them properly again. So reducers repeatedly try to get rid of one party or the other, with results that are never really intelligible.

What is needed has to be something more like a double-aspect account, in which *we do not talk of two different kinds of stuff at all, but of two complementary points of view*: the inner and the outer, subjective and objective. Human beings are highly complex wholes, about which we really don't know very much. We get the partial knowledge that we do have of them in two ways: from the outside and the inside. In general, neither of these ways of knowing has any fixed precedence over the other. They are both useful for different purposes, just as, for instance, sight and touch are useful in different ways for our knowledge of the external world. And, as we mentioned earlier, there are some situations, such as delight, pain, grief, and the like, where the subjective angle is central. Thomas Nagel, in his book *The View from Nowhere*, has proposed that relating these view-points properly is a central philosophical problem, one that has been distorted repeatedly by various kinds of dualism. He writes:

> I want to describe a way of looking at the world and living in it that is *suitable for complex beings without a naturally unified stand-point*. It is based on a deliberate effort to juxtapose the internal and external or subjective and objective views at full strength, in order to achieve unification when it is possible, and to recognize clearly when it is not. Instead of a unified world view, we get the interplay of these two uneasily related types of conception, and the essentially incompletable effort to reconcile them.[5]

MORAL CONSIDERATIONS

It is important to notice that a decision to emphasise either the subjective or the objective angle in our thought has serious consequences. We cannot simply toss up and choose at random. On some moral issues there is serious reason for giving precedence to one of these angles. In our tradition, a central motive for materialist reduction has been moral indignation against the Church. Most of the great philosophical reducers have been violently anti-clerical, often with excellent reason. Hobbes's central concern was to discredit the horrible seventeenth-century wars of religion. Hume's was to attack repressive Christian morality, especially the tyranny of the eighteenth-century Calvinistic Scottish Church. Nietzsche's was to puncture the complacent sentimentality of his Lutheran upbringing. And so on.

Now atheism and anti-clericalism do not actually require materialism. Atheistic idealism like Hume's is a perfectly possible option and it may be a more coherent one. At the end of the nineteenth century many serious sceptics thought it the clearer choice. (Russell's lifelong ambivalence is quite interesting here.) At present, however, materialism strikes most atheists as a more straightforward path, and it can, of course, more easily tap the prestige of physical science.

Both reductive materialism and reductive idealism have converged to suggest that reductivism is primarily a moral campaign against Christianity. This is a dangerous mistake. Obsession with the churches has distracted attention from reduction employed against notions of human individuality, which is now a much more serious threat. It has also made moral problems look far simpler than they actually are. Indeed, some hopeful humanist reducers still tend to imply that, once Christian structures are cleared away, life in general will be quite all right and philosophy will present no further problems.

In their own times, these anti-clerical reductive campaigns have often been useful. But circumstances change. New menaces, worse than the one that obsesses us, are always appearing, so that what looked like a universal cure for vice and folly becomes simply irrelevant. In politics, twentieth-century atheistical states are not an encouraging omen for the simple secularistic approach to reform. It turns out that the evils that have infested religion are not confined to it, but are ones that can accompany any successful human institution. Nor is it even clear that religion itself is something that the human race either can or should be cured of.

This kind of secularist motive for reductivism is, then, something of limited value today, something that needs more criticism than it often gets. But there are other motives for it, much less noticed, that are really dangerous: primarily, those concerned with the power-relations between the reducing scientists and the reduced people who are their subject-matter, such as the psychiatric patients just mentioned. When the question is about how a particular person is to be treated, then that person's own viewpoint on the matter has a quite peculiar importance. Psychological theories, such as behaviourism, which exclusively exalt the objective standpoint cannot possibly do justice to that importance. Indeed, they exist to bypass it.

Behaviourism was seen as admirably scientific and austere just because it was reductive. Its reductiveness was believed to make it scientifically impartial. Behaviourists dismissed attention to the subjective angle as an irrelevant extravagance, a sentimental luxury that ought to be renounced in the name of science. But this high opinion of its scientific status was not itself a piece of science. It was a propaganda exercise on behalf of a special moral position. The position itself was never defended in the appropriate moral terms, but always as being in some mysterious sense 'scientific'. The preference for the outside angle remains a dangerous piece of dogma, which has most unfortunately outlasted the official demise of behaviourism.

I suggested earlier that, when we encounter claims to intellectual austerity, such as this one, we should always look for the pay-off. Here, that is not hard to find. It is both convenient and flattering for psychologists to regard other people as mechanisms and themselves as the freely-acting engineers appointed to examine and repair them. To ignore the subject's own views about his or her state naturally makes the work much simpler. It also greatly increases the practitioner's power. No doubt psychologists are often sincere in claiming to act for the good of their 'subjects' – a word with interesting associations. But the principles underlying this approach simply leave no room for the subjects' own view about what their own good might consist in. Those principles legitimise manipulation unconditionally. No doubt that is one reason why this way of doing psychology is no longer quite so widely favoured as it once was.

PROBLEMS OF THE SOUL

There is, however, a different and more serious difficulty about reductive psychological projects such as that of behaviourism. They cannot easily be combined with that other favourite project of the later Enlightenment: atheism.

The problem is this. If indeed it is true that there are no spiritual forces acting on human beings from the outside – if our spiritual experiences are entirely generated from within – then what goes on in our spiritual life is unavoidably psychological business. It can no longer be handed over to theology. A parsimonious, God-free metaphysic is simply not compatible with a miserly psychology. Instead, it demands a wide, hospitable, sensitive enquiry into the inner life, to take up a mass of business that has now become empirical rather than metaphysical.

Bernard Williams puts this point well. Discussing religious morality, he writes,

> Granted that its transcendental claim is false, human beings must have dreamed it, and we need an understanding of why this was the content of their dream. (Humanism – in the contemporary

sense of a secularist and anti-religious movement – seems seldom
to have faced fully a very immediate consequence of its own views;
that this terrible thing, religion, is a *human* creation).[6]

And since this aspect of human life – which of course is by no means
confined to areas traditionally claimed by the religions – has a great deal
of influence on behaviour, psychologists ought to take its phenomena seriously. Yet this cannot possibly be done without profound attention to
reports of subjective experience.

Freud saw this difficulty and dealt with it briskly in his book *The Future
of an Illusion*. He dismissed this whole aspect of life as pathological, ruling
that God was simply a by-product of the Oedipus complex, exploited by
wily priests. But even the wiliest of priests cannot exploit successfully without
suitable material to work on. And, as Jung pointed out, even within the
Judaeo-Christian tradition the spiritual life involves a great deal more than
father-imagery. This kind of experience is not confined to any official religion, though of course official religions outside the western tradition explore
provinces of it that are unfamiliar here. Nor can it plausibly be reduced
to illicit wish-fulfilment for an afterlife. Greek religion offered little hope
of an afterlife and Judaism for a long time actively denied it. Spiritual experience is simply an aspect of normal experience, and even elements in it
that actually are neurotic still belong to the subject-matter of psychology.
It necessarily uses symbols just as other imaginative activity does, and those
symbols deserve just as much attention.

This was why Jung proposed that psychology should enlarge itself to deal
adequately with these wider territories. Since his day, however, academic
psychologists have systematically resisted such suggestions, seeking instead
to contract their discipline so as to look more like a physical science. (For
instance, the normal training of psychiatrists today includes no reference
to spiritual problems, though these are often of the greatest interest to
their patients.) In a variety of ways, of which behaviourism was only the
most dramatic, psychologists have pursued a reductive ideal of rationality,
striving to cut their vast subject-matter down to size. We will look at some
of the difficulties this campaign has posed in the next few chapters.

7

MOTIVES, MATERIALISM
AND MEGALOMANIA

———•◆•———

PSYCHOLOGICAL REDUCTION

Besides the reduction of mind to matter, psychological reducers have
another possibility open to them, which can prove even more gratifying.
Besides reducing other people's motives to mechanical movements, they
can also reduce them to other, underlying, motives which are cruder than
those usually admitted. Now the relation between these two enterprises is
not clear. If the physicalist reduction works, it is not obvious how the
purely psychological one can find room to work as well, or why it is needed.
If (for instance) Huxley and Skinner are right to say that the chapters in
this book have just written themselves as a result of a blind movement of
particles – that the author's thoughts didn't affect the process at all – it
is rather hard to see how they have also (actually) been produced by unbridled self-aggrandisement and dynastic ambition.

Both methods, however, have been practised together since the dawn of
modern reduction, without any clear notice of how they should be related.
Hobbes constantly uses both. He insists equally that life itself is but motion
and that, for instance, 'No man giveth, but with intention of Good to
himself, because Gift is voluntary, and of all Voluntary acts, the Object is
to every man his own Good.'[1] Freud also uses both methods, though he
prefers the psychological one: 'Parental love, which is so moving and at
bottom so childish, is nothing but the parents' narcissism born again.'[2]

Now I don't at all want to say that this kind of diagnosis of underlying
motives is always wrong or unjustified. On the contrary, I think it is often
called for, and it can be practised responsibly to great profit. But I do
want to point out the enormous inducements there are to practise it indis-
criminately and wildly instead. The pleasure of showing other people up
as moral frauds, combined with the intellectual satisfaction of extending
one's guiding theory more and more widely, is a pay-off that theorists find
it very hard to resist.

Thus even straightforward psychological reduction of motives is a tricky business, by no means always austere and well guided. But what is far worse is a bastard mixture of this with the physicalist reduction, losing all the advantages of both. This muddle is endemic among sociobiologists. Thus David Barash, updating Freud:

> Parental love itself is but an evolutionary strategy whereby genes replicate themselves . . . We will analyse parental behaviours, the underlying selfishness of our behaviour to others, even our own children.[3]

And E. O. Wilson:

> Human behaviour – like the deepest capacities for emotional response which drive and guide it – is the circuitous technique by which human genetic material has been and will be kept intact. Morality has no other demonstrable ultimate function.[4]
>
> The evolutionary theory of human altruism is greatly complicated by the ultimately self-serving quality of most forms of that altruism. No sustained form of human altruism is explicitly and totally self-annihilating. Lives of the most towering heroism are paid out in the expectation of great reward, not the least of which is a belief in personal immortality.
>
> Compassion is selective and often self-serving . . . it conforms to the best interests of self, family and allies of the moment.[5]

These passages are bizarre because, officially, sociobiology is not supposed to have any views about motives at all. Its business is only with behaviour, with the statistical probability that certain types of action will affect the future distribution of an agent's genes. Disastrously, however, sociobiologists have chosen to describe this harmless topic in the language of motive, using words like 'selfishness', 'spite' and 'altruism' as technical terms for various distributive tendencies. (Both this passage from Barash and the one from Dawkins quoted earlier, by the way, occur in the first pages of their books, *before* the special, technical definition of selfishness has been explained.)

Because this language of motive is so natural and habitual in its ordinary sense, these authors constantly slip into mixing the two systems and thus supposing that they have radically explained human psychology. Dreams of still wider academic empire, involving the reductive conquest of all other studies, naturally follow:

> It may not be too much to say that sociology and the other social sciences, as well as the humanities, are the last branches of biology waiting to be included in the Modern Synthesis. One of the

44

functions of Sociobiology, [just *one*] then, is to reformulate the foundations of the social sciences in a way that draws these subjects into the Modern Synthesis.

Stress will be evaluated in terms of the neurophysiological perturbations and their relaxation times. Cognition will be translated into circuitry. Learning and creativeness will be defined as the alteration of specific portions of the cognitive machinery regulated by input from the emotive centres. Having cannibalized psychology, the new neurobiology will yield an enduring set of first principles for sociology.[6]

None of this would have looked plausible if a hasty combination of physicalist and psychological reductions had not given these writers the impression that they had finally summed up human psychology. If passages like these don't constitute megalomania, I don't know what does. About them, I rest my case.

The other region of fantasy that seems relevant here is the range of predictions now being made, not just by ordinary prophets but by eminent scientists, about an eventual human conquest of the entire universe. Essentially, these predictions are Lamarckian, extrapolating what is seen as a rising graph of evolution that will exalt the human race to the skies, giving it an increasingly glorious, and perhaps unending, future. These predictions postulate highly successful space travel and an even more successful transfer of human consciousness (whatever that is) to machines. They have no support from current Darwinian biology, which flatly rejects the Lamarckian upward graph. Instead they rest on highly abstract arguments drawn from cosmology, from dubious probability theory, and from certain areas of artificial intelligence.

The prophecies were first made half a century back by J. B. S. Haldane and J. D. Bernal, two very distinguished and imaginative scientists who were devout dialectical materialists. Marxism had accustomed both of them to debunking everyday concepts by sternly reductive rhetoric, and also to using the promises of a remote and splendid future in order to justify ignoring the crimes and miseries of the present. These two unlucky habits are surely what betrayed them into their compensatory dreams of a distant future. Bernal's little book has been admiringly quoted by several modern proponents of this compensatory myth.[7] It combines strongly the two elements I have been noting: harsh, austere contempt for ordinary ways of thinking, and unbridled indulgence in power-fantasies. In particular, Bernal shows an extraordinary, paranoid revulsion from the human body:

Modern mechanical and modern biochemical discoveries have rendered both the skeletal and metabolic functions of the body to a great extent useless . . . Viewed from the standpoint of the mental

activity by which he (man) increasingly lives, it is a highly ineffi-
cient way of keeping his mind working. In a civilised worker, the
limbs are mere parasites, demanding nine-tenths of the energy of
the food and even a kind of blackmail in the exercise they need
in order to prevent disease, while the body organs wear themselves
out in supplying their requirements . . . Sooner or later the useless
parts of the body must be given more modern functions or
dispensed with altogether.[8]

Is that austere enough for us? We can't take time here to examine the
modern versions of this story. I have quoted Bernal because his forceful
style shows so clearly the strange ambivalences of reductive rhetoric. His
chilling, deadpan tone crushes diffident readers into accepting his openly
ludicrous visions as if they were sober, practical proposals. This passage,
along with the one quoted earlier, may serve to point out what I chiefly
want to say: namely that, though reduction is often a useful tool, not all
reductions are either useful or sensible.

8

WHAT ACTION IS

———— •◆• ————

INSIDE AND OUTSIDE VIEWS

Conceptual monoculture cannot work because, in almost all our thought, we are dealing with subject-matters that we need to consider from more than one aspect. That is why we constantly face the difficulty that I have compared to the problem of relating two different maps of the same country or two windows in the aquarium.

This problem can arise in many different contexts, wherever two different languages are used to describe the same phenomenon. In practical terms, it crops up whenever different agencies (such as the police and the proba-tion service) have to tackle a single problem (for instance, juvenile crime or child-abuse). And in theoretical terms it can arise between different branches of the various sciences wherever they share a topic. But there is one kind of question on which at present all of us – not only specialists – are in constant trouble about it, and that is our understanding of the nature of our own actions and the actions of those around us.

Here our current world views present us with an unnerving double-vision as we try to use two different approaches. Ought we to be explaining those actions in terms provided by the physical sciences, or are we still allowed to describe them in terms that make some kind of sense to the actors them-selves? Can it be legitimate, in a world where physical science is deeply respected and seems to claim omnicompetence, to go on construing human action in the non-scientific terms that allow us to understand them from the inside?

ACTIVE VERSUS PASSIVE

The question is: do we ever really act? When we say that we have *acted* delib-erately, rather than just drifting or being driven, we mean that we have done

47

something on purpose. And when we do that, our actions can be explained – often successfully – by reference to our conscious thinking, especially to our purposes.

It is sometimes suggested, however, that this kind of explanation by purpose is unreal, it is just an illusion. The true cause of our action is always a physical event, usually (of course) an event that we ourselves never even hear of. Those apparently successful explanations by purpose are just mistakes.

We ourselves are (then) never really active agents at all. We are always passive, always *being driven – like people hypnotised or possessed by an alien force*. Indeed, this metaphor of driving was the one that Richard Dawkins used when he wrote, in the first paragraph of the preface to *The Selfish Gene*, 'we are survival machines, robot *vehicles* blindly programmed to preserve the selfish molecules known as genes'. Cars don't have their own purposes. They need someone else to drive them.

Dawkins's language seems to imply, somewhat mysteriously, that the gene itself *is* a real agent, a kind of active hypnotist doing the driving. (It's not clear quite what he means by this. Once the concept of activity – of agency – is removed from its normal use, it should surely vanish altogether. There is then no longer any use for the contrast between active and passive at all.) But the idea certainly is that the human being that we take ourselves to be is passive, not in charge, not affecting events by its thought. Rather more persuasively, Colin Blakemore and other contemporary writers have suggested a similar arrangement in which agency is transferred, not to the genes but to the brain. Blakemore puts it like this:

> The human brain is a machine which *alone* accounts for all our actions, our most private thoughts, our beliefs. It creates the state of consciousness and the sense of self. It makes the mind. . . . To choose a spouse, a job, a religious creed – or even to choose to rob a bank – is the peak of a causal chain that runs back to the origin of life and down to the nature of atoms and molecules. . . . We feel ourselves, usually, to be in control of our actions, but that feeling is itself a product of our brain, whose machinery has been designed, on the basis of its functional utility, by means of natural selection. . . . All our actions are products of the activity of our brains. It seems to me to make no sense (in scientific terms) to try to distinguish sharply between acts that result from conscious attention and those that result from our reflexes or are caused by disease or damage to the brain.[1]

Here it is the brain that seems to be personalised and credited as a distinct agent. The message is that we should no longer say that *we* 'use our brains' or think *with* our brains, just as we say that we see with our eyes and walk with our legs. We should no longer consider the brain as one organ among others. Instead, we are now to consider *ourselves* as beings who are separate from it and are driven by it, as if it were a kind of hypnotist. This third-person agent is to displace the first person altogether from effective control of decision-making.

This is not just a slight verbal change. It would crucially affect social life because, normally, the distinction between deliberate activity and mere passive drifting is of the first importance to us. We need to know whether the people we deal with are in full charge of their actions or are in some way passive to outside forces – whether, for instance, they are drunk or psychotic or have just been blackmailed or hypnotised. We have to deal with them as conscious, responsible agents whose thoughts direct their actions, not as mere whirring lumps of matter.

Our notion of responsibility centres on our understanding of people's purposes. And responsibility is not just a legal matter. It covers a far wider area of life than mere blame and punishment. It covers the whole ownership of actions, the notions that we form of people's characters, the grounds of our entire social attitude to them. In considering these things, we constantly concentrate on what we believe them to be thinking.

THE QUEST FOR SIMPLICITY

Since this centrality of the first-person point of view is a matter of common experience, theorists would obviously not have tried to eliminate such a crucial tool of thought if they hadn't thought they had a good reason for it. The reason that moves them is, pretty clearly, *a particular notion of what explanation is* – a conviction that all explanation must be causal and that the only legitimate form of causal reasoning is one that cannot be extended to cover purpose.

As we have seen, that form is the simple seventeenth-century model of causation, attributing all real causation to collisions between the ultimate solid particles studied by physics. Other sciences, which traced other kinds of connection, were only speculating at a superficial level. They dealt in appearances and could always be mistaken. Physics alone could plunge down to the rock of reality. (The metaphor of *surface* and *depth, shallowness* and *solidity* is essential to the model's seduction).

MANY QUESTIONS, MANY ANSWERS

As we have seen, since that time it has become clear that we don't need that kind of metaphysical simplicity. We no longer have those handy ultimate solid particles, with their single simple habit of colliding. Physics has become more complicated, which is why physicists themselves are now much less devoted to the old sweeping model than many biologists and social scientists are.

The deeper reason for the change is, however, that *we now have a much more realistic conception of what explanation itself involves*. We have begun to understand that the real world actually is complicated, and particularly that the people in it are so. Because they are complex, we need to ask many kinds of question about them, not just one. To answer them, we need to use many different ways of thinking, and this is why we need to use many different disciplines. They are tools adapted to resolve distinct problems, not rival monarchs competing for a single throne. In fact, this isn't a monarchy at all, but a republic. There is space for all of them. We can't reduce them to a single fundamental science and we don't need to. The relation between them is not linear but convergent.

THE VANISHING SOUL

We badly need to be clear about this point today because the stop-gap device which used to obscure the need for it is vanishing. When Descartes first introduced this model, it notoriously had another component who was supposed to take care of the first-person viewpoint: the immortal soul, the seat of consciousness. That soul was still an accepted part of the model in Newton's day. But it has always been an unsatisfactory device. It was too simple to deal with the manifold functions of consciousness, and too disconnected from the physical mechanisms to be capable of driving them. So it was gradually sidelined.

I suspect that it is this kind of soul that Blakemore and his colleagues are attacking. Quite rightly, they insist that a brain doesn't need this extra, disembodied entity to drive it. Brains work as they do because they are parts of living bodies. But then, our ordinary notion of the active self isn't the notion of such a disembodied soul either. It's a notion of the whole person – not divided into separate body and mind – of whom the brain is just one working part.

The disembodied soul was not helpful and we do not now invoke it. *But without it, the rest of the seventeenth-century pattern doesn't really make sense*. The Machine that was tailored to fit the Ghost cannot work on its own. We need a new model that does justice to the many different kinds of question that we ask and the ways in which they all converge.

EXPLAINING THE THINKER

Consider somebody who is working on a really hard problem. It might be Darwin or Einstein or Jane Austen or Hildegarde of Bingen or Napoleon or Boudicca planning a campaign; it might be the chairperson of the Mafia organising a heist, it might be someone busy on an article for the *Journal of Consciousness Studies* or working on any of the difficult choices that Blakemore has listed. The details of the problem don't matter. What matters is that it is a hard one, hard enough to need careful attention, thus too hard to be solved off-stage by our old friend the Unconscious – and that it is something on which it will eventually be necessary to act, so that our question about the nature of action will finally be relevant. On ordinary assumptions, what is decided here will determine later action and will thus directly affect the outside world. If Napoleon decides this afternoon to invade Russia, then Russia is what he will invade, not (for instance) Andorra or the Outer Hebrides. This is surely correct.

As this person sits and thinks, we can imagine the converging, but not necessarily competing, lines of explanation as raying out from him or her on all sides. These lines don't represent forces charging in to 'drive' the thinker like a passive vehicle. Instead, they are lines of sight for the observer – viewpoints – angles from which we can look at a most complex process. They are positions that we might take up if we – as outside observers – want to understand his or her thinking.

If we are taking that thinking seriously, the first thing that we shall try to do is to grasp his own point of view on the problem that confronts him. We try to follow his reasoning as he himself understands it. If it seems satisfactory, we may simply accept it as our own. It is only if it does not that we will see reason to move to one of the other points of view, so as to find out what else is needed.

In the crudest case, if the ideas involved seem really crazy, we may wonder whether the thinker is seriously disturbed, perhaps ill. We may then look at the medical angle; might there be a brain tumour? We can also, if we see the need, ask questions about his background, about a wide range of factors that may have influenced him. But this kind of supplementation is not normally appropriate unless we think that the views themselves do not fully make sense. Before resorting to it, we bring in various conceptual schemes simply to fill in gaps that we find in his thought, to extend it and to see whether we can understand it better – conceptual schemes that bear on the subject-matter he is dealing with, rather than on his own peculiarities.

Thus, in Napoleon's case, economic historians might find themselves at odds with political and military ones because they use different abstractions to concentrate on different aspects of his problem. They would then use all manner of economic theories. In a case like Darwin's, there is huge scope for these conflicts because his ideas are so wide-ranging that they raise questions for a whole gamut of disciplines, offering a corresponding number of opportunities for clashes. For instance, in his own day his biological suggestions conflicted with important doctrines of physics, since (as Lord Kelvin pointed out) before the discovery of nuclear reaction it did not seem possible that an earth as old as the one that Darwin envisaged could possibly have kept its heat long enough to allow the development of life.

The point of my analogy with the relation between different maps is to draw attention to just this kind of clash between conceptual schemes. Though there is indeed only one world, the various disciplines necessarily describe it differently by abstracting different patterns from it. While they ignore each other, they can commit themselves to views that turn out to conflict. When this is noticed, both parties need to work to make their conclusions somehow compatible. In Darwin's case it was physics that was wrong, but very often changes are needed on both sides. Making those changes does not, however mean getting rid of the difference between their methods so that they end up with a single pattern. Nor does it mean that one discipline will eliminate the other. They continue to present different pictures, like the different maps of the world, but now with a better understanding of how they should be related.

'FUNDAMENTAL'?

In the case of our worried thinker, then, no one of the enquiries that we can make is going to give us a 'complete explanation' of the thought. Indeed, it is not clear what a complete explanation would be, since there are an infinite number of questions that might be asked about it. Each enquiry necessarily shows only one aspect of what is going on. If we want a fuller view of what's happening, we will have to put a number of them together.

Is there any reason to expect that one of these kinds of explanation should be more fundamental than the rest? Is any such hierarchy necessary? In particular, is there any reason, when we talk about action, to prioritise facts about the brain over other explanatory facts?

It is not clear why such a hierarchy should be needed. When we pick out one explanation as being 'fundamental', we normally mean that it is specially relevant to the particular enquiry that we want to make. If indeed we are neurologists and our enquiry is about whether (for instance) Einstein's brain was really different from other people's, then we might reasonably call the details of that brain fundamental. But for most other purposes we simply take it for granted that a well-functioning brain is needed as a background condition of all thought – as is also the rest of the nervous system and the other organs – and we assume that, so long as it functions properly, the details of its working do not matter.

This approach does not reflect any underestimation of neurology. It is an assumption that we have to make because thought does not remain a private matter. It leads to speech and to other action in the world, and these must be intelligible to other people besides its originator. The ideas that a thinker comes up with must be ones that these others can understand too, not ones that would only fit a brain that is physically like his own. Original thinkers, in explaining their ideas to others, do not proceed by sending out diagrams of their own brain-states, but by speech and actions in the public world. Thus, no amount of information about Einstein's brain would enable a neurologist who was ignorant of physics to learn anything from that brain about relativity theory.

WHY PLURALISM IS NEEDED

We have been considering the case for cognitive pluralism: for the view that all explanation, and particularly the explanation of human action, quite properly uses many non-competing but convergent methods, because it involves answering questions that arise from different backgrounds, and that this is why explanation cannot be reduced to a single fundamental method.

Let us now return to Colin Blakemore's alternative formulation and notice the difficulties raised by its more reductive approach, difficulties that I think show why something pluralistic is needed. The trouble here begins with the word 'alone' in his first sentence ('The human brain is a machine that alone accounts for all our actions'). Certainly a suitable brain is needed as one causal factor in all human action. But how could it be considered as the only one?

As just noticed, if we want to account for somebody's action – that is, to explain it – the first thing that we need to know about will be their own point of view on the facts that they face, their beliefs about it, their skills and conceptual schemes, their motives, their background, and of course the subject-matter that they are trying to deal with. Without understanding the problems that face Napoleon, we can get no handle on his thinking. After that, we shall also need to know more about the options open to him, which means examining the whole social and physical life around him.

The 'causal chain that runs back to the origin of all life and down to the nature of atoms and molecules' that Blakemore mentions is not really just one chain passing through this agent's brain. It is a network that runs crossways through every aspect of his life and much of the surrounding world. If, when we have investigated it, we still find his or her action unintelligible, we may then start to enquire about the state of the agent's body, including the brain, to see whether some illness is distorting his judgment. But normally, the explanation of actions goes on successfully without any investigation of brain-states at all.

It should be noted that the neurological kind of reduction is not the only one available here. It would be just as possible (and just as misleading) to say that the realm of background thought in the world determines the whole thing. For instance, it could be argued that Einstein's next move was fully determined by the state of physics in his day: by the totality of moves made by previous physicists, which left only one path open. That intellectual realm would then provide its true explanation. This is the kind of suggestion that is put forward by reductivists of a different stripe, those who want to interpret all phenomena in terms of patterns of information. And of course, with hindsight, explanations of this sort are often useful. But they too obviously depend on illicit abstraction, on picking out a single favoured pattern as sovereign and neglecting the rest of the world.

What, then, does this mysterious word 'alone' mean? It is my impression that it is really intended to negate only one other possible cause, namely, conscious thought, first-person activity, which is ruled out as a causal factor in producing action because it is believed to involve a detached Cartesian soul.

This seems clear when Blakemore writes, 'It seems to me to make no sense (in scientific terms) to try to distinguish sharply between acts that result from conscious intention and those that are pure reflexes or are caused by disease or damage to the brain.'

It is surely rather strange to dismiss this distinction as unscientific, since it is one that any consultant neurologist who was examining a patient would undoubtedly think central, and indeed one that is needed in many other areas of medicine. Certainly the distinction is not always *sharp*. There are areas of overlap, cases where more than one kind of cause is involved. But to suggest that it does not arise at all – that there are no clearly distinguishable 'acts that result from conscious intention' – is to suggest that, for all we know, the writing of *The Origin of Species* may not have been a consciously intended act of this kind but just a series of inadvertent spasms, comparable to a reflex. And this is really not convincing.

SUBJECTIVITY IS AN OBJECTIVE FACT

The philosophical conclusion that emerges here is that conscious thought has a legitimate and essential place among the causal factors that work in the world. It is not a spooky extra but a natural process. In a species such as ours, it is an integral part of normal behaviour. Descartes was wrong to export it to a metaphysical ghetto. Our inner experience is as real as stones or electrons and as ordinary an activity for a social mammal as digestion or the circulation of the blood. The capacity to have this conscious experience, and to use it effectively in making choices, is one that has evolved in us, and in many other species, just as normally as our capacities to see, hear and walk.

As already mentioned, we need to notice how unlikely it is that such a capacity could have evolved – as Blakemore suggests – merely as an idle epiphenomenon, surface froth, a shadow-show with no effect in the real world. Natural selection can only work on real consequences. It can only promote things that have effects. There is no way in which it could have got a grip on such an ineffectual shadow – could have made conscious thought a normal and central accomplishment in the species, which it certainly now is – if it had been idle. The reason why this power of practical thinking has been able to evolve is that it is actually a useful way of producing well-judged action.

This conclusion does not, then, involve any extravagant metaphysics. When we say that someone acts freely, deliberately and responsibly, this does *not* mean that a separate soul in him does so, cut off from the influences around it. It simply means that he or she does this action as a whole person, attending to it and being well aware of what he is doing – not (for instance) absent-mindedly or madly or under some outside pressure such as hypnosis. Of course this agent needs to have a brain – and no doubt some genes – in good order to make this choice. But it is the whole person who uses that brain, just as he uses his legs to walk with and his eyes and his hand in writing.

9

TIDYING THE INNER SCENE
Why Memes?

————·•·————

THOUGHT IS NOT GRANULAR

We have been considering the aims and workings of reductivism in general. In doing this, we have come across a number of ways in which reductions – originally devised for the physical world – have been applied to the world of thought and feeling, and we have seen certain difficulties that tend to haunt this enterprise. It is time now to look at a current project of this kind which is offered as being particularly successful and scientific.

In considering such schemes we naturally ask, what does it mean to understand the workings of human thought, or of human culture? What kind of understanding do we need here? Is it the kind that might be achieved by atomising thought, by analysing it into its ultimate particles and then connecting them up again? Or is it, rather, the kind of understanding that we normally mean when we speak of understanding an attitude, a suggestion, or a policy, or a word by placing it in a context that makes it intelligible – by supplying an appropriate background and entering into what it means for those who hold it?

In general, of course, these two patterns are not alternatives. Normally, we use both together as complementary aspects of understanding. Both in science and in everyday life, we reach equally readily for either tool, either method as the case requires. Difficulties can arise equally about the inner structure of items and about their contexts, and we count whatever resolves each particular difficulty as an *understanding* or an *explanation*.

Of late, however, it has been strongly suggested that, in studying thought, the atomising approach is the only truly scientific one and should take precedence over other methods. Accordingly, Richard Dawkins has suggested that the scientific approach to culture is to split it into standard units called *memes* which are in some ways parallel to its atoms, in others to its genes, and to study their interactions.[1]

That proposal is entirely understandable in view of the success of these methods in physical science. It is always natural to hope that a method that works in one area will help us in another. All the same, it is not obvious how this line of thought can help us in this quite different situation. The trouble is that thought and culture are not the sort of thing that can have distinct units. They do not have a granular structure for the same reason that ocean currents do not have one – namely, because they are not stuffs but patterns.

There is nothing mystical or superstitious about this. Sea water is indeed a stuff or substance with units. It can be divided – not, indeed, into the hard indivisible little grains that Renaissance physicists expected, but still into distinct, lasting molecules and atoms. But, by contrast, the currents themselves are *patterns of movement* – ways in which the water flows – and they form part of a wider system of such patterns, which surrounds them. To understand the currents one must first investigate these wider patterns.

Of course the microstructure of the water itself can sometimes be relevant here, but usually it is just a standing background condition. The microscope is not the first tool that scientists reach for when they want to understand the distribution of sewage in the oceans or, even more obviously, when they are analysing patterns of traffic-flow. The first movement of understanding in such cases has to be outward, to grasp what is happening in the context. But thought and culture too are moving and developing patterns in human behaviour, ways in which people think, feel, and act. They are not entities distinct from those people. Since such patterns are not composed of distinct and lasting units at all, it is not much use trying to understand them by tracing reproductive interactions among those units.

Incidentally, the name 'meme' itself is of some interest. Dawkins explains that he abbreviated it from *mimeme*, meaning a unit of imitation, and both words are evidently modelled on *phoneme*, which is a term invented by linguists early in the twentieth century to describe a unit of sound. 'Phoneme' however quickly turned out to be the name of a problem rather than of a fixed ultimate unit. As the Professor of General Linguistics at the University of Edinburgh put it in 1970,

> Most linguists, until recently at least, have looked upon the *phoneme* as one of the basic units of language. But they have not all defined phonemes in the same way (and have frequently arrived at conflicting analyses of the same data). Some linguists have described phonemes in purely 'physical' terms; others have preferred a psychological definition. Some have argued that grammatical considerations are irrelevant in phonological analysis; others have maintained that they are essential. These are among the issues that have divided the various schools of phonology in recent years . . . [2]

This problem has certainly not got any simpler since that time. In short, the sound of speech as we hear it turns out not to be granular, not to have definite units. It is a continuum which can be divided up in various ways for various purposes. The original hope of atomising it seems to have flowed from a general confidence in atomising which was rather prevalent at that epoch. One might compare Loeb's notorious concept of *tropisms* as an ultimate unit that would explain all motion in plants and animals.[3] In most fields this approach has not turned out to be useful and there seems no clear reason to revive it today.

TROUBLE WITH RESIDUAL DUALISM

The meme project has, however, been quite widely accepted because it was exactly what our tradition was waiting for. For two centuries, admirers of the physical sciences – a category that includes most of us – had wanted somehow to extend scientific methods over the whole field of thought and culture. They wanted it for the good reason that they wanted to reunify our thinking, to heal the breach in our world view made by Descartes's division between mind and matter, between the physical sciences and humanistic ways of thinking.

The methods used have not, however, gone half deep enough. What was needed was genuinely to abandon the dualistic approach, to stop considering a human being as two things jammed together and to treat it as a whole that can properly be examined from many different aspects. Instead of doing this, theorists have tended still to assume that they were dealing with two separate, parallel kinds of stuff or substance, namely, mind and matter. This residual dualism makes it seem that – if we don't just write the mind off altogether – we can unify the two by simply extending the methods that we have used so successfully on matter to the parallel case of the other stuff, mind.

Thus it offers a way to fulfil Auguste Comte's positivist programme of moving human thought steadily away from religion through metaphysics until it consists of science alone. But that programme is not really an intelligible one. It only looks plausible because of an ambiguity on the idea of *science*. As a helpful historian puts it,

> The [French] Philosophes believed that enlightenment had been vouchsafed to them by the discoveries of the seventeenth century, particularly those of Newton, which had illuminated the nature of the physical universe, and those of Locke, which had done the same for the mind. ... Their ultimate purpose was to spread the belief that human behaviour, like the material universe, was amenable to scientific investigation, and that society and government should be studied scientifically in the interests of human happiness.[4]

But at that time the meaning of 'studying things scientifically' was much wider than it is today, as is plain at once from the bracketing of Newton with Locke. Centrally, the term 'scientific' still had the very general meaning of thinking things out for oneself in a suitable manner rather than relying on tradition or authority. Later, the rising success of the physical sciences gradually biased its meaning towards presenting them as the only model. And the opposition that some Enlightenment prophets proclaimed between science and religion, casting religion as the representative both of tradition and of political oppression, intensified this bias.

Newton's example, too, tended to be used as a justification for any simplification on social subjects, as if the physical sciences always proceeded merely by making things simpler. As we have seen in Chapter 6, David Hume justified his reduction of all human motives to utility in this way. But Newton's greatness did not lie merely in simplifying the scene. It was rooted in the prior work that enabled him to see *which* generalisation to back, which simple system to design. Science progresses just as often by making distinctions as it does by abandoning them.

Hume, then, was being misled by a surface likeness, imitating a superficial form of thought rather than penetrating to its point. But he was not alone in this. Many theorists during the later Enlightenment were fired with the ambition to become Newtons of psychology, of morals or of political thought. They claimed scientific status for a wide range of simplifications pursued from various ideological angles, so that eventually, the excesses of allegedly scientific prophets such as Marx, Freud and Skinner caused serious alarm. This is why, in the mid-twentieth century, serious admirers of science, led by Karl Popper, narrowed the meaning of the term 'science' in a way designed to cover only the physical sciences themselves.

THE HOPE OF STANDARDISATION

This was a natural move, but it raises a difficulty about the status of other kinds of thinking, a problem that has not yet been properly faced. Though Popper's campaign was aimed primarily against ideologists such as Marx and Freud, on the face of things it also disqualifies the social sciences and humanities from counting as fully 'scientific'. And since the term 'scientific' remains a general name for academic excellence, people conclude that these cannot be serious, disciplined ways of thinking about the world. Social scientists and humanists therefore often feel that they ought to make their reasonings *look* as like physical science as possible. This is the demand that memetics satisfies.

But the right way to remedy the Cartesian split is not for one half of the intellectual world to swallow the other. It is to avoid making that split in the first place. A human being is not a loosely joined combination of two radically different elements but a single item – a whole person. We do not, therefore, have to divide the various ways in which we think about that person into two rival camps. These various ways of thinking are like a set of complementary tools on a workbench or a set of remedies to be used for different diseases. Their variety is the variety of our needs. The forms of thought needed for understanding social dilemmas are distinct from those that we need for chemistry and those again from historical thinking, because they answer different kinds of question. They are bound to have different standards of validity.

These kinds of need for thought are actually just as diverse as our physical diseases are. In medicine today, the idea of a universal patent medicine such as was advertised in Victorian times, equally potent to cure colds, smallpox, rheumatism and cancer, would not seem plausible. Nor are supposedly universal tools much welcomed on the workbench. The sort of unity that thought actually needs is not the formal kind that Daniel Dennett tries to impose by inflating Darwinism into a universal system.[5] It is a unity that flows adequately from the fact that we are studying a single world – the one that we live in – and that our thought arises from a single source, namely, our joint attempt to live in that world. The fact that all our ways of thinking deal with that one world unifies our thought sufficiently, just as the science of medicine is sufficiently unified by the fact that all its branches deal with the human body.

10

THE SLEEP OF REASON
PRODUCES MONSTERS

———•◆•———

THE QUEST FOR A UNIVERSAL ACID

Is it possible to provide any stricter, more formal kind of unity than the convergence that results from discussing a single world and a single range of experience? The great rationalist thinkers of the seventeenth century were obsessed by the ambition to drill all thought into a single formal system. Descartes himself, as well as Spinoza and Leibniz, tried inexhaustibly to mend the mind/body gap by building abstract metaphysical systems powered by arguments akin to their favoured models of thought, logic and mathematics. They were answered, however, by empiricists such as Locke and Hume who pointed out how disastrously this project ignores the huge element of contingency that pervades all experience. We are not terms in an abstract calculation but real concrete beings. We do not live in a pure world of necessary connections but in one shaped, over countless ages, by countless events of which we know very little. We deal with this pervasive contingency by ways of thinking – such as historical methods – which provide crucial forms for our understanding of this strange world, but which cannot be reduced to a single form.

Although both rationalists and empiricists tried to claim a monopoly for their own chosen forms of thinking it has become clear, from Kant's time onward, that the tool-bench of thought must allow for a wider variety of methods. The subject-matter is far more radically complex than the seventeenth century supposed. It cannot be drilled to show a single empire. Daniel Dennett, however, persistently tries to dodge this awkward fact by imposing uniformity. He describes what he calls Darwin's 'dangerous idea' – that is, the idea of development by natural selection – as a 'universal acid . . . it eats through just about every traditional concept and leaves in its wake a revolutionised world view, with most of the old land-marks still recognisable, but transformed in fundamental ways'.[1] This is, however, evidently a selective acid, trained to eat only other people's views while leaving his own ambitious project untouched:

Darwin's dangerous idea is reductionism incarnate, promising to unite and explain just about everything in one magnificent vision. Its being the idea of an algorithmic process makes it all the more powerful, since the substrate neutrality it thereby possesses permits us to consider its application to just about anything . . . [including] all the achievements of human culture – language, art, religion, ethics, science itself.[2]

He sees this as a revolutionary move. Yet this attempt to frame a Grand Universal Theory of Everything is markedly old-fashioned. It flows from just the same kind of casual, misplaced confidence that led physicists of the Aristotelian school to extend purposive reasoning beyond the sphere of human conduct, where it worked well, to explain the behaviour of stones, where it did not. Still more damagingly for Dennett's claims, it also resembles closely the vast metaphysical structures that Herbert Spencer built by extrapolating evolutionary ideas to all possible subject-matters, thus producing, as his followers admiringly said, 'the theory of evolution dealing with the universe *as a whole*, from gas to genius'.[3] Darwin, though he remained polite in public, hated 'magnificent visions' of this kind. As he wrote in his *Autobiography*,

I am not conscious of having profited in my work from Spencer's writings. His deductive manner of treating every subject is wholly opposed to my frame of mind. His conclusions never convince me. . . . They partake more of the nature of definitions than of laws of nature.[4]

In short, Darwin understood that large ideas do indeed become dangerous if they are inflated beyond their proper use: dangerous to honesty, to intelligibility, to all the proper purposes of thought. For him the concept of natural selection was strictly and solely a biological one and even in biology he steadily rejected the claim that it was a universal explanation. He re-emphasised this point strongly in the sixth edition of the *Origin*:

As my conclusions have lately been much misrepresented, and it has been stated that I attribute the modification of species exclusively to natural selection, I may be permitted to remark that in the first edition of this work, and subsequently, I placed in a most conspicuous position – namely at the close of the Introduction – the following words: '*I am convinced that natural selection has been the main, but not the exclusive, means of modification*'. This has been of no avail. Great is the power of steady misrepresentation.[5]

THE SEARCH FOR SCIENTIFIC FACADES

Where does this history leave us today? How can we fit the science that is now so important to us into the general pattern of our lives without distorting anything?

Sages find it hard now to imitate the caution of the founders of modern science, who carefully avoided applying physical concepts to mental or social questions. The temptation to expand the empire of science is much stronger now that it is so successful. The social sciences have for some time tried to acquire its coinage by adapting its methods in more or less realistic ways to their subject-matter. But the Popperian narrowing of the concept has redesigned that coinage in a way that usually disqualifies such more realistic methods from counting as real 'science'. Standards are now set that concentrate on form, not on suitability to the subject-matter. This makes it necessary to use methods which closely imitate the forms of physical science. And among those forms, a prime favourite is, of course, atomism.

This, then, is the principle that requires us, if we want to understand culture, somehow to find its units. But is culture the sort of thing that divides up into units? Edward O. Wilson sternly declares that it is. In his book *Consilience*, which seriously tries to mend the culture-gap, he proposes this atomisation as the means of reconciling the humanities and social sciences with science by bringing them into its province. Culture (he says) must be atomisable because atomising is the way in which we naturally think:

> The descent to minutissima, the search for ultimate smallness in entities such as electrons, is a driving impulse of Western natural science. It is a kind of instinct. Human beings are obsessed with building blocks, for ever pulling them apart and putting them back together again. . . . The impulse goes back as far as 400 BC when Leucippus and Democritus speculated, correctly as it turned out, that matter is made of atoms.[6]

The year 400 BC scarcely seems long enough ago to certify an instinct. Granted, however, that people do often break things into units and that this is sometimes useful, is culture a suitable candidate for the treatment? Well, says Wilson, it has to be understood somehow. But *what does it mean to understand it*? What questions are we asking? Wilson reveals his odd stance here by saying that the best way to understand culture would be, not to investigate the thoughts and intentions of the people practising it, but to know how it developed in the course of evolution. That, however, is not really possible because we don't have the evidence. The next best way of understanding 'gene-culture coevolution' must therefore be

63

to search for the basic unit of culture. . . . Such a focus may seem at first contrived and artificial, but it has many worthy precedents. The great success of the natural sciences has been achieved substantially by the reduction of each physical phenomenon to its constituent elements followed by the use of the elements to reconstitute the holistic properties of the phenomenon.[7]

Again, this argument reproduces, in a reverse direction, the same mistake that Aristotelian physics made when it extended explanation by purpose from the human sphere to the sphere of inanimate matter. Stones do not have purposes, but neither do cultures have particles. The example of physics cannot be a reason for imposing its scheme on a quite different kind of subject-matter.

ARE THEY ATOMS OR GENES?

Are there, perhaps, reasons of conceptual convenience forcing us to impose this apparently unsuitable pattern on thought? That must depend on what we are trying to do, and various memologists seem to have different aims. At times, Wilson himself clearly means to keep quite close to the pattern set by the discovery of physical particles. He hopes to find *minutissima*, ultimate units of thought, and to connect them eventually with particular minimal brain-states so as to provide (as he says) a kind of alphabet of a brain-language underlying all thought. This is an almost inconceivably ambitious project, a wild kind of cosmic expansion of Leibniz's quest for a universal language. But it is unmistakably a search for units of *thought*, not for units of culture. As he says, 'I have faith that the unstoppable neuroscientists will . . . in due course . . . capture the physical basis of mental concepts through the mapping of neural activity patterns.'[8]

At other times, however, Wilson forgets this project entirely and describes his particles just as readily as 'units of culture'. And the examples that other memologists give mostly conform to this quite different model. Richard Dawkins, their first begetter, lists as his 'units of cultural transmission' 'tunes, ideas, catch-phrases, clothes-fashions, ways of making pots or of building arches' to which he adds popular songs, stiletto heels, the idea of God and Darwinism – certainly not the kind of things which could figure as Wilsonian ultimate units of thought.[9] Dawkins, however, insists that they are not merely convenient divisions of culture either but fixed, distinct natural units.

> There is something, some essence of Darwinism, which is present in the head of every individual who understands the theory. If this were not so, then almost any statement about two people agreeing

with each other would be meaningless. An 'idea-meme' might be defined as an entity which is capable of being transmitted from one brain to another. . . . *The differences in the way that people represent the theory are then, by definition, not part of the meme.*[10]

Unluckily, however, this isn't how the history of thought works at all. Such fixed essences are not found. Questions about just where the centre of a particular doctrine lies are exactly the ones that constantly divide people who are interested in that doctrine. These people often express strong views on the matter, but in doing so they are taking a moral stand, not detecting a solid cultural atom. Marx notoriously said that he was not a Marxist. As we have seen, Darwin would probably have taken the same line were the question put to him and perhaps Christ might have done the same. Agreement is a much more subtle matter than this formula suggests.

It is clear, however, that by this account memes are still intended as *minutissima*, ultimate divisions, though here they are particles of culture rather than of thought. Daniel Dennett is equally insistent that these units are distinct and lasting, natural divisions not just conventional ones. 'These new replicators are, roughly, ideas . . . the sort of complex ideas that form themselves into distinct memorable units.'[11] Giving a list of examples even more mixed than Dawkins's, in which he includes *deconstructionism*, the *Odyssey* and *wearing clothes*, Dennett comments:

> Intuitively we see these as more or less identifiable cultural units, but we can say something more precise about how we draw the boundaries . . . the units are *the smallest elements that replicate themselves with reliability and fecundity.* We can compare them, in this regard, to genes and their components. A three-nucleotide phrase does not count as a gene for the same reason that you can't copyright a three-note musical phrase.[12]

But the literary conventions that define items like the *Odyssey* are artefacts devised for civic convenience, not fixed natural units. *Wearing clothes* is not any sort of minimum unit but a general term used to cover a vast range of customs. *Deconstructionism* is a loose name covering a group of ideas that stand in some sort of historical relation, a group that certainly has no fixed core. *Darwinism* only looks more plausible because of its unifying reference to Darwin. It is really a very complex group of ideas with no agreed outline. Views about what is central to such groupings vary and are normative, not factual. As dictionary-makers find, they usually cannot be defined by any single nugget of meaning. Again, the *Odyssey* contains many elements that are memorable on their own, such as the stories of the Cyclops, of Scylla and Charybdis, and of the Wandering Rocks. It can hardly be a minimal unit.

What is now the point of the whole proposal? If memes really corre-spond to *genes* of culture they cannot be its units. These are completely different ideas. Considered as genes, they would not be the cultural phenomena themselves but, instead, a set of hidden entities which were their causes. In that case they must indeed be fixed units, unchanging causes of the changing items that appear in the world. But all the exam-ples we are given correspond to phenotypes. They are the apparent items themselves. Moreover, most of the concepts mentioned cannot possibly be treated as unchanging or even as moderately solid. Customs and ways of thinking are organic parts of human life, constantly growing, developing, changing and sometimes decaying like every other living thing. Much of this change, too, is due to our own action, to our deliberately working to change them.

In one of his characteristic sudden spasms of acute critical insight Dennett himself notes this difficulty:

> Minds (or brains) . . . aren't much like photocopying machines at all. On the contrary, instead of just passing on their messages, correcting most of the typos as they go, brains seem to be designed to do just the opposite, to transform, invent, interpolate, censor, and generally mix up the 'input' before yielding any 'output'. . . . We *seldom* pass on a meme unaltered. . . . Moreover, as Stephen Pinker has stressed . . . much of the mutation that happens to memes (how much is not clear) is manifestly *directed* mutation. 'Memes such as the theory of relativity are not the cumulative product of millions of *random* (undirected) mutations of some original idea, but each brain in the chain of production added huge dollops of value to the product in a non-random way.' . . . Moreover, when memes come into contact with each other in a mind, they have a marvel-lous capacity to become adjusted to each other, swiftly changing their phenotypic effects to fit the circumstances.[13]

So what, if anything, does this leave of the parallel with genetics which has quietly replaced that of atoms? How seriously is that parallel now intended? If memes are indeed something parallel to genes, as the last sentence of this quotation certainly implies, if they are hidden causes of culture rather than its units, *what sort of entities are these causes supposed to be*? They are not physical objects. But neither are they thoughts or ideas of the kind that normally play any part in our experience. They seem to be occult causes of those thoughts. How then do they manifest them-selves? What makes us think they are there? It does not help to say that they are bits of information located in the infosphere.[14] Information is not a third kind of stuff. It is not an extra substance added to Cartesian mind and body or designed to supersede them. It is an abstraction from them. Invoking such an extra stuff is as idle as any earlier talk of phlogiston or animal spirits or occult forces. Information is facts about the world, and we need to know where, in that world, these new and causally effective entities are to be found.

11

GETTING RID OF THE EGO

———•◆•———

MORAL JUSTIFICATIONS FOR ATOMISING

Unless some clear picture emerges, showing what kind of entity memes are supported to be, the parallel between them and genes surely vanishes, and the claim to scientific status with it. Meme-language is not really an extension of physical science. As so often happens, it is an imagery which is welcomed, not for scientific merit but for moral reasons, as being a salutary way of thinking. At one point Dawkins himself speaks of it simply as an analogy 'which I find inspiring but which can be taken too far if we are not careful'.[1] Dennett, while making much stronger claims to scientific status, also adds that 'whether or not the meme perspective can be turned into science, in its philosophical guise *it has already done much more good than harm*'.[2]

What kind of good has it done? Dennett explains that the idea of memes corrects our tendency to exaggerate our own powers, reminding us that we are not, as we 'would like to think, godlike creators of ideas, manipulating them and controlling them as our whim dictates and judging them from an independent, Olympian standpoint'. As he rightly says, we are not always 'in charge'.[3]

This admission, however, can easily be made in other ways, without inventing a special set of mysterious occult beings to replace us. Susan Blackmore, who has lately taken up the cause of memes, gives this moral point a special twist by grafting it, somewhat unexpectedly, on to the Buddhist doctrine that the self is an illusion: 'We all live our lives as a lie . . . belief in a permanent self is the cause of all human suffering'.[4] But such dismissals of everyday concepts have a quite different meaning, depending on just what new item the dismisser offers as a substitute. What Buddhism offers is a deeper freedom, one that is held to flow from abandoning stereotypes about one's personality and recognising the 'Buddha nature' within one. This nature is held to unite all living beings, without

68

compromising their individual power to feel and act. It thus calls on us strongly to live in harmony with the rest of creation. By contrast, memetics offers only the news that we are (as Blackmore herself puts it) 'meme machines', constructions produced by alien viruses for their own purposes and incapable of having any purposes of our own. If anyone actually did try to believe this it is hard to see what practical consequences could follow other than helpless fatalism, quickly followed by general breakdown. It is clear that the suggestion is, like so many other learned suggestions about selves, merely a paper doctrine about other people, not one by which anyone could live.

The chief reason why Blackmore accepts a belief in memes seems to be that she thinks it is the only possible alternative to Descartes's crude idea of a substantial self co-extensive with consciousness. She is much impressed by the experiments of Benjamin Libet, who notoriously also saves himself trouble by constantly shooting at this outdated target. To replace it, she commends Dennett's 'multiple drafts' model of the self as proposed in his book *Consciousness Explained*. That model, however, cannot serve her purpose. It is a genuine attempt to depict the mind's own creative activity. It leaves no room for memes and cannot accommodate them, even though Dennett himself has since taken up meme-talk. Dennett's remark there that the idea of the self is a 'benign user illusion' misleads her. It is actually only a bit of residual Cartesian dualism, a suggestion by Dennett that the 'self' is always conceived as a Cartesian disembodied ghost. But 'self' is in fact a highly complex idea with many different uses. Nothing can be gained, morally or metaphysically, by trying to shoot it down in favour of this tinpot successor.

In general, the moral point that she shares with Dennett – the demand for a correction of human vanity, the insistence on a more realistic notion of our species' place in nature – is a healthy and reasonable one. It is quite true that western culture has systematically exaggerated both the power and the importance of *Homo sapiens* relative to the rest of creation. Thinkers such as Dawkins and Wilson have done really useful work in correcting this absurdity, in making us more aware of our relative insignificance both in time, in the evolutionary perspective, and in the vast array of life forms that still surrounds us.

LITERALLY PARASITISING BRAINS

The value of that correction, however, depends on the reality of the particular causal background that is then introduced to replace human activity. About evolution, the correction works because it points to real forces in the world, forces that are responsible for the results that people had supposed were due to human effort. In order to make the meme proposal parallel to this case, it would be necessary to show that memes, too, were genuine external forces, alien puppet-masters previously hidden from us but revealed now as the true causes ruling our life. That indeed is the dramatic picture that Dawkins originally suggested, quoting a remark of Nick Humphreys:

> Memes should be regarded as living structures, *not just metaphorically but technically*. When you plant a fertile meme in my mind you *literally* parasitise my brain, turning it into a vehicle for the meme's propagation in just the way that a virus may parasitise the genetic mechanism of a host cell.[5]

This was the sort of language that made the proposal seem so exciting and important in the first place. If the alleged discovery had been a real one, it would indeed have been important – but, of course, also disastrous since it would have entailed helpless fatalism. Dennett tries to disinfect the imagery somewhat by shifting the metaphor to symbiosis, citing as a close parallel

> the creation of eukaryotic cells that made multicellular life possible . . . one day some prokaryotes were invaded by parasites of sorts and this turned out to be a blessing in disguise, for . . . these invaders turned out to be beneficial and hence were *symbionts* but not parasites.[6]

But however soothing this change may be emotionally it still does not give these entities any sort of intelligible status. In order to conceive ideas, or their mental causes, as separate organisms existing in their own right before infesting minds, we would need to forsake empiricism and build a very bold – perhaps Hegelian? – framework of objective idealism, allowing mental entities this independent status outside particular minds. And idealism is as far as possible from Dennett's philosophical style.

It seems extraordinary that a thinker as committed as Dennett to the continuity of evolution should choose to build this metaphysical wall in order to keep mental entities separate from us instead of treating our thoughts and customs as what they obviously are – namely, forms of activity which our species has gradually developed during its history to supply its needs. As William of Occam observed, *varieties of entities should not be multiplied beyond necessity.* When human beings think and act, no extra entities need to be present in them besides themselves.

Dennett explains that his main point is that our thoughts do not always do us any good and must therefore not be thought of – as (he rather surprisingly says) humanists think of them – as entities aiming at our advantage, but as aiming at their own:

The meme's eye perspective challenges one of the central axioms of the humanities ... we tend to overlook the fundamental fact that 'a cultural trait may have evolved in the way it has simply because it is *advantageous to itself*.[7]

... competition is the major selective force in the infosphere and, just as in the biosphere, the challenge has been met with great ingenuity. ... Like a mindless virus, a meme's prospects depend on its design – not its internal design, whatever that might be, but the design it shows the world, its phenotype, the way it affects things in its environment [namely] minds and other memes.[8]

We therefore need memetics to help us understand the strategies by which memes contrive to infest us even when they are not useful to us, for example: 'the meme for faith, which discourages the exercise of the sort of critical judgement that might decide that the idea of faith was, all things considered, a dangerous idea.'[9]

Thus (it seems) if we want to know why people have faith in something – for instance, why western people today often have faith in the pronouncements of scientists – we ought not to ask what reasons, good or bad, these people have for that confidence. Instead, we should simply note that the idea of faith is an efficient parasite. But how would that get us any further?

This is the kind of example that enables memeticists to overlook the oddity of their story by using the example of ideas that they already disapprove of, usually religious ones. (See for instance Dawkins's article 'Viruses of the Mind',[10] where he asks 'Is God a Computer Virus?') But – as they occasionally notice – if the theory is really universal, it must be extended to all thought, including our own. The deplorable habit of explaining away one's opponents' views as mere symptoms of their folly, rather than trying to understand them, now becomes the only way of explaining any thought anywhere – including (of course) our own thought by which we have just drawn this very conclusion. The urgent need that there is, in studying social change, to understand what other people think they are doing – to grasp the advantage that they see in acting as they do – vanishes. The only advantage involved is one to a bizarre metaphysical parasite. Thought itself becomes, at this point, entirely inexplicable and has to be abandoned.

MOTIVATION IS NOT A NEW TOPIC

At this point we need to say something obvious. The fact that our thoughts and customs are not always to our advantage is not a new scientific discovery. It is a familiar platitude, both in daily life and in traditional humanistic thinking. We know all too well that our thoughts and customs often lead us to act foolishly, destructively, even suicidally. And the crucial point about this self-destructive tendency – the thing that makes it most distressing – is that in these cases the conflicting motives which lead to the trouble are indeed all our own. They do *not* arise from possession by some kind of external parasite. They are warring parts of ourselves.

Far from this recognition being alien to the humanities, it has always been one of their central themes. It is central in literature, where it lies at the root of both tragedy and comedy. And when we study history, our interest in this human tendency to self-destructiveness is crucial because it directs our curiosity about the past, because we need to know why things go so badly wrong much more urgently than we need to celebrate our successes. It is also the starting-point of our reflection about the deep practical dilemmas that give rise to moral philosophy.

In the humanistic disciplines so far, enquiry about self-destructive behaviour has mostly concentrated on the attempt to understand human motivation. That is not at all the area to which memologists direct our attention, but it is one that does indeed hold hidden causes of thought and action. Those causes, however, are not *hidden* ones in the sense in which DNA was hidden before it was discovered. They are not facts in the outer world which merely happen not to have been researched yet. They are facts about motives, and they are obscure largely because we find it so hard and painful to attend to them. They are facts that we cannot understand properly unless we are prepared to make some serious imaginative effort of identification with the actors in question.

That is why literature is such an important part of our lives, why the notion that it is less important than science is so mistaken. Shakespeare and Tolstoy help us to understand the self-destructive psychology of despotism. Flaubert and Racine illuminate the self-destructive side of love. What we need to grasp in such cases is not the simple fact that people are acting against their interests. We know that; it stands out a mile. We need to understand, beyond this, *what kind* of gratification they are getting from acting in this way. If, instead of looking for this factor directly and imaginatively by studying their conduct, we were to shift our attention to the alleged interactions between populations of memes, as Dennett advises, we would lose a crucially important source of knowledge in order to pursue a phantom.

EXPLAINING WITCH-HUNTING

The effect of this exchange can be interestingly seen by looking at the kind of example where, at a casual glance, we might find memology most persuasive, namely, in cases where large numbers of people do act irrationally for motives that seem really obscure. For instance, consider the witch-craze which prevailed in Europe from the fifteenth to the seventeenth centuries. This craze was not, as is often supposed, simply a survival of ancient superstition caused by ignorance and finally cured by the rise of science. To the contrary, in the Middle Ages there were few prosecutions for witchcraft because the church authorities thought that witchcraft was rare (though real) and they discouraged witch-hunting because they saw the danger of false accusation. It was in the Renaissance that things changed. At that time, as a recent historian puts it:

> The Europeans did three things which set them far apart from most other peoples at most other times and places. Between 1500 and 1700 they set sail in tall ships and colonised the far corners of the globe. They made stunning strides forward in the sciences. And they executed tens of thousands of people, mainly women, as witches.[11]

The attack of frenzy coincided, then, with the increase of knowledge rather than being cured by it. And, as these authors show, when it finally subsided it did not do so because science had shown that bewitchment was physically impossible, but because people gradually came to find it psychologically incredible that there was such an organised host of demon-worshippers. Writers of various kinds greatly helped to nourish this incredulity, but scientific arguments do not seem to have contributed anything particular to it.

I cite this case because (as I say) it is one that really does need explanation and one where explanation by memes would look so easy. We need only posit a new meme successfully invading a population that has no immunity to it, a meme that declines later as that immunity develops. Its success is then due to its own reproductive strategy – presumably produced by a mutation – not to any fact about the people concerned. We need not look at those people. We need not relate the meme to these people's intentions. We certainly need not look at human psychology generally or look into our own hearts to see what we might learn there about such conduct. We simply place the whole causation outside human choice, thus avoiding that overestimation of our own powers that so disturbs Dennett. This effort to avoid pride would of course land us in a quite unworkable kind of fatalism.

But, on top of that, the meme story simply fails to give us any kind of explanation at all. What we need to understand in such a case is how people could begin to think and act in this way in spite of the beliefs, customs and ideals that had prevented them from doing so earlier. We need, in fact, to understand the psychology of persecution and xenophobia. We need to penetrate paranoia. We need this, not just in relation to the witch-craze but for understanding the oddities of human conduct at other times and places too, not least in our own lives. *Understanding* it does not mean discovering, by research, new facts about the behaviour of an imaginary alien life form. It means essentially self-knowledge, an exploration of what de Tocqueville called 'the habits of the heart'. Examining the evolutionary strategies of mythical culture-units cannot save us from this awkward form of investigation.

12

CULTURAL EVOLUTION?

————•◆•————

WHAT CHANGES THE WORLD?

Memetics is only one of a number of schemes that have lately been put forward to explain our mental lives in terms of evolution. This symbolic language has immense appeal just now, indeed, it may well be a necessary counterpoise to the obsession with atomism. If the detailed patterns supplied by atomisers are to make sense and be used, some wider perspective is needed within which they can be deployed. That perspective is now supplied by the notion of cultural evolution. It is worth while to ask, just what does this idea do for us?

I thought about this when I lately came across a mug inscribed with the following remark, which it attributed to Margaret Mead: 'Never doubt that a small group of thoughtful, committed citizens can change the world; indeed, it's the only thing that ever does.' It struck me at once that this was a mug badly at odds with current thinking; indeed, it cannot lately have been attending to the media as an educated mug should. These days, the message that we chiefly hear is that changes in the world are due to something on a much larger scale – perhaps economic causes, perhaps a shift in the gene pool, perhaps cultural evolution – certainly something far grander than a few people worrying in an attic. Is the mug therefore wrong?

This seems to me rather an important issue. We always have a choice about the perspective from which we will look at human affairs, whether we will examine them from the inside, as participants, or from some more distant perspective, and if so, which of many distant perspectives we will choose. Or can we combine these angles? In theory, we know that these points of view are not really alternatives but complementary parts of a wider enquiry. Yet current thinking urges us to find, somehow, one key explanation, a single standpoint that is guaranteed right because it is scientific.

In seeing how to use concepts such as cultural evolution, I think it is worth while to look briefly at some of the other long perspectives that have been offered in recent times as key explanations of historical change. How useful have they been?

The most obvious of these alternative angles in recent times is the Marxist conception of history. That approach simply told historians that, instead of getting mired in personal transactions such as the quarrels and marriages of kings, they should concentrate on large economic factors such as inventions, diseases, changes of crops and climate, land tenure, labour conditions and expansions or contractions of trade. This was surely a most liberating and illuminating move, a move whose importance we now take for granted, though we may not always thank Marx for it. It had the characteristic advantage of all such distancing moves. It made large-scale tendencies that had been obscured by the distracting human dramas in the foreground visible at last. It showed up non-human background factors that are crucial to the shaping of human life. And since it did all this in the name of science, it carried a prestige that seemed to set it above other possible kinds of explanation.

That special prestige was, however, bought at a heavy price. It imposed a fatal narrowness, an exclusiveness that tended to stop people developing the new insights effectively.

IS FATALISM TRUE?

The history of Marxism lights up two misfortunes that are liable to afflict a story about social development when it claims scientific status. The first and most notorious of these is fatalism. Dialectical materialism extended the determinist assumptions commonly made in the physical sciences to cover human life and especially its own predictions. This made it obscure why anybody should take the trouble to work inexhaustibly – as Marx and Engels themselves did – on political projects whose outcome was already foredoomed. The remote perspective that was so useful for studying long-term economic trends simply could not be used for examining practical questions about what to do next, nor for moral questions about what to aim at. Marxist propaganda therefore oscillated between demanding the proletarian revolution urgently as a cure for current iniquities and trying to make people accept it by saying that, in any case, it could not be prevented.

This is the point where my mug's predictions surely become of interest. On the face of things, what the mug says has undoubtedly happened. We might instance the Invisible College, the group of influential thinkers who met in London in the mid-seventeenth century and whose discussions developed into the Royal Society. This group included several distinguished scientists, but its interests ran far beyond physical science and gave it a much wider influence. As Robert Boyle put it:

The 'Invisible College' consists of persons that endeavour to put narrow-mindedness out of countenance by the practice of so extensive a charity that it reaches unto everything called man, and nothing less than a universal goodwill can content it. And indeed they are so apprehensive of the want of good employment that they take the whole body of mankind as their care.

But . . . there is not enough of them.[1]

Or we could think of Wordsworth and Coleridge and the other Romantic poets, whose new thinking shaped our sensibilities through the Romantic Revival. Or of John Stuart Mill and his colleagues the sanitary reformers, who insisted, in the face of huge opposition, on putting drains into British cities. Or of the Buddha and the five friends with whom – after much hesitation – he shared the revolutionary view of life that he had reached in meditation. Or indeed of Marx and Engels themselves and the people, including their opponents, who helped them to shape their theories. There is also the little matter of the Apostles.

When supporters of the long perspective are asked to explain examples like these, they commonly reply that these people made no real difference. The changes that followed would have come about in any case. Sometimes there is something in this. In cases such as the drains it may well be mainly right. Cholera epidemics might have left little choice about that in any case. But in most cases the particular form that the change takes can make an enormous difference.

For instance, it may well be true that, even if Newton and Locke and Boyle had never been born, some group of people in a commercial country like Britain would have set about developing the physical sciences in the late seventeenth century and would have adapted the background beliefs of the time so as to make room for them. But was it inevitable that these people would have developed and propagated the Augustan ideology that shaped the peculiar British version of the Enlightenment – that exact mix of rationalism, empiricism, Whiggish politics, Anglican theology, pragmatism and misogyny that the champions of science in that age devised – the mix that, under the flag of Reason and Newton, proved benign enough to dominate thought in Britain throughout the eighteenth century?[2]

Again, in a very general way, perhaps it might have been predicted that the narrowness of that ideology would eventually produce some such reaction as took place at the Romantic Revival. A celestial observer might have foreseen vaguely the negative side of that reaction. But the positive suggestions about replacements for it varied hugely from one country to another and involved real original thinking. They were not the kind of thing that could ever be considered inevitable. And they have profoundly affected the way in which English-speaking people still live and think. Besides

Wordsworth and Coleridge there was Blake – an extraordinary and quite unpredictable person – and his group of friends. These included Godwin, Mary Wollstonecraft and Tom Paine, who later went off to play his part in that other rather influential group, the Fathers of the American Revolution.

HOPES OF SCIENTIFIC OBJECTIVITY

Besides fatalism, the second and less obvious drawback that can attend such long perspectives is the illusion of impartiality. The findings of the physical sciences are supposed to be objective, that is, free from bias. A social theory that joins them in gaining the status of a science may therefore seem to qualify for exclusive dominion. Approaches that conflict with it can seem to be necessarily *un*scientific – that is, wrong. Though Marx himself seems not to have been specially keen to claim the authority of physical science, Engels did stress that claim, insisting that Marxist doctrine was unique in being a scientific structure in the narrow sense, something solidly founded on the findings of biology and physics. This encouraged Marxism to become a narrow church, an orthodoxy that denounced its critics as fiercely as any earlier religion, instead of listening to them and learning from them.

It is worth while to notice how the illusion of impartiality worked here. Marxist thinkers saw themselves as objective physical scientists because their reasoning was materialistic. They dealt in physical causes such as crops and climate, rather than in ideas. But of course they were selecting these particular causes out of many other equally physical ones in accordance with their own system of thought. That system centred on simple and dramatic ideas about the class war: ideas generated during the failed revolutions of 1848 and confirmed by Engels's experience of conditions in Manchester. It posited a polarisation of humanity in which (as the Communist Manifesto put it) the workers of the world would shortly unite, since they had nothing to lose but their chains. It aimed to complete the violent reshaping of human society that had been envisaged in 1848 by simply reversing the class situation that existed under western capitalism.

Though this seemed like large-scale thinking, it had, as usual, a local bias. It has been suggested that the class war might have looked very different to Engels if he had studied it in Birmingham, where numerous small workshops were conducted in a much more cooperative way than the huge, despotically run Manchester cotton mills. More seriously, the Marxist account entirely ignored factors outside the human species, and indeed most factors outside Europe. Marx was not concerned about the exploitation of natural resources. He thought those resources were infinite, a belief that was widely accepted in countries which adopted his views. He saw capitalist imperialism simply as the oppression of one set of humans by another, not as a source of ecological disaster. And of course, even within human affairs, his theory grossly oversimplified the problem. Marx was very astute in diagnosing many of the evils of capitalism, but he was mistaken in supposing that it was about to cure those evils by collapsing.

In rehearsing this familiar story, the point I want to stress is the illusion of impartiality that can result from taking this long perspective. Marxist theory moved from an immensely abstract general principle about causation – that all changes proceed from conflict – to deduce results about a particular political conflict in which its founders had already taken sides. The abstractness of the universal principle seemed to guarantee the impersonality that belongs to physical laws, impersonality of a kind that could not be found in the usual run of historical causes. But this impersonality was deceptive because the principle was being understood from the start in a biased way that predetermined its application to that case.

SPENCERIAN ABSTRACTIONS

This deception is even more obvious in the social Darwinist project that has been Marxism's main rival and that seems to have outlived it, persisting vigorously today as a belief in the supremacy of market forces. Its prophet, Herbert Spencer, derived his views from a single grand and highly abstract Law of Evolution;

> Evolution is an integration of matter and concomitant dissipation of motion; during which the matter passes from an indefinite, incoherent homogeneity to a definite, coherent heterogeneity; and during which the retained motion undergoes a parallel transformation.[3]

Like many of us who have been struck by a promising idea, Spencer then began to see this happening everywhere. As he said, 'Bearing the generalisation in mind, it needed only to turn from this side to that side, and from one class of facts to another, to find everywhere exemplifications.'[4]

In case anyone might think his law too vague to provide practical guidance, Spencer drew from it at once the simple and satisfactory political conclusion that heterogeneity called for the utmost political freedom and that this meant, above all, free trade. Commercial freedom would ensure (in the disastrously ambiguous phrase that he invented) 'the survival of the fittest'. He named this as the basic principle of 'evolution', a word whose meaning he was largely responsible for developing and which Darwin carefully avoided. Accordingly (said Spencer), the working of this principle must on no account be disturbed by charitable attempts to help the unfit – that is, the poor:

The whole effort of nature is to get rid of such, to clear the world of them, and to make room for better. . . . If they are sufficiently complete to live, they do live. If they are not sufficiently complete to live, they die, and it is best that they should die.[5]

As James Moore explains, Spencer reasoned that:

All heterogeneity, all individuality, is the inevitable product of natural forces and a manifestation of universal progress. Thus, where markets are freely competitive, where government is decentralised . . . there, one could be sure, human beings are co-operating with the forces that mould their hopeful destiny. And where else were these conditions more fully realised than in the United States? Business was booming, untrammelled by regulation, and the fittest were proudly surviving in a competitive marketplace.[6]

What evolution demanded was, then, universal imitation of the current methods of American capitalism. Whether this conclusion would have been ranked as 'scientific' if Spencer had not decided that *The Origin of Species* supported his doctrine is not altogether clear. After making that decision, however, he always claimed to be an enthusiastic promoter of Darwin's theory, which he thought was equivalent to his own. It was thus under the banner of Darwinian science that Spencer reached, and converted to his views, a large and receptive audience, especially in the United States.

That is why what is really Spencerism received, and still bears, the name 'social Darwinism'. It is also a main reason why a different, but large, section of American opinion still sees Darwinism itself as thoroughly immoral and science in general as sinister. As we have seen, Darwin himself actually rejected Spencer's metaphysical approach. The trouble lay, as Darwin saw, in the quick transit between the vast principles and the particular cases. If we ask why Spencer and his converts were so sure that their principle of heterogeneity demanded specially *commercial* freedom – rather than (say) the freedom of workers to control their working conditions or of citizens to protect their environment – the principle itself supplies no answer. That choice actually flowed from economic ideas current in the day and had its source in Adam Smith's objections to the rather confused excise system of the late eighteenth century. Again – as with Marxism – a large black box intervened here between abstract principle and application, a box that hid an unexamined jumble of local and personal influences.

The intervention of this black box – this arena for self-deception about bias – seems to me to be the most serious drawback that is liable to dog attempts to view social change 'scientifically' from a long perspective. Spencerism provides a clear example of this drawback. Others may be found in the supposed 'laws of history' proposed by theorists such as Spengler and Arnold Toynbee.

In all these cases, as in Marxism, serious ideals were at work. Important half-truths were being stated; the trouble lay in their being euphorically universalised. Marxists were usually moved by a genuine indignation about social injustice. And Spencer's insistence on individual freedom was itself an honourable one, part of the Enlightenment's long campaign against oppressive customs stemming from feudalism. There was also something very good about his attempt to view human life and the rest of nature in a single perspective. The trouble is that this is an enormously harder enterprise than Spencer and his followers ever realised. Our culture had deliberately set up strong walls between humanity and other species for many centuries, allowing quite unrealistic ideas to develop about the foreign country outside the species-barrier. The apparatus of thought that needed to be used in order to generalise across it was therefore shaky and misleading. Apparently simple words like 'animal', 'natural' and 'selection' turned out to carry an unexamined load of explosive meaning.

This same combination of good ideals and dubious results can be found, too, in the earlier system which lay behind both these ideologies – the first real attempt at universal historical explanation and the source of their shared emphasis on conflict – the Hegelian dialectic. This was primarily an account of how ideas develop through opposition, each thesis being resisted by its antithesis and a higher synthesis eventually growing which combines the good points of both.

This idea has the enormous advantage of undermining bigotry. It forces contenders to accept that they have no monopoly on the truth. Despite the persistent pugnacity of scholars, it has had a lasting good effect in civil- ising controversy by making people look for truths outside their own camp.

The downside of all this emerges, however – as in the other cases – in the choice of the theses that are supposed to be in conflict. For instance, for a long time in European history many people thought that the only choice about religion lay between Catholicism and Protestantism. Within these camps, too, the choice could seem even narrower, for instance between Calvin and Luther. The Hegelian perspective tends to concentrate attention on these existing duels, rather than on new directions. In this way it can lock people into existing thought-patterns rather than help them to move out of them. This was what Kierkegaard said had happened to Danish society in his day, where people well satisfied with bourgeois opinions circled round rehar- monising them on Hegelian patterns. He wrote his book *Either/Or* to remind them that it is sometimes necessary to make real choices instead.

Similar pros and cons attended the still earlier paradigm of accounting for all puzzling changes as the dispensations of God. This had the obvious draw- back that it could easily lead to fatalism. But it also provided the much more useful option of treating the new situation as a challenge: what the Quakers called a Chariot, an opportunity sent by Providence for new and laudable activity. Thus there is always an up and a down side to these projects.

13

SELECTING THE SELECTORS

———•◦•———

IS EVOLUTIONARY THINKING DIFFERENT?

So much for past paradigms, earlier ways of explaining social change. What about the latest candidate? What are the special advantages and drawbacks of explaining these changes by natural selection?

Clearly it has the great advantage of treating human life as part of nature, not as something mysteriously set apart from it. It celebrates our continuity with the world we spring from rather than trying nervously to disown it. That continuity is a central fact of life. Human dignity does not call on us to claim to have been blank paper at birth, pure cognitive beings shaped only by something called Society or Culture and able to change the rest of the world as we please. That muddled notion of human freedom is still powerful in the social sciences, even if slightly less so than it used to be, so the evolutionary model does us a great service by insisting that culture itself is part of nature. It must be seen as somehow continuing natural patterns.

But which patterns? It is easier to say this as a general matter of faith than to work out how, in detail, we should fit together the ways of thinking that we have developed for describing the natural world from the outside – as spectators and exploiters – with the ways we use for dealing with our social life from the inside, as participants. Many sages are now offering evolutionary gear-mechanisms to connect these two approaches. In doing this they are riding the wave of current fashion even as they also direct it. Evolutionary talk is the flavour of the age and will be with us for a long time yet.

My doubts about it – which are closely related to Darwin's – are certainly not going to make this enthusiasm go away. In so far as it is really useful, I shall be doing no harm by criticising it. I hope that, by mentioning my worries about it, I may perhaps help its proponents to make it clearer.

SELECTION OF WHAT BY WHAT?

The central difficulty here is surely that of getting a forest into a pint pot. The things that we think of as elements in culture are so various in form that it is hard to see straight away how we can find a single pattern of change that suits them all without Procrustean distortion. Is there a way of reducing them to a taxonomy, making them in some way parallel to the known elements of biology such as species, individuals, populations and genes?

What does the evolutionary model actually demand here? John Ziman, introducing his collection of essays entitled *Technological Innovation as an Evolutionary Process*, writes that he and his fellow contributors, when they say that artefacts have *evolved*, 'mean more than that they have developed gradually. We are indicating that this development has occurred through genetic variation and natural selection.' He goes on to ask, 'Do *all cultural entities* evolve in this sense – that is, change over time by essentially the *same mechanism*?' In the last chapter of the book, he and his team give their reply to this question: 'We have come to see the evolutionary perspective as an indispensable tool of thought, highlighting a vital aspect of *all historical processes*. Our contributions to this book . . . show *the effectiveness of "selectionism" as a unifying paradigm of rationality*'.[1]

This is a big claim, going far beyond the technological examples that they actually deal with. It seems important to know how it is to be cashed out in practice. In any given case, what kinds of competing entities ought to form the population that is the raw material for this process of selection? *How do we find our units of selection?* We might ask this (for instance) about some of the more prominent items that constantly get mentioned as 'rising' during the history of the western world in the last two centuries. This seems a reasonable case to take, since what rises may surely be said to evolve, and these are in fact fair examples of the kind of historical process that we often need to explain. Among these 'rising' items historians commonly list such things as: individualism, the middle class, the commercial spirit, the factory system, mechanisation, urbanisation, egalitarianism, imperialism, the standard of living, rapid transport, feminism, literacy and population, while other things such as feudalism, faith and skill in handicrafts are said to have correspondingly declined.

The worrying thing here is not just the wide variation among the kinds of things that these words denote but the prior process of deliberate choice that has to go on before such abstractions are ever named in the first place. Words like this are not simple names of given entities, like the names of particular existing animal species which might be seen as competing to survive. They are abstractions, terms arrived at by cutting up the continuum of history in particular ways in order to bring out particular aspects of what has been happening. And these ways are not arbitrary or imposed by natural selection but deliberate. To use such words is already to have taken

83

a position on questions about what is important there. These terms are *selective* in the quite literal sense of involving actual human choice. How is it possible to mesh that situation with metaphorical talk of 'selectionism' involving selection from without by forces in the environment?

Is it indeed true that there is always 'a vital aspect' of such cases which can usefully be seen as a selection: a competition between a set of rival contenders, ending in a victory for the 'fittest'? No doubt, if we have a special confidence in the value of this pattern, we can often manage to see it in the events we study. But the point I want to stress is that the decision to apply it to a particular social change already involves a particular view about the meaning and importance of that change. It is essential to be aware of this perspective.

For instance, it is certainly possible to view 'the rise of the middle class' simply as a case of the survival of the fittest: the victory of one given, existing set of people over a given range of other sets because it fits better with the given environment. But this is to commit oneself to a static, essentially Marxist view of class conflict. It misses the possibility that what is going on may be better described as a wide change in the ways in which people make their living – a different spread of occupations, producing different customs and different value-judgments for everybody.

When a middle class 'rises' noticeably, it receives many recruits both from above and from below, changing its own constitution along with that of its fellows. The result is that everybody ends up viewing both themselves and the whole social hierarchy rather differently and the boundaries between classes become less sharp. There is not (apart from outside physical factors) a fixed, neutral 'environment' to which such a fixed, aspiring class has to adapt. It might therefore seem more natural to say that, if anything is evolving, it is really the whole social structure. More boldly still, it might be equally plausible to say that all the 'rising' items I have listed above are merely aspects of a single big historical process – a wider slice of social evolution. But on both these suggestions it gets even harder to view the process as one of 'Darwinian' (or Spencerian) selection among a given set of candidates.

ARE THERE CULTURAL SPECIES?

How do we actually pick out from the cultural scene our main units, the entities that we can usefully describe as evolving? This is easiest in the case of artefacts, which are what Ziman and his team mostly discuss. Cathedrals, railway carriages and samurai swords are definite kinds of item, almost as clearly demarcated as natural species. The purposes for which they are made can be complex and can sometimes change, but are usually relatively limited. Their makers usually assume that these purposes are clear, and those who study them can normally take them for granted. There is often no need to discuss them. And while those purposes remain unchanged, the pattern of selection among various candidates can often be used.

Even here, however, we can run into problems. Should Victorian railway stations and modern skyscrapers be taken as further stages in the evolution of the cathedral? Or are they rather new species, life forms that have competed with it and taken its place? Do they occupy the same ecological niche or a different one? In such cases, the change in purpose quickly becomes the central issue. It arises in Gerry Martin's fascinating article on samurai swords in *Technological Innovation*, when he feels moved to add an apologetic note:

> (Good reader, at this point I ask for your sympathy and understanding; we are discussing an object constructed with consummate and loving skill, revered, collected and exhibited in the world's greatest museums, but whose sole purpose is to violently cut up living human beings. I cannot start to reconcile these conflicting attributes.)[2]

But if he carried his study further to consider the way in which these swords eventually gave place to later weapons, the change in the roles that these new weapons played in society would surely make it hard to treat them as simply more efficient adaptations to the same environment. And if he were writing about the development of modern weapons or methods of torture, this kind of question might become central.

It becomes more pressing still if one is writing about explicit abstractions such as individualism or feminism or imperialism rather than weapons. It does not seem to be possible to mention such items without implying value-judgements, and these judgments make a chronic difference to how you identify the items in the first place and so to what can count as their 'evolution'. People do not usually talk of something as evolving at all unless they are viewing it in some sort of positive light. They do not commonly speak of the evolution of crime, or drunkenness, or careless driving. Yet surely increases in these things too are among the 'historical processes' that Ziman mentions. My question is: Is there some reason why they do not qualify as 'evolutions'?

The evaluative element in the word 'evolution' was surely one of the central reasons that made Darwin avoid it. This element comes out interestingly in the first example that the OED gives for the biological sense of the term. In his *Principles of Geology* Charles Lyell wrote, 'The testaceae of the ocean existed first, and some of them by gradual evolution were *improved* into those inhabiting the land'.[3] When we are discussing social change, this value-laden way of talking does not, of course, commit us to approving of the particular development that we are discussing. But it does mean that we are picking it

85

out as an enterprise, a project that people are somehow trying to promote, rather than as something that just happens to them (as the 'meme' pattern implies). We therefore need to interest ourselves in their own notion of what they are doing, not just in the outside forces that may be working on them. It also means that we have some reason for thinking the topic in question important enough to analyse. If, however, one picks out any of the *isms* in my list as a project of this kind, one is saying something about the whole of society, not just about a single element in it. De Tocqueville, when he invented the word 'individualism', was talking about a pervasive change in the entire American social attitude, not a limited element that had happened to prevail over a given set of rivals.[4]

'MECHANISMS'?

In trying to understand such large and various changes, I am not persuaded that the best course is to look for a single 'mechanism' that may be supposed to have brought them all about. (This is where Darwin's objection to wide extrapolation from limited examples seems to me quite right.) In discussing large-scale matters we are inevitably talking in terms of large abstractions that we have already formed. The 'mechanism' to be found – which is presumably a common form of development – must therefore work at the level of these abstractions. This means that it already incorporates our previous biases. And we know how quickly those biases change from age to age, constantly altering the language that we use to describe social matters. There is, unfortunately, nothing here like the antiseptic, artificially unchanging language of physics. There are no neutral, naturally given units of selection as there are when we talk about the evolution of an animal species.

This does not mean that we cannot deal rationally with these matters. Our one-sidedness is not fatal so long as we are aware of it and make it explicit. All our opinions are, of course, our own opinions, expressing certain views on what is important. But we can articulate those views and offer them openly to others as contributions to the general stock. The trouble only comes in if, instead, we dogmatically universalise our own generalizations and promote them (as Spencer and Marx and Toynbee did) as laws of nature.

To avoid this, it seems fairly important to remember that the entity directly responsible for causing a given social change – aside from the physical conditions – has to be the actual people involved, not their doctrines. Our various *isms* are shorthand ways of describing the activities of human beings, not those of abstractions. To understand these activities, we have to get some idea of what they had in mind, what they thought they were doing, which may be quite different from what they finally achieved. And if we are discussing some contemporary change, some dilemma where we now need to choose a way forward, talking as if a set of competing abstractions were the agents in charge can only land us in fatalism.

As we have seen, this instant flight from concrete to abstract entities is one of the most misleading features of the 'meme' pattern that is now popular as a proposed explanation of social change. Meme-talk simply extends to bizarre lengths the typical faults of explanations that try to use the long perspective when looking at something as close to us as the motivation for social change. But the respect with which this suggestion has been treated shows how strong the bias towards such methods is today.

In resisting that bias, I may, of course, just be showing one of those extraordinary blind spots that we find so entertaining when we study the history of thought. I can only repeat that my objection is not at all to the bringing of human affairs into the same perspective as the rest of nature. That is a move I strongly support. What worries me is the hasty use of certain patterns that have been found useful in biology to explain human affairs where they have only a somewhat artificial application, at the expense of the directly relevant study of human motives.

In this context, any attention to these motives tends to get dismissed as mere unscientific 'folk psychology'. This dismissal bypasses the mass of valuable information that we collect in our lives from dealing with our conspecifics as participants in the social process. The quick move to evolutionary thinking trades this immediate data for the more indirect and patchy kind that we would have to use if we were dealing with species that were quite remote from us. This is a policy of looking at human life through the wrong end of the telescope, making it seem far less intelligible than it actually is.

14

IS REASON SEX-LINKED?

THE SURPRISING PERSISTENCE OF MIND

We have been considering some current myths that are designed to bring the life of the mind within the province of scientific method. It is, however, surprising in a way that these are still felt to be necessary after so much trouble has been taken to get rid of that disturbing entity altogether. As Steven Pinker has put it,

> The concept of mind has been perplexing for as long as people have reflected on their thoughts and feelings. The very idea has spawned paradoxes, superstitions and bizarre theories in every period and culture. One can almost sympathise with the behaviourists and social constructionists of the first half of the twentieth century, who looked on minds as enigmas or conceptual traps that were best avoided in favour of overt behaviour or the traits of a culture.[1]

If there is obviously nothing *but* a body, mind/body problems need not arise. The body does not then have to relate to anything. If (as we have seen) certain confusions do result from Descartes's having sliced human beings down the middle, many people feel at heart that the best cure is just to drop the immaterial half altogether.

The early behaviourists said this explicitly; mind and consciousness were unreal. And under the surface this suspicion is still very widespread. It is felt that reductive techniques should not merely atomise the mind. They should get rid of it altogether, translating whatever needs to be said about thoughts into statements about bodies. And eventually, their translations will be experimentally checked in the laboratory.

As we have seen, it is uncertain whether this proposal could ever make sense. But certainly the thing cannot be acceptably done in our culture *at large* today, for moral reasons. It clashes with the moral position that is central to the very attitude that calls for this scientific reduction. It offends against individualism.

When the sages of the Enlightenment deposed God and demystified Mother Nature, they did not leave us without an object of reverence. The human soul, renamed as the individual – free, autonomous, and creative – succeeded to that post, and has been confirmed in it with increasing confidence ever since. Though it is not now considered immortal, it is still our pearl of great price. Thus, paradoxical as it may seem, our 'materialist' culture takes for granted an entity that its reductive philosophy has no room for.

Can a plausible way of describing this awe-striking object reductively, as a mere function of the body, be found? This is hard, because freedom and independence from the compulsions of that body are seen as crucial to its special value. The individual, according to an influential view spawned by the Enlightenment, is essentially a will using an intellect. This individual is still widely conceived as eighteenth-century sages conceived it, as active reason, asserting itself in a battle against passive feeling, which is seen as relatively subhuman – a merely animal affair emanating from the body. (We shall consider the force of animal imagery here in Chapters 21 to 23.) The dignity of the will rests on controlling and conquering that feeling.[2]

The dominance of this model has been serious philosophical business, but it cannot be dealt with only by citing academic philosophy. Indeed, as the model wanes in attractiveness to professional philosophers, its general cultural appeal appears, ironically, to grow. Big conceptual schemes like this work at every level in our lives. The conceptual framework is indeed its skeleton, but skeletons do not go about nude. Concepts are embodied in myths and fantasies, in images, ideologies and half-beliefs, in hopes and fears, in shame, pride, and vanity. Like the great philosophers of the past who helped to shape our tradition, we need to start by taking notice of these.

THE NEED TO TAKE SIDES

The mind/body division evokes the general human tendency to dramatise conflicts. If asked 'what does a human being consist in?' theorists readily pick out two elements that seem to oppose each other, because such opposition is striking, and indeed often does need our attention. We do often have to deal with inner conflict.

This is not the only way to start thinking about human personality, but it has been very active in our tradition. Paul the Apostle, following Plato, wrote 'the flesh lusteth against the Spirit, and the Spirit against the flesh: and these things are contrary the one to the other: so that ye cannot do the things that ye would' (Galatians 5: 17), and the idea became a moral commonplace.

The notions of both mind and body have therefore been shaped, from the start, by their roles as opponents in this drama. Without this, the sharp division between them may lose much of its point. 'Perhaps', one might want to say, 'a human being is a whole and acts as a whole, in spite of these inner conflicts. Never mind for the moment what may happen after death; in this life what matters is to look beyond conflicts to the integration of the personality.'

Indeed, the notion that mind opposes body, when baldly stated, may sound rather puritanical today. Yet the idea that such a drama is essential to human dignity is still powerful. The actions by which the will is to show its independence may indeed now be different ones. We now praise a bold adultery rather than a martyrdom. But this is not really a concession to the flesh. What is admired is the boldness. The ideal of asserting one's own will rather than doing what comes naturally is as strong as ever. The force of this model can be seen in a hundred theoretical battles. It appeared notably in the violent objection to 'biological determinism' that greeted the sociobiologists' suggestion that human motivation might owe something to genetic causes.

There were certainly other things badly wrong with sociobiological thinking but this particular complaint was bizarre. Why should biological causes be specially objectionable among the many sorts of causes which – on any view – set the scene for human action? Why were genetic influences more offensive than social conditioning, whose presence nobody doubted? Was it really supposed that hormones did not affect our moods, or that babies started life with no feelings and no tendency to develop any particular sort of feeling? Was our whole emotional and imaginative life then sheer imitation, a set of behaviour-patterns imprinted from outside on passive material by a mysterious supra-personal entity called society? Or, if we occasionally escaped from those influences, were we always performing some existential miracle of self-assertion, without source in the world around us? Had genius (for instance) no roots in the individual physical constitution? Do our *bodies* play no part in our personal lives except as an inert vehicle, a dough, or occasionally an impediment?

These are, I think, positions that no one would accept today on their own merits. Yet many people of good will have thought them both factually true and morally necessary. Their appeal flows from powerful imaginative patterns used by the sages of the Enlightenment. Those patterns have served us well, but they are now reaching the limits of their usefulness.

We have seen that Enlightenment thinking was not, any more than any other style of thinking, wholly impartial, detached, rational, and impersonal. It was, in fact, as practical, as local, as much coloured by particular political and social programmes, and by the private quirks of its inventors, as any other body of thought. Since we have by now taken in much of what is good in it, we need to attend now to these foreign bodies.

90

THE SOLITARY WILL (AND THE FORGOTTEN BODY)

The central question is about personal identity, about what 'I' essentially am. The view of Enlightenment rationalism about this was badly flawed. Crudely – and we have to be crude here to bring the matter out into the open – this notion showed the essential self as consisting in reason. That meant an isolated will, guided by an intelligence, arbitrarily connected to a rather unsatisfactory array of feelings, and lodged, by chance, in an equally unsatisfactory human body. Externally, this being stood alone. Each individual's relation to all others was optional, to be arranged at will by contract. It depended on the calculations of the intellect about self-interest and on views of that interest freely chosen by the will.

This is, fairly clearly, not an uncontentious or *obvious* picture of the human condition. How came it to be widely accepted? The answer is, of course, that it was devised largely for particular, quite urgent, political purposes connected with civic freedom and the vote. The social-contract conceptual scheme was a tool, a wire-cutter for freeing us from mistaken allegiance to kings, churches, and customs. Like other such tools, this way of thinking was carefully not used in places that did not suit those purposes. In particular, it was originally applied only to men, and any later attempts to extend it to women aroused painful indignation and confusion. Each man – each voter – was conceived as representing and defending his household. There was no question of its other members needing to speak for themselves.

WHY GENDER IS RELEVANT

This is not a perverse or irrelevant point. It is no trifling matter that the whole idea of an independent, inquiring, choosing individual, an idea central to western thought, has always been essentially the – somewhat romanticized – idea of a male. It was so developed by the Greeks, and still more by the great libertarian movements of the eighteenth century.[3] It was no accident that their cry was for 'the rights of man' and for 'one man, one vote'. For implicit in these developments was a covert identification of the individual will with the male, and of the neglected body (and feeling) with the female. Rousseau himself, the great architect of modern social-contract thinking and champion of individual freedom, denied firmly that any such ideas could be extended to women. 'Girls', he explained,

> should early be accustomed to restraint, because all their life long they will have to submit to the most enduring restraints, those of propriety . . . They have, or ought to have, little freedom . . . As a

woman's conduct is controlled by public opinion, so is her religion ruled by authority . . . Unable to judge for themselves, they should accept the judgment of father and husband as that of the church.[4]

So wrote the man who owed his whole career to the devoted, intelligent, educated encouragement of Mesdames de Warens, d'Épinay, and others, in the book (*Émile*) whose main theme is the need for complete freedom in the education of boys. As for equality, that too, he said, was solely a male affair. 'Woman is made to submit to man and to endure even injustice at his hands'.[5]

At the end of the eighteenth century, Mary Wollstonecraft suggested in her *Vindication of the Rights of Woman* that this was odd, and that Rousseau's ideals should extend to both sexes. Horace Walpole voiced the general fury by calling her 'a hyaena in petticoats'. And, throughout the nineteenth century, proposals to educate and enfranchise women continued to produce similar frenzy. They were not just opposed as troublesome and inconvenient, but as monstrous – a view supported by amazingly feeble arguments.

THE LIE IN THE SOUL

It surely emerges that the original, sex-linked idea of a free and independent individual had not been thoroughly thought through. Despite its force and nobility, that idea contained a deep strain of falsity. The trouble is not just that the reason why it should apply only to one half of the human race was not honestly considered. It is that the supposed independence of the male was itself false. It was parasitical, taking for granted the love and service of non-autonomous females and also, for some time, of the less enlightened male non-voters who provided for the needs of bodily life. It excluded most of the population while pretending to be universal.

Mutual dependence is central to all human life. The equivocal, unrealistic dismissal of it does not just inconvenience women. It distorts morality by a lop-sided melodrama. It causes the virtues that we need for giving and receiving love and service (and indeed for catering for everyday bodily needs) to be uncritically downgraded, while those involved in self-assertion are uncritically exalted – except, of course, when they are displayed by women. The point is not just that heroic male virtues are getting exalted over 'passive' female ones. It is that, in truth, both sexes need, and can practise, all the virtues. Though there are real (some would still say 'natural') differences between men and women, as I have argued elsewhere,[6] they do not have this drastic moral consequence. The official, wholly separate, ideal of manhood as disembodied will is a distorted one. It damages men's lives as well as women's. The supposed gender-division of moral labour is, and always was, a lie.

92

Mary Wollstonecraft's protest was maddening to her contemporaries because it was so plainly justified. She was not changing the rules. The individualistic tradition, being supposedly radical and universal, did indeed demand to be extended to females. But it had been so shaped that it could not be. It rested on an unreal, stereotyped notion of the relation between gender and the virtues. Though stark, honest realism had always been the watchword of the rationalist tradition, on this matter it was riddled by evasion, bias, and self-deception.

To put the point another way: 'feminism' is not the name of some new doctrine, imported into controversies for no good reason. That name stands for the steady, systematic correction of an ancient and very damaging bias. Its opposite, which may be called virism, had always reigned unnoticed. Correcting it is not a single, simple move. It demands different emphasis in different places because the bias has worked unevenly. Like other corrections, feminism might hope in the end to become unnecessary and so to put itself out of business. But that end is still a long way off.

15

THE JOURNEY FROM
FREEDOM TO DESOLATION

———— •◆• ————

NIETZSCHE, SARTRE, AND THE
PRIVATISATION OF MORALITY

The gender-partiality mentioned in the last chapter has been specially crippling in the strain of extreme individualism that is generally seen as belonging to the Left: the near-anarchistic strain that descends from Rousseau through Nietzsche and Heidegger to Sartre, and to a wide variety of present-day egoistic individualism, as well as the more right-facing kinds expressed in monetarism and sociobiology.[1] Modern feminists, unfortunately, initially put a lot of confidence in this tradition, and did not at once subject Nietzsche to anything like the well-deserved acid bath that they gave Freud.[2] (Simone de Beauvoir's veneration for Sartre probably protected him.) It is worth reflecting on how this strand of tradition significantly (if indirectly) bears on the mind/body problem.

What Nietzsche did was to move the good will, which Kant had placed at the centre of morals, from a social to a solitary habitat. For Kant, the good will was the rational will. It respected all other rational beings, and agreed to moral laws that they too could find reasonable. It was united with them in the 'Kingdom of Ends' – not, of course, an actual state, but an ideal, imagined community in which all could in principle agree on values.

Nietzsche, though deeply impressed with Kant's assertion of the dignity of the will, rejected this communalism. On the one hand he was far too sceptical about moral reasoning to suppose rational agreement possible. On the other, he – himself a solitary – was merely disgusted by Kant's ideal of social harmony and communal virtue:

> A word against Kant as moralist. A virtue has to be *our* invention, our more personal defence and necessity; in any other sense it is merely a danger . . . 'Virtue', 'duty', 'good in itself'; impersonal and universal – phantoms, expressions of decline, of the final exhaustion

of life, of Königsbergian Chinadom. The profoundest laws of preser-
vation and growth demand the reverse of this; that each one of us
should devise his own virtue, his own categorical imperative.[3]

This, he said, would naturally lead any enlightened person in the modern
age to live alone, despising his contemporaries and rejecting claims by
others on fellowship or compassion, feelings that he regarded as shameful
weaknesses. Nietzsche advertised this ideal strongly as a virile one, and
buttressed it by a great deal of spiteful misogyny in the style of Rousseau
and Schopenhauer. He did not, apparently, see that solitude might as easily
be a refuge for weakness as an assertion of strength, nor that childish
boasting about one's own superiority makes this interpretation rather likely.

Nietzsche was, of course, in many ways an impressive and serious thinker.
But he was an astonishingly uneven and unselfcritical one. His chosen
solitude made it hard for him to spot defects in his thought, and – exactly
as happened with Rousseau – in that protected environment his neuroses,
flourishing like green bay trees, often seized his pen and distorted his
metaphysics.

It is not possible to make literal, explicit sense of the idea of many
private, personalised moralities, all quite separate from each other. Nietzsche
may indeed not have meant us to take it literally, for he always worked
through rhetoric and often laughed at systematic theorists. But, since he
has become a recognised sage, people do take it literally. Fantasies like this
are, of course, quite as influential as completed systems, and Nietzsche
certainly meant them to be influential.

The respectful way to treat him is not to put all his views politely in a
museum, but to do as he did himself and point out sharply which of the
things he said have living value, and which are – like this one – poppy-
cock. (I have discussed Immoralism further in my book *Wickedness*.[4])

INVENTING VALUES

This Nietzschean moral fantasy is surely the source of Sartre's similar suggestions that we need, in some sense, to create or invent our own values. Values
might in principle be anything. 'One can', he says, 'choose anything, but
only if it is upon the plane of true commitment'. Someone might, he adds,
object that ' "your values are not serious, since you choose them yourselves".
To that I can only say that I am very sorry that it should be so, but if I
have excluded God the Father, there must be somebody to invent values.'[5]

So what happens (as the philosopher Philippa Foot once asked) if I
choose that the only value shall be not-treading-on-the-lines-of-the-paving-
stones, or perhaps sneezing-every-ten-minutes?[6] Would this then become
a value? Certainly it is not one at the present, but then that is just why I

have had to invent it. If I show true commitment – devote my life to doing these things – will that constitute these as my invented values? Or does commitment perhaps also involve vigorous efforts to convert others to doing them too?

FREE FROM WHAT?

The interesting question is, what is wrong with this example? Plainly, we would not in fact see it as an instance of moral freedom, but of obsession, that is, of being made *unfree* by an arbitrary compulsion, extraneous to the personality.

What is the difference? Philippa Foot pointed out that, though perhaps anything could, in principle, be said to have value, not everything can be so described intelligibly. The question always arises, what kind of value does it have? When people praise something that we do not see the point of, we ask for that point, and often we are given it. This is necessary, not just to convince others, but for our own satisfaction.

The sneezer or paving-stone-avoider might explain their precepts as religious rituals, or perhaps as promoting health. But they would have to make it clear why they were so, and they would depend, both for satisfying themselves and for convincing anyone else, on a pre-existing, shared understanding of the sort of value that health or religion themselves have. Language is not private. What makes the moral judgement intelligible is a background range of values and ideals, furnished partly by our culture, but also, more deeply, by our common species-repertoire.

Kant, in fact, was not being silly in emphasizing the communal background needed for morality. No doubt he was too narrow in his ideas of what was actually moral conduct, and also too confident about the role of reasoning, as opposed to feeling, in producing agreement. But he was right that background agreement was necessary, and that new, free thinking must be intelligibly related to what it grew out of. Moral insights are not explosions, interrupting all previous thought. They are organic growths, continuing existing lines. However startling they may be, they always arise from a community, and they always aspire to go on and influence a community.

How seriously were these professions of solipsistic moral independence actually meant? They have certainly been of enormous use to adolescents at the stage of life when they need to develop away from their homes. (At that point it may sometimes even be necessary to forget for the moment one's dependence on others.) They also have a particular value in public situations such as Sartre's – that of the French Resistance during the Second World War – where outside circumstances force a sudden, drastic change in the moral options open to people. But at other times it is hard to see what they could amount to.

In actual life, both Sartre and Nietzsche were men of principle, who in fact took a great deal of trouble to justify their actions to others, and sometimes vigorously to promote particular public causes. In doing this, they used the common moral vocabulary without embarrassment, and appealed to existing notions of value. They did indeed show originality in making new moral suggestions, in a way which can well be described as refining or extending or reshaping values. But what could it mean to invent a new one? And if this were somehow done, how could it appear as the work of the will rather than of the imagination? More significantly, for our present purposes, what had become of the body?

WHICH WAY IS LEFT?

The whole idea of centring human personality on the (disembodied) will is, I think, imaginative and moral propaganda rather than a piece of dispassionate psychological analysis. It is an image designed to move people from certain current positions, an image that ought never to have been let harden into a metaphysical doctrine about what a human being essentially is. Up to a point, no doubt, all such ideas are coloured in this way. That is why it is essential to understand what their message is – how they are intended to work. Politically, this exaltation of the individual will has in the past been popular on the 'Left' in so far as Leftness means innovation, because the will was needed in order to break free from the emotional bonds of convention. Besides, demands for individual freedom – of a modest, political sort, not extreme Sartrean internal freedom – are another mark of Leftness.

The Right/Left antithesis is, however, confused and unhelpful on this topic, as on many others. It is not clear where, on that political spectrum, we should place the unspoken creed which runs, 'I believe only in the independent, creative individual. The one certain human duty is to avoid interfering with that individual, and it is a duty demanded particularly from women.' If there is such a spectrum, its ends run round behind and join each other.

On the recognised Right, the ideal of a free spirit as a heroic individual, a stern ruler poised above the foolish multitude, has been very powerful. Nietzsche liked it, but its most eloquent proponent was Carlyle, who is worth hearing on our present topic. After his wife's death, Carlyle told Tyndall broken-heartedly 'how loyally and lovingly she had made herself a soft cushion to protect him from the rude collisions of the world'.

How could someone whose lifelong theme was heroism, and who held great audiences spellbound by celebrating it, make such a claim and such an admission? Why did he need his 'cushion'? Clashes between ideals never bothered Carlyle much, since he thought consistency rather a fiddling consideration anyway. But he also had a real advantage here over many theorists of his time and ours in that he had never claimed to subscribe to the ideals of liberty, equality, and fraternity. Could people who did subscribe to them take the same line about women? It might seem hard, but most of them managed it. As Mill remarked,

> The social subordination of women stands out, an isolated fact in modern social institutions . . . a single relic of an old world of thought and practice exploded in everything else, but retained in the one thing of most universal interest; as if a gigantic dolmen, or temple of Jupiter Olympius, occupied the site of St. Paul's and received daily worship, while the surrounding Christian churches were resorted to only on fasts and festivals.[7]

Women (that is) were still called on to remain hierarchical, feudal, emotional, 'bodily', and biological, in order to make it possible for the men to become totally free, equal, autonomous, intellectual, and creative.

IMAGES IN MANY MIRRORS

Although life in many parts of the world is still conducted on this assumption, there are now considerable difficulties about defending it in the West. Too many women have noticed the absurdity of the demand, and are impolite enough to mention it. They cannot all be put down by being called hyenas. Politically speaking, then, the choice now is between promoting everybody – equally – to the position of the Hobbesian or Sartrean solitary individual, or rethinking that notion of individuality radically from scratch.

It is cheering to see that feminists are now proving very critical of the moves toward the first solution, which were rather common a few decades back.[8] Undoubtedly, the rethinking option is the one we shall have to try. Much good feminist writing now is devoted to attempting it, and this is, of course, what I am trying to do now. But the way forward is by no means clear.

Why, however (you are still wondering) do I persist in talking about the relations between the sexes instead of getting down directly to the mind/body problem? I answer: *because mind/body problems, being queries about ourselves, never do present themselves to us directly.* They are always seen reflected indirectly in some mirror or other, and the distortions of the particular mirror are crucial to understanding them. They always appear in our lives in terms of myth, and the current myths are shot through with dramas about gender.

Consider, for instance, these remarks from Sartre, when, in his exaltation of the will, he has occasion to denounce physical matter as alien to it, and therefore to our essential being. We could hardly hope for a more explicit connection of the physical or bodily and the 'feminine'. He describes the material world as 'viscous', clinging to us in order to entrap us:

> The For-Itself is suddenly *compromised*. I open my hands, I want to let go of the slimy and it sticks to me, it draws me, it sucks at me . . . It is a soft, yielding action, a moist and feminine sucking . . . it draws me to it as the bottom of a precipice might draw me . . . Slime is the revenge of the In-Itself. A sickly-sweet, feminine revenge . . . The obscenity of the feminine sex is that of everything which 'gapes open'. It is an *appeal to being*, as all holes are . . . Beyond any doubt her sex is a mouth and a voracious mouth which devours the penis.[9]

This shows how extraordinarily easy it is, when trying to talk about the whole human condition, to project one's fantasies on to this vast screen, and how dominant, among such fantasies, is the kind of conflict which readily presents itself both as one of reason versus feeling and also as one between the sexes.

Certainly, this is an unguarded passage, not the sort of thing that would appear in sober Anglo-American philosophical journals. Of course I have chosen it for that reason. But these bizarre statements about the isolation of the will are useful just because they are unguarded. We have grown so used to the greyer, more moderate forms that they pervade our thinking and are hard to notice. For instance, R. M. Hare's highly respectable, academic, 'prescriptivist' account of morals[10] may have roots in a notion of individual moral freedom not wholly unlike Sartre's existentialist one (despite all the differences). Could it therefore be that it owes its success to the fact that its readers had, at some imaginative level, already accepted the more colourful existentialist account? The point I have been raising here is what package of assumptions goes along with such a view? What unspoken prejudices about bodiliness and femaleness? These questions are always worth probing.

THE APOTHEOSIS OF THE INTELLECT

So far, I have been dealing chiefly with the notion of the essential self as the will. The will has, however, always been thought of as accompanied by, and using, the intellect. 'Reason' in the eighteenth-century sense included both; indeed, as Kant put it, the will simply is practical reason. Today, this idea has branched away from straightforward exaltation of the will to produce a rival diagnosis of personal identity as centring on the scientific intellect.

This is now a powerful idea, especially where people interested in artificial intelligence want to blur the differences between people and computer programs. Space allows me only a single example of this syndrome, and for reasons already given I choose a lurid one, which is, however, backed by some highly respected scientists.[11]

It has for some time been proposed that *Homo sapiens* should colonise space, and should, for convenience in this project, transform himself mechanically into non-organic forms. This project is now held to look increasingly feasible, on the grounds that computer software is the same whatever kind of hardware it runs on, and that minds are only a kind of computer software. Thus, as the eminent Princeton physicist Freeman Dyson puts it:

> It is impossible to set any limit to the variety of physical forms that life may assume . . . It is conceivable that in another 10^{10} years life could evolve away from flesh and blood and become embodied in an interstellar black cloud . . . or in a sentient computer . . . [12]

Our successors can thus not only avoid ordinary death, but also survive (if you care to call it surviving) the heat-death of the universe, and sit about in electronic form exchanging opinions in an otherwise empty cosmos. This, Dyson thinks, would restore the meaning to life, which has otherwise been drained from it by the thought that final destruction is unavoidable.

Could fear and hatred of the flesh go further? Behind this lies Bernal's prophecy, which we have noted earlier, a prophecy to which Dyson acknowledges his debt, that,

> As the scene of life would be more the cold emptiness of space than the warm, dense atmosphere of the planets, the advantage of containing no organic material at all . . . would be increasingly felt . . . *Bodies at this time would be left far behind* . . . [13]

Reason, in fact, can at last divorce the unsatisfactory wife he has been complaining of since the eighteenth century, and can live comfortably for ever among the boys playing computer-games in the solitudes of space. Is that not touching?

PERSISTENT GHOSTS

Of course the cult of the cerebral has milder, less frantic aspects than this and did not originally require such aberrations. But it has hypertrophied, and today it generates them. The individual will and intellect are exalted in a way that can make any interference with them – even that of the other features of the organism they belong to – seem an outrage.

Moral solipsism is on offer. It is not just that rational choice is exalted high above the emotions. It has also been sharply separated from them, treated as the central, necessary part of the personal identity while the emotions are a chance, extraneous matter. This analysis is not just inhumane, it is incoherent. Choice and thought cannot be separated from feeling and imagination; they are all aspects of personality. Exalters of choice and of the intellect are not free from feeling; they are unconsciously led by one set of feelings rather than another, often to very strange and disagreeable places. The division between mind and body, conceived as essentially one between reason and feeling, is not necessary. There is no set of perforations down the middle of a human being directing us to tear at this point.

Contemporary philosophers have noted this in a variety of useful discussions.[14] Unlike the popular mythologies we have been examining, recent philosophy of mind has done its best to see off the disembodied hero of the Enlightenment. Its preference remains, overwhelmingly, for a 'materialist' account of the mind/body relation, however subtly phrased.[15] What is ironic, however, about this ostensible rejection of 'dualism' by most contemporary philosophers of mind, is the persistence in their thinking of shades of the Enlightenment ghost they thought they had routed. For, when they discourse about the 'mind/body' relation, they rarely consider anything in that 'body' below the level of the neck. Either they focus exclusively on the mind's relation to the brain, or, more generally, on its relation to the physical world *tout court*. Flesh and bones (and, unsurprisingly, women's minds) are still relatively neglected subjects in the field. Nor do thinkers find it easy to bring thought and feeling together realistically so as to make sense of the relation between them. We will look at this difficulty in our next chapter.

16

BIOTECHNOLOGY AND
THE YUK FACTOR

—— ·•· ——

THE BIFURCATION OF MORALS

We have been noticing that human beings are not loosely composed of two separate items. There is no perforation down the middle that reads 'Tear here to detach body from mind'. Nor, as is also sometimes suggested, do they consist of only one of these items, the other having been thrown away.

In observing this, we have noticed, too, the absence of another suggested perforation in these beings, one which would be marked 'Tear here to detach reason from feeling'. In real life, we tend not to find that reason and feeling are separate items. They are interdependent aspects of a person, divisible only for thought. But attempts to separate these factors and set them at war have been extremely common. It is worth while to see how they are working now on some current issues that concern many of us.

We might ask, then, What kinds of moral objections are there to interventions such as xenotransplantation, genetic engineering, and bio-engineering generally? In answering such questions, ethicists often like to divide moral arguments firmly into two sets, ones that point to dangerous consequences and ones that say the act itself is intrinsically wrong. But unless the two angles are brought together again at some point, this division can split the subject disastrously.

It is often hard to consider probable consequences on their own, since we really do not know what they are likely to be. On the other hand, trying to consider intrinsic objections on their own, apart from consequences, seems unrealistic. We feel that these direct objections must be irrational because the only rational way to judge things *is*, as utilitarians suggest, by weighing their consequences. People are inclined to dismiss intrinsic objections as emotional, subjective, something that can't really be justified or argued about at all. But, as just noticed, the probable consequences themselves often are not clear enough to make reasoned conclusions possible either. So both lines of enquiry fail.

It is not very helpful to see debates in this way as flat conflicts between thought and feeling because, usually, both are engaged on both sides. In the case of bio-engineering, I think this approach has been specially unfortunate. People often have the impression that reason quite simply favours the new developments although feeling is against them. This stereotyping paralyses them because they cannot see how to arbitrate between these very different litigants.

In fact, however, debate hardly ever really is between these two. Feelings always incorporate thoughts – often ones that are not yet fully articulated – and reasons are always found in response to particular sorts of feelings. On both sides, we need to look for the hidden partners. We have to articulate the ideas behind emotional objections and to note the emotional element in claims that are supposed to be purely rational. The best way to do this is often to start by taking the intrinsic objections more seriously. If we look below the surface of feeling we may find thoughts that show how the two aspects are connected.

In the case of biotechnology, such thoughts do indeed emerge. What is really worrying the objectors is not, I think, the detail of any particular proposal. It is the hype, the scale of the proposed project, the weight of the economic forces now backing it, and the sweeping change of attitude that is being demanded. Biotechnology on the scale that many people are now demanding it does not appear to be compatible with our existing concepts of nature and species – concepts that are part of our current science as well as of everyday thought. A new ideology is being proposed that would remodel those concepts to fit the new technologies, envisaging species as unreal and nature as infinitely malleable.

Hard experience may, of course, cut these vast aspirations down to size anyway. The hopes offered may be disappointed, as happened with earlier technological miracles such as nuclear power. But whether they are or not, we need to be critical of attempts like this to remodel our whole idea of nature on the pattern of one particular, currently favoured technology. We know that seventeenth-century mechanists were mistaken in supposing the world to be made of clockwork, and a twentieth-century repetition of their overconfidence does not seem likely to work out any better. So questions about biotechnology raise wide issues, not just about the relation of thought to feeling and of acts to consequences but also about where our world pictures come from and what needs to happen when we change them.

GETTING WHAT WE ASK FOR

To begin, however, with the question of acts and consequences: it is interesting to note that some consequences are not just a matter of chance. Acts that are wrong in themselves can be expected to have bad effects of

103

a particular kind that is not just accidental. Their badness follows from what is wrong in the act itself, so that there is a rational, conceptual link between them and their results. These consequences are a sign of what was wrong with the act in the first place.

I shall suggest later that this kind of connection between act and consequence does indeed help us to make sense of the objections raised to bio-engineering. But we should notice first that this kind of reasoning isn't something new and sinister. It is commonplace in other realms of morals. For instance, it is no accident that habitual and systematic lying, or habitual and systematic injustice, have bad effects in human life. These habits can be expected to destroy mutual trust and respect, not accidentally, but because accepting those consequences is part of the act. Acts of lying or injustice are themselves expressions of disrespect and untrustworthiness, so they unavoidably call for more of the same.

Similarly, institutions such as torture, or slavery, or any gross subjection of one class to another, have moral consequences that are not accidental. We can expect those consequences to follow, not because of a contingent causal link (like expecting that a tornado may kill someone) but because they are effects that anyone who acts in this way invites and is committed to accepting. Slavery asks for resentment, bitterness, and corruption, attitudes that cannot fail to produce the sorts of acts that express them. In a most intelligible phrase, those who institute slavery *get what they are asking for*. Hubris calls for nemesis, and in one form or another it's going to get it, not as a punishment from outside but as the completion of a pattern already started.

This language of 'getting what you asked for' seems to me important. It has been heard on all sides and from all kinds of people in Britain lately about 'mad cow disease'. That disease apparently arose because, in order to save expense, sheep's brains, along with other animal waste, were used as an ingredient in cattle feed. This device seems to have transferred a disease of sheep to great numbers of cattle, who had to be slaughtered. The disease then spread to humans who had eaten the beef, giving an indefinite and still increasing number of people a new and disastrous form of an illness known as Creutzfeldt-Jacob disease.

People who say that this kind of consequence might have been expected are not, of course, saying that there is a particular causal law to the effect that 'feeding animal waste to herbivores always gives them an illness that can ravage the meat industry and then destroy humans'. Nor are they saying that 'wickedness is always punished'. Their thought is less simple and has both a moral and a causal aspect. It runs, I think, something like this: 'You can't expect to go on forever exploiting living creatures if you don't pay some attention to their natural needs. You ought not to be trying to do that in the first place. Neglecting the species-nature of cows is wrong in itself. It is a gross insult to the life of the animals. So it should be no surprise that this insult upsets their health, with unpredictable further consequences. These consequences are not, then, an accident. They flow directly from the moral obtuseness that goes with greed.'

THE ROLE OF FEELING IN MORALS

I have not said anything yet about how far this way of objecting is justified. I am merely explaining it. Later on I want to look more closely at some of the ideas involved in it, especially at the key concepts of 'species' and 'nature'. But just now I want simply to spell out its reasoning, pointing out that it is not just a formless emotional cry. These people are not, as is sometimes suggested, merely expressing an inarticulate disgust at the unfamiliar by exclaiming 'yuk'. Their further conversation shows that they are saying something intelligible, something that needs to be answered. To state the point briefly, they are objecting to attacks on the concept of species. And I think there is good reason for that objection.

This point needs to be made because direct, intrinsic objections to bio-engineering often are seen as being beneath the level of the real argument. They are described as 'the yuk factor'. They may still be treated with respect for political reasons, because they are known to be influential. And they may also be tolerated because of a general belief that all ethics is irrational anyway – a notion that feeling is always separate from reason – so that their wildness is not particularly surprising. Often, too, these objections are expressed in religious language, and many people now seem to think that religious language cannot be understood by outsiders. Religious thought is conceived as being so isolated from the rest of our reasoning as scarcely to count as thought at all, so this, too, can make them seem undiscussable. (For that reason I shall avoid religious language in this discussion, trying to keep it entirely in secular terms.) Thus current forms of relativism and subjectivism can generate a mindless approach to morals, a sort of weary tolerance of sensible and foolish scruples alike.

I think we can do better than this. We can try to understand them.

In the first place, I am suggesting generally that the 'yuk factor', this sense of disgust and outrage, is in itself by no means a sign of irrationality. Feeling is an essential part of our moral life, though of course not the whole of it. Heart and mind are not enemies or alternative tools. They are complementary aspects of a single process. Whenever we seriously judge something to be wrong, strong feeling necessarily accompanies the judgement. Someone who does not have such feelings – someone who has merely a theoretical interest in morals, who doesn't feel any indignation or disgust and outrage about things like slavery and torture – has missed the point of morality altogether.

UNNATURAL?

Of course we know that these feelings are not an infallible guide. Of course we need to supplement them by thought, analysing their meaning and articulating them in a way that gives us coherent and usable standards. Unanalysed feelings sometimes turn out to be misplaced. Disgust can spring from chance associations or unfamiliarity or mere physical revulsion, such as a horror of cats. We always have to look below the surface. We must spell out the message of our emotions and see what they are trying to tell us. And we have actually quite a good, flexible vocabulary for doing this, for articulating their meaning and seeing how much it matters.

For instance, if somebody says that agriculture or contraception or keeping animals as pets is unnatural, others can understand what objection they are making even if they disagree. A reasonable argument can follow, weighing pros against cons. It is true that agriculture was indeed the first move in shifting human life away from the approximate balance with its surroundings that seems to have marked a life spent in hunting and gathering. And contraception is indeed a considerable interference with a central area of human social and emotional life. These are real objections that can be spelled out, made clearer, and set against other considerations. All parties can then consider the balance and ask what matters most, which is where the thinking comes in. Gradually, given time and good will, agreement is often arrived at. This has happened about countless issues in the past, often resulting in the whole issue being forgotten. The work may be hard, but in principle these are matters that can be decided in rational terms – not ones that must be left to a brute clash of inarticulate feelings, even though they arose from feelings in the first place.

Nor is the notion of something's being wrong because it is *unnatural* an empty one. Suppose that someone suggests that it is unnatural to bring up children impersonally without individual bonds to carers, as Plato proposed, and as modern theorists like Shulamith Firestone and the behaviourist J. B. Watson have also demanded. Or, that it is unnatural to prevent children from playing or to keep them in solitude. Most of us are likely to agree with this objection, to accept its language, and to feel outrage if these things are seriously proposed.

Of course the notion of *human nature* has often been distorted and misused. Yet it is clear that we need it and rely on it on such occasions. The same is true of the notion of *human rights*, in spite of many obscurities. That too is supposed to follow simply from membership in our species. These rights are not cancelled by culture, as they would be if we were simply moulded by our society and had no original nature. They are rights that are supposed to guarantee the kind of life that all specimens of *Homo sapiens* need: a kind different from what might suit intelligent kangaroos or limpets or pure disembodied minds. That is why people complain that human beings who are badly treated have been 'treated like animals'. It is taken for granted that we know what a distinctively human nature demands.

This point is often hard to remember today simply because the notion of human nature has so often been misused for political purposes by people wanting to resist reform. The whole idea has been well pummelled during the Enlightenment. But that doesn't mean we can do without it.

Of course this notion, like many other important ones, is many-sided, wobbly, and often obscure. It is so because our nature is complex and makes conflicting demands, between which we have to arbitrate. But we cannot dispense with the idea. It is a standard we must use whenever we want to assess and criticise our institutions. We need some conception of the human nature that we think they ought to fit as a criterion for judging them. We are always developing and updating that notion, but we never try to do without it. We need it for understanding both our own moral reactions and other people's, rather than merely fighting about them. Accordingly, when people who are worried about new technologies complain that they are unnatural, we should try to understand what they are objecting to. We might find something serious.

A notable example of this in our tradition occurred when people began to be sensitive about cruelty, which they really had not been before. In the sixteenth century a few bold people, such as Montaigne, began to express disgust and outrage about judicial torture and the use of cruel punishments, and also about the abuse of animals. They said that these customs, which had largely been taken for granted as perfectly normal and justified before, were *monstrous, unnatural,* and *inhuman.* Because of the strength of their indignant feeling, other people listened and gradually began to agree with them. The notion of what is *human* took a surprising turn to include this kind of response to suffering.

This meant that, during the Enlightenment, the 'humane' movement gathered strength, articulated its objections, and became a real political force. People began to think seriously that it was a bad thing to inflict suffering when they didn't need to. They no longer felt that they ought to repress their sympathetic feelings as unmanly. Attention to that range of sympathetic feelings stirred up reasoning that altered our world view. It called for different ideas about the entire status of humanity and of the natural world that we inhabit, ideas that are still being developed and are still very important to us today.

17

THE NEW ALCHEMY

———•◆•———

HOW SOLID ARE SPECIES?

Let us turn, then, from this general discussion to listen for a moment to the people who now express their disgust about bio-engineering and ask what these objectors are thinking, rather than merely what they are feeling. There are, after all, quite a lot of them, many of them thoughtful people, who have strong views about it. As Jean Bethke Elshtain put it in an article on cloning:

> This is an extraordinarily unsettling development. ... It was anything but amusing to overhear the speculation that cloning might be made available to parents about to lose a child, or having lost a child to an accident, in order that they might reproduce and replace that lost child. This image borders on obscenity. ... The usual nostrums are no use here. I have in mind the standard cliché that, once again, our ethical thinking hasn't caught up with technological 'advance'. This is a flawed way to reflect on cloning and so much else. The problem is not that we must somehow catch up our ethics to our technology. The problem is that technology is rapidly gutting our ethics. And it is *our* ethics. Ethical reflection belongs to all of us – all those agitated radio callers – and it is the fears and apprehensions of ordinary citizens that should be paid close and respectful attention.[1]

This is surely a reasonable demand, whether we are eventually going to agree with their objections or not. And their thought is not, I think, particularly obscure. It centres on the concept of the *monstrous*. Bio-engineering, at least in some forms, is seen as monstrous or unnatural, in a sense that means a great deal more than just unusual or unfamiliar. This sense is very interesting and needs to be examined.

The natural element that is seen as threatened here focuses on the concept of a species. Our tradition has so far held that this concept should be taken pretty seriously, that the boundaries of a species should be respected. One obvious example of this is the objection generally held to sexual inter-course with other animals. At a popular level, too, this conviction is reflected in the symbolism of our myths. Traditional mixed monsters – minotaurs, chimeras, lamias, gorgons – stand for a deep and threatening disorder, something not just confusing but dreadful and invasive. Although benign monsters such as Pegasus and archangels are occasionally found, in general the symbolism of mixing species is deeply uncanny and threatening. Even less mixed monsters, such as giants and three-headed dogs, are so framed as to violate the principles of construction that normally make life possible for their species. They too are usually seen as alien and destructive forces.

Science too has up till now supported this tradition by taking species seriously and in general still does so today. Of course scientific ideas about it have changed in one very important respect. We now know that species are not permanent, timeless essences – that they have been formed and can change and decay – and also that a few species hybridise and mingle at their borders.

All the same, on the whole biologists still see species as profoundly shaped by the niches that they occupy. Fertile hybrids are known to be rare and usually unsuccessful. Current biology tends to stress rather strongly the extent to which each species is adapted to fit its niche and must keep its parts exactly suited to each other if it is to survive. Biologists are now much given to studying *evolutionary functions*: to asking why creatures have just this or that set of characteristics and explaining how this set is needed to fit them for their own peculiar way of life.

On the whole, then, today's evolutionary biology tells us that however much we might want to have a world filled with novelties and monsters, chimeras and winged horses and three-headed dogs, we can't, because in the real environment these would not be viable life forms. We can make mice with human ears on their backs in the laboratory, but they could not survive in the wild. Similarly, the lion-tiger hybrids that can sometimes be bred in zoos could not make a living in the habitat of either parent species. Their muddled mix of inherited traits unfits them for either parent's lifestyle. In fact, it seems that actually very few evolutionary niches are available at any given time, and that these are normally far apart, accommodating only the rather widely varied creatures that now occupy them. Most of the range of apparent possibilities between is not habitable. That is why there have been so many extinctions; threatened species could not usually find some-where else to go. Any change that is not directly demanded by altered outside circumstances is likely to be lethal. Evolution, in fact, knows what it is about when it puts together the repertoire of characteristics that marks a species.

TAKING CHARGE OF NATURE

Lately, however, some distinguished champions of bio-engineering have started to tell a different story, claiming that this whole idea of firm divisions among species is out of date. Not only (they say) can some characteristics be moved about among species, but there is no reason in principle why all characteristics should not be so moved. Species are not serious entities at all, merely fluid stages on a path along which organisms can always be shifted and transformed into one another. This transformability is called *algeny*, a name modelled on alchemy but this time (it is claimed) not a mistake but a genuine advance. (The name has not been devised as a joke by outside critics. It comes from Joshua Lederberg, a Nobel laureate biologist and past president of Rockefeller University who is a powerful champion of bio-engineering.[2])

Algenists propose, then, that just as the alchemists thought of all chemical substances as merely stages on an unbroken continuum, so biologists should see living species as stages on a continuum along which, in principle, they can always be moved and exchange their properties. As in alchemy, this process has a direction, the word 'alchemy' itself being apparently derived from an Arabic word for 'perfection'. For the alchemists, all metals were in the process of becoming gold. Alchemists saw themselves as midwives accelerating this natural process of improvement. And, notoriously, this was for them not just a commercial enterprise but also a mystical and religious one. When Meister Eckhart wrote that 'copper is restless until it becomes gold'[3] he was speaking figuratively of the soul's struggle for salvation, a way of thinking that still impressed Newton.

In the same way today, the mystics of the genetic revolution see themselves as experts engaged in completing nature's work and especially in the business of ultimately perfecting humanity. As Robert Sinsheimer puts it,

> The old dreams of the cultural perfection of man were always sharply constrained by his inherited imperfections and limitations. ... The horizons of the new eugenics are in principle boundless – for *we* should have the potential to create new genes and new qualities yet undreamed of. ... Indeed this concept marks a turning-point in the whole evolution of life. For the first time in all time, a living creature understands its origin and can undertake to design its future. Even in the ancient myths man was constrained by essence. He could not rise above his nature to chart his destiny. Today we can envision that chance – and its dark companion of awesome choice and responsibility.[4]

More recently, Gregory Stock has carried this banner further in a widely-sold book called *Redesigning Humans: Choosing Our Children's Genes*.[5] In his first chapter, which is called 'The Last Human', he remarks that 'we are on the cusp of profound biological change, poised to transcend our current form and character on a journey to destinations of new imagination'. This journey, as he later explains, has become possible because

> the technological powers we have hitherto used so effectively to remake our world are now potent and precise enough for us to turn them on ourselves ... With our biological research we are taking control of evolution and beginning to direct it ... Ray Kurzweil, the inventor of the Kurzweil reading machine, the Kurzweil music synthesizer and other high-tech products, ... [predicts that] 'We will enhance our brains gradually through direct connexion with machine intelligence until the essence of our thinking has fully migrated to the far more capable and reliable new machinery' ... By 2029, computer technology will have progressed to the point where 'direct neural pathways have been perfected for high-bandwidth connection to the human brain' ... As Hans Moravec ... points out in *Mind Children* ... once we build human-equivalent computers, they will figure out how to build superhuman ones ... One day we will manipulate the genes of our children in sophisticated ways, using advanced germinal choice technologies ... The desire and the perceived need are clear.[6]

This last point is important to Stock because he realises that not all his readers will at once agree that they feel this irresistible desire. He meets that difficulty with two alternative strategies which are both familiar legacies from the Marxist Utopian tradition. Part of the time, he assures us that we probably do want these changes even if we aren't aware of it yet. But it doesn't much matter if some of us don't want them, because everybody else does, so these things will happen anyway. The rest of the time, he concedes that perhaps we don't quite want them yet, but urges us to get over this weakness by nerving ourselves to follow our spiritual destiny – not because we know what it is but, on the contrary, just because we don't:

> Ironically, embracing the challenges and goals of these transformative technologies is an act of extraordinary faith. It embodies an acceptance of a human fate written both in our underlying nature and in the biology that constitutes us. We cannot know where self-directed evolution will take us, nor hope to control the process for very long ...
>
> *In offering ourselves as vessels for potential transformation into we know not what, we are submitting to the shaping hand of a process that dwarfs us individually* ... From a spiritual perspective, the project of humanity's self-evolution is the ultimate embodiment of

our science and ourselves as a cosmic instrument in our ongoing emergence . . . We know all too well our limitations, our ineptitudes and weaknesses. No wonder the idea that we would attempt to fashion not only our future world but our future selves terrifies many people . . . We would be flying forward with no idea where we are going and no safety-net to catch us . . . If, instead of blinding ourselves with Utopian images we admit that we don't know where we are headed, maybe we will work harder to ensure that the process itself serves us, and in the end that is what we must count on.[7]

This vision would, of course, look more impressive if it was really *ourselves* that we were offering up as vessels to this mysterious process rather than our unfortunate descendants. But in that case we should, of course, probably be even less willing to sign up for it. The pronoun *we* operates very oddly in these contexts.

Stock also quotes, though a little less confidently, from the 1992 manifesto of a sect called The Extropians, so named because they don't believe in entropy. It is a letter to Mother Nature:

Mother Nature, truly we are grateful for what you have made us. No doubt you did the best you could. However, with all due respect, we must say that you have in many ways done a poor job with the human constitution. You have made us vulnerable to disease and damage. You compel us to age and die – just as we're beginning to attain wisdom. And, you forgot to give us the operating manual for ourselves! . . . What you have made is glorious, yet deeply flawed . . . We have decided that it is time to amend the human constitution . . . We do not do this lightly, carelessly or disrespectfully, but cautiously, intelligently and in pursuit of excellence . . . Over the coming decades we will pursue a series of changes to our own constitution . . . We will no longer tolerate the tyranny of aging and death . . . We will expand our perceptual range . . . improve on our neural organization and capacity . . . reshape our motivational patterns and emotional responses . . . take charge over our genetic programming and achieve mastery over our biological and neurological processes.[8]

If we 'reshape our motivational patterns and emotional responses', presumably making them different, how do we know that we shall then want to go on with these projects that we have started? Where is this confidence in I-know-not-whattery supposed to come from? Faith is certainly in great demand in these quarters, and it is not in short supply. Similarly, species-transformations are confidently seen as being quite straightforward. Thus Thomas Eisner writes,

As a consequence of recent advances in genetic engineering, [a biological species] must be viewed as ... a depository of genes that are potentially transferable. A species is not merely a hard-bound volume of the library of nature. It is also a loose-leaf book, whose individual pages, the genes, might be available for selective transfer and modification of other species.[9]

18

THE SUPERNATURAL ENGINEER

——— .•. ———

IMAGES OF ALIENATION

What does this idea of separable leaves amount to? Scientifically, of course, the idea doesn't work. This language reflects an unusable view of genetics, so-called 'bean-bag genetics' of the crudest kind: one gene, one characteristic. From the metaphorical angle too, the implications of these pictures are not encouraging. The idea of improving books by splicing in bits of other books is not seductive because in books, as in organisms, ignoring the context usually produces nonsense. Nor is the parallel with the chemical elements, which is more seriously meant, any more hopeful. Of course it is true that atomic scientists did, up to a point, confirm the alchemists' suspicion that it was possible to break the boundaries between elements. They broke them at Los Alamos and Hiroshima and on a number of other occasions since, for instance at Chernobyl. But these events did not generate any general recipe for breaking them safely and successfully. Nor did researchers discover that the elements evince any general progress toward ultimate perfection, either in gold or in *Homo sapiens*.

Another more powerful image, however, lurks behind this one. It is the image constantly suggested by the word 'engineering': the simple analogy with machines. Cogs and sprockets can in principle be moved from one machine to another since they are themselves fairly simple artefacts, and the working of these machines is more or less fully understood by their designers. Those who use this analogy seem to be claiming that we have a similar understanding of the plants and animals into which we might put new components. But we did not design those plants and animals. This is perhaps a rather important difference.

The really strange and disturbing thing about all these images is the alienation of the human operator from the system he works on. He appears outside the system. He is an autonomous critic, independent of the forces that shape everything around him, a fastidious reader in a position to reshape books to suit his own taste, a detached engineer redesigning a car to his own satisfaction. Even when the book or car in question is a human body – perhaps his own – this designer stands outside it, a superior being who does not share its nature. Readers can always get another book if they don't like the first one, and car-owners are not much surprised at having to get another car.

What sort of being, then, is this operator supposed to be? He (it surely is a he) can only be a Cartesian disembodied soul, a ghost working on the machine. He 'lives in his body' only in the sense in which a yachtsman might live in his boat. Like so much of the science fiction that has influenced them, these images are irremediably dualist, implying a quite unreal separation between ourselves and the physical world we live in. Today we are supposed to have escaped from Descartes's dualistic prison, but some of us don't even want to try to.[1]

NEW TECHNOLOGIES, NEW WORLD VIEWS

How seriously ought we to take these algenic manifestos? Need we really worry about their strange metaphors?

Of course, not all bio-engineers sign up for this bizarre ideology, or want to. They may well not speak or write in these terms. All the same, it surely does seem that they are often acting in those terms, whether consciously or not. The scale on which the whole work is going forward, the colossal confidence expressed in it, the way in which it distracts attention from other possible enterprises, the rate at which money flows into it rather than in other directions, all seem to imply a belief that its possibilities are unparalleled – potentially infinite. It is taken for granted that this is the best way to solve our problems. It is expected, quite generally, that social questions will have this kind of biochemical solution.

This is surely what appals the objectors. What they are essentially rejecting is not any particular single project. It is this huge uncriticised impetus, this indiscriminate, infectious corporate overconfidence, this obsessive one-way channelling of energy, fired by a single vision. The speed and scale involved are crucial. Single projects, introduced slowly, tentatively, and critically, would not necessarily disrupt our whole idea of nature. We have got used to many such changes in human history. But it always takes time to learn to live with them, to get a realistic idea of their pros and cons, to fit new things into our lives without wasteful misdirection. It is already taking us a long time to do that with existing inventions such as contraception and rapid transport.

Anyone who doesn't think this kind of delay is necessary – anyone who wants people to rush with aplomb into this mass investment of mind and resources – does have to be calling for a drastically changed view of nature as a whole, a view that claims that our power and knowledge are such that we can rationally expect to alter everything. To feel this kind of confidence, we would need to stop seeing the natural world as a colossally complex system with its own laws, a system that we, as a tiny part of it, must somehow try to fit into. We would need, instead, to see it simply as a consignment of inert raw material laid out for our use.

To say that this change is *unnatural* is not just to say that it is unfamiliar. It is unnatural in the quite plain sense that it calls on us to alter radically our whole conception of nature. Our culture has of course already moved a long way in the direction of making that shift, from Bacon's trumpet calls in the seventeenth century to Henry Ford's in the twentieth. Of late, however, environmental alarms have sharply slowed that triumphalist movement, making us try to be more realistic about our own vulnerability and dependence. The ideology of algeny is clearly a step backward from that painful struggle toward realism.

In fact, our culture is at present trying to ride two horses here. It is poised uneasily between two views of nature. The confident, contemptuous Baconian view already pervades many of our institutions, notably in intensive farming, where the feeding arrangements that produced mad cow disease are nothing exceptional. Market forces see to it that short-termism and institutionalised callousness already rule the way in which we rear animals for food. Seeing this, proponents of bio-engineering sometimes ask why we should object to moving further in this direction. Doesn't consistency demand that we extend the conquest that we have begun and mechanise our lives completely?

Consistency, however, is notoriously not always a virtue, as the public is uneasily aware. The fact that you have cut off somebody's arm is not always a reason why you have to cut off their leg as well. It is one thing to have drifted into having faulty institutions that one doesn't yet see how to change. Deliberately adopting an ideology that entirely obscures what is bad about them is quite another.

That ideology is what really disturbs me, and I think it is what disturbs the public. This proposed new way of looking at nature is not scientific. It is not something that biology has shown to be necessary. Far from that, it is scientifically muddled. It rests on bad genetics and dubious evolutionary biology. Though it uses science, it is not itself a piece of science but a powerful myth expressing a determination to put ourselves in a relation of control to the non-human world around us, to be in the driving seat at all costs rather than attending to that world and trying to understand how it works. It is a myth that repeats, in a grotesquely simple sense, Marx's rather rash suggestion that the important thing is not to understand the world but to change it. Its imagery is a Brocken spectre, a huge shadow projected on to a cloudy background by the shape of a few recent technological achievements.

The debate then is not between Feeling, in the blue corner, objecting to the new developments, and Reason in the red corner, defending them. Rhetoric such as that of Stock and Sinsheimer and Eisner is not addressed to Reason. It is itself an exuberant power fantasy, very much like the songs sung in the 1950s during the brief period of belief in an atomic free lunch, and also like those in the early days of artificial intelligence. The euphoria is the same. It is, of course, also partly motivated by the same hope of attracting grant money, just as the earlier alchemists needed to persuade powerful patrons that they were going to produce real, coinable gold.

But besides these practical considerations, in each case there is also a sincere excitement, a devout faith, a real sense of contacting something superhuman. The magician becomes intoxicated with the thought that he is at last getting his hands on a power that lies near the heart of life.

This kind of exaltation has a significant history. In our culture it arose first in the seventeenth century, when theorists became fascinated by the burgeoning marvels of clockwork automata. This was the point at which technology began to shape the imagery by which people depicted their world and so to *dictate their metaphysic* – a process that continues and that has profound effects. On each occasion, prophets have gone far beyond the reasonable expectation of useful devices from the new form of work. Each time, they have used this new form to reshape their whole vision of the world, and of themselves, on the pattern of what was going on in their workshops.

In the case of clockwork, Descartes, Newton, and the eighteenth-century mechanists managed to shape a powerful vision that displayed the whole material world as one vast clock, claiming that the right way to understand any part of it was simply to find its 'mechanism', that is, the part of the machine that drove it. The cogs of this machinery were supposed to work always by direct physical impact. That imagery was so strong that, when physicists themselves began to move away from it at the end of the nineteenth century, their attempt raised deep distress in the profession. Einstein and many others felt that rationality itself was threatened. And a general belief in this kind of clockwork undoubtedly remains today, in spite of the shift to electronic machinery. We still talk of 'mechanisms', and we are still not really happy about action at a distance, as in gravitation. And we are still using this language when we talk of 'bio-engineering'. But for the last century we have not been in a position to suppose, as Laplace did, that clockwork is literally the universal structure of the world.

THE RELEVANCE OF 'GOD'

The difficulties of the physicists' shift from strict mechanism show up as a problem that cannot help recurring. How can people who see the world as a reflection of their current favourite technology handle the change from one technology to another? The status of a world view that revolves around a particular technology must vary with that technology's practical success and failure. Yet world views are expected to be permanent, to express timeless truths. Finality is expected when they are supposed to be religious and no less so when they are supposed to be scientific.

The mechanistic picture was both religious and scientific. From the religious angle it did not, in its original form, mark any sharp break from earlier views, since God was still the designer. The stars were still busy, as they were in Addison's hymn,

> For ever singing as they shine
> 'The hand that made us is divine'[2]

This ambiguity was what enabled the pattern to catch on so widely, allowing the general public to accept Pope's celebration of it:

> Nature and Nature's laws lay hid in night,
> God said 'Let Newton be' and all was light.[3]

On the clockwork model the world thus became amazingly intelligible. God, however, gradually withdrew from the scene, leaving a rather unsettling imaginative vacuum. The imagery of machinery survived. But where there is no designer the whole idea of mechanism begins to grow incoherent. Natural selection is supposed to fill the gap, but it is a thin idea, not very satisfying to the imagination.

That is how the gap that hopeful biotechnicians now elect themselves to fill arose. They see that mechanistic thinking calls for a designer, and they feel well qualified to volunteer for that vacant position. Their confidence about this stands out clearly from the words I have emphasised in Sinsheimer's proposal that 'the horizons of the new eugenics are in principle boundless – for *we* should have the potential to create new genes and new qualities yet undreamed of. . . . For the first time in all time *a living creature* understands its origin and can undertake to design its future.'[4]

Which living creature? It cannot be human beings in general; they wouldn't know how to do it. It has to be the elite, the biotechnologists who are the only people able to make these changes. So it emerges that members of the public who complain that biotechnological projects involve *playing God* have in fact understood this claim correctly. That phrase, which defenders of the projects dismiss as mere mumbo jumbo, is actually a quite exact term for the sort of claim to omniscience and omnipotence on these matters that is being put forward.

The God-shaped hole in question has, of course, been causing trouble for some time. After the triumphal Newtonian spring, physics got increasingly complicated, to the point where J. C. Squire revised Pope's epitaph, complaining that

> It could not last; the Devil howling 'Ho!
> Let Einstein be!' restored the status quo.[5]

ATOMS, COMPUTERS AND GENES

At this point a new world picture ought to have emerged, a picture drawn, this time, not from technology but from science itself. But, as Squire said, the public found these new physical theories so obscure that nobody managed to express them in a convenient image. The idea of 'relativity' only generated a social myth, a vague cultural relativism about human affairs. Not till after the Second World War did three new, much more colourful images emerge in rapid succession. They all reached the general public, and they were all reflections of new technologies. They are the ones that occupy us today.

First, at the physical level, the idea of the atom was dramatised by bombs and by the promise of atomic power, so that the world seemed to consist essentially of atoms. Second, in human social life, computers emerged, and it was promptly explained that everything was really information. And third, on the biological scene, genetic determinism appeared, declaring that (among living things at least) everything was really genes and we were only the vehicles of our genes, but that (rather surprisingly) we nevertheless had the power to control them.

It has proved quite hard to relate these three different world-pictures, all of them reductive, but requiring different reductions. In theory, of course, they should not conflict. As far as they are scientific, they should, properly speaking, all find their modest places within the wider field of science. But world-pictures like this are not primarily science. The science that is supposed to justify them is quite a small part of their content. They are actually metaphysical sketches, ambitious maps of how all reality is supposed to work, guiding visions, systems of direction for the rest of our ideas. And because these visions draw their strength from particular technologies in the outside world, belief in them fluctuates with the success of their parent technology and particularly with its disasters.

The news of Three Mile Island and Chernobyl took much of the steam out of the atomic myth. Though we still know atoms are important, we do not turn to them today for salvation. Bio-engineering has not yet had a similar disaster; if it does, the consequence will surely be the same. As for artificial intelligence, hard experience has cut back many of the claims that were made in its early days. But computers are still becoming more and more central in our lives and the metaphysical notion that 'everything is really information' gains strength with acceptance of them. Thus, today nobody is surprised to read in a book written by two (otherwise respectable) cosmologists the following strange jumble of metaphysical claims:

> An intelligent being – or more generally, any living creature – is fundamentally *a type of computer*. . . . A human being is *a program* designed to run on a particular hardware called a human body. . . . A living human being is *a representation of a definite program*.[6]

Thus in a way that is surely very remarkable, our technology and our economics combine to shape our world view. As Jeremy Rifkin reasonably points out:

> Every new economic and social revolution in history has been accompanied by a new explanation of the creation of life and the workings of nature. The new concept of nature is always the most important strand of the matrix that makes up any new social order. *In each instance, the new cosmology serves to justify the rightness and inevitability of the new way human beings are organizing their world by suggesting that nature itself is organized along similar lines.* . . . Our concepts of nature are utterly, unabashedly, almost embarrassingly anthropocentric. . . . The laws of nature are being re-written to conform with our latest manipulation of the natural world. . . . The new ideas about nature provide the legitimizing framework of the Biotech Century. . . . Algeny . . . is humanity's attempt to give metaphysical meaning to its emerging technological relationship with nature.[7]

POSSESSED BY A TECHNOLOGY

Of course technology is an important part of our life. Of course each new technology does teach us something about the world around us – often something very important. We can rightly draw from these lessons models to help us understand wider phenomena, so far as those models are actually useful.

The trouble only comes in with the obsession with a particular model that drives out other necessary ways of thinking. The objectors are saying that the luminous fascination of bio-engineering is making us constantly look for biochemical solutions to complex problems that are not biochemical at all but social, political, psychological and moral. For instance, much of the demand for liver transplants is due to alcohol. But it is a lot harder to think what to do about alcohol than it is to call for research on transplants. Similarly, infertility is largely caused by late marriage and sexually transmitted diseases. But changing the customs that surround these things calls for quite different and much less straightforward kinds of thinking. Again, food shortages throughout the world are caused much more by faulty systems of distribution than by low crop yields, and – in the opinion of most experienced aid agencies – the promotion of patented transgenic crops in poor countries is calculated to increase the faults in those distribution systems, not to cure them.

I touch on these examples briefly and crudely here, merely to show that objectors who are moved by strong emotion are not necessarily being merely irrational and negative. My aim throughout has been to point out the solid thoughts that may be found underlying this particular emotion and to suggest that – here as in other issues of policy – we had better take such thoughts seriously. Strong feeling no more invalidates these contemporary protests than the equally strong feeling that accompanied early protests against slavery and torture invalidated those campaigns. In all such cases we need to understand what the excitement is about, not simply to dismiss it. And here, if we look into what is causing the alarm, we shall find that this is not a mere local or passing issue. These remarkable proposals flow from a long-standing, unrealistic attitude to the earth, of which we are often unaware. It will be as well to look at it next.

19

HEAVEN AND EARTH

an Awkward History

———•◆•———

PROBLEMS OF UP AND DOWN

How has it come about that we have identified ourselves so carefully with
our will, or with our intelligence? And why have we detached those entities so meticulously from the bodies that support them? Many factors have
certainly contributed to this narrowness. But among them has been our
suspicious attitude to the earth itself.

People in our civilisation have viewed their planet in a variety of ways.
Sometimes they have worshipped it, thought of it as their mother, felt
awe and gratitude towards it for the gifts it gave them. At other times,
however, they have despised and feared it. They have seen it chiefly as
the opposite of heaven, as a mean and degraded realm that entraps them
and stops them fulfilling their true destiny. Thus, the Oxford Dictionary
gives as the meaning of 'earthy', 'Heavy, gross, material, coarse, dull, unre-
fined ... characteristic of earthly as opposed to heavenly existence ...'
If we look up 'dirt' we find, '(1) Excrement; (2) Unclean matter, such as
soils any object by adhering to it, especially the wet mud or mire of the
ground'. And if we go to 'soil' we find '(1) A miry or muddy place, used
by a wild boar for wallowing' and we soon arrive at '(4) Filth, dirty or
refuse matter'.

Until very lately, this more hostile view was the more prevalent in our
culture, and not only in religious thinking. I don't think we have noticed
this bias, but it has been effective in many parts of our thinking, even in
the sciences. For a long time it prevented us from seeing the earth as an
intelligible system at all. This obstruction is only now beginning to lift.

Fear and distrust of the earth draws much of its force from the strong
natural imagery that links the up-down dimension with difference of value.
Earth is 'lower' than us, the sky is 'higher'. The earth is, of course, also
darker, while the sky is the source of light. Light and the upward direction always tend to stand for greater nobility.

This sort of thinking may seem naive, but it is remarkably strong. It still has an influence today far beyond the sphere of traditional religion. For instance, propagandists for space travel commonly take it for granted that aspirations towards what is literally higher – to what takes us away from the earth – are also spiritually 'higher', that is, nobler than anything that we can find below.

Is this way of talking just fantasy, just the casual extension of a figure of speech, or is there more to it? If we want to grasp its meaning, we may do well to look back briefly at the history of the symbolism to see how we have got here.

In our culture, heaven, the seat of God, was of course long placed literally in the sky. Pre-Copernican cosmology developed this idea in some detail. It set heaven, containing God and his angels, outside a set of transparent concentric spheres that carried the sun, moon, stars and planets. All these bodies were made of a special substance – *aether* – distinct from the four elements with which we are familiar below. They all moved, too, with a circular motion, which was thought to be the most perfect of all motions, by contrast to the crude motion in a straight line downwards which is found on earth.

Plato explained in the *Timaeus*[1] that our brains themselves are revolving systems modelled on these heavenly circles, and our thoughts, as they go round, echo these cosmic motions. The earth, by contrast, was merely the dead point at the centre of the system, the place to which things fall if they can't go upwards. Its central position was not a sign of importance but just marked its low status, its distance from everything of high value. After all, as Dante showed, what lay at the centre of Earth itself was Hell.

SOULS BECOME OBSERVERS

The business of Christian souls was, then, always to move upwards, away from this planet towards their true home. They were only visitors here, in a transit-camp created mainly as a stage for their interactions with God and especially for the drama of their salvation.

This meant that, when Copernicus displaced the earth from its central position, the humiliation that is often said to have accompanied this move was not fully felt. Though there was certainly a sense of confusion and insecurity, the citizenship of human souls in heaven remained and their salvation was still central business for the cosmos. Moreover – what is really interesting – this sense of complacent independence from the earth even managed to survive the Enlightenment's discrediting of religion.

When secular westerners stopped seeing themselves as Christian souls subject to judgement, they did not conclude, humbly, that they were only rather gifted earthly animals. Instead, they managed to see themselves in

Cartesian terms as pure intellects: observers, set above the rest of the physical world in order to understand and control it. Anyone who wants to see how this image works today should have a look at the Strong Anthropic Principle, which proposes that the entire universe is essentially a device whose sole purpose is to foster intellectual beings of this kind – that is, us, or at least the physicists among us. Not surprisingly, these anthropicists stage their cosmic drama largely in outer space, treating the earth and its fauna as more or less obsolete and expendable.[2]

GLORIFYING ASTRONOMY

This association between spiritual grandeur and the actual sky has meant that scientific enquiries about the heavenly bodies have long been held in particularly high esteem. The special reverence for astronomy goes back (again) to Plato's *Timaeus*, which declared that the celestial bodies were themselves divine beings, animated by intelligences that could find their way around the sky, following the rational plan that ruled the universe.[3] (The planets, of course, needed to be particularly smart in order to follow their complex paths, while the earth, which only had to stay still, did not need to be so clever.)

Studying the heavens was (then) directly studying the divine, and was therefore a specially noble occupation. Today, people would probably not give that reason for prioritising astronomy. But the notion that this enquiry has a special spiritual value is still often expressed, for instance by astro-physicists such as Steven Weinberg, who celebrates this study as furnishing a central justification for human life in his epilogue to *The First Three Minutes*:

> The more the universe seem comprehensible, the more it seems pointless.
>
> But if there is no solace in the fruits of our research, there is at least some solace in the research itself. Men and women are not content to comfort themselves with tales of gods and giants, or to confine their thoughts to the daily affairs of life; they also build telescopes and satellites and accelerators, and sit at their desks for endless hours working out the meaning of the data that they gather. The effort to understand the universe is one of the very few things that lifts human life a little above the level of farce and gives it some of the grace of tragedy.[4]

It is interesting to ask, is there really any reason why we should regard (say) research on a topic like black holes as essentially more noble than research on something earthly, such as parasites or black beetles?

THE GODS OF THE KITCHEN

This hierarchy of value among the sciences goes back a long way in our tradition. When Aristotle started to write his book *On the Parts of Animals*, he had to apologise for discussing such a vulgar subject. He wrote:

> Having already treated of the celestial world . . . we proceed to treat of animals [not leaving out] to the best of our ability, any member of the kingdom, however ignoble. For if some have no graces to charm the sense, yet even these, by disclosing to intellectual perception the artistic spirit that designed them, give immense pleasure to all who can trace links of causation, and are inclined to philosophy . . . We therefore must not recoil with childish aversion from the examination of the humbler animals. Every realm of nature is marvellous.

He then tells a story. Heraclitus (he says) was visited by some strangers who hesitated to come in because they found him warming himself at the stove in the kitchen. Heraclitus, however, at once told them

> not to be afraid, as even in that kitchen divinities were present. Just so, we should venture on the study of every kind of animal without distaste, for each and all will reveal to us something natural and beautiful.[5]

In fact (said Aristotle) there are gods in the kitchen as much as anywhere else, and scientists ought to learn not to turn up their noses at them. A real scientist ought to be able to say, as James Lovelock does, 'I speak as the representative of the bacteria and the less attractive forms of life, who have few others to speak for them'.[6]

Aristotle never managed to get this point about the importance of the kitchen gods through to his own philosophical tradition. After his death, none of his followers ever developed his carefully planned research programme for the scientific development of zoology, though they dealt with almost every other aspect of his thought. Later scholars ignored it entirely.

TAKING WORMS SERIOUSLY

Nor had things changed much in 1882, when Darwin, then in the last year of his life, gave lunch to Edward Aveling, the translator of Karl Marx. Aveling, who was an eager campaigner on behalf of Darwin's evolutionary theories, asked him what he was working on now. Darwin said he was investigating the behaviour of earthworms. Shocked at this frivolity, Aveling, asked him what could possibly have led him to interest himself in a subject so insignificant? Darwin replied simply, 'I have been studying their habits for forty years.'

It clearly had not struck Aveling that Darwin could never have produced his wider and more epoch-making theories without that kind of attention to zoological details. He had already spent eight years working on the classification of barnacles and this work had, as he said, been a great help to him in writing *The Origin of Species*. Aveling would have been still more upset if he had known how thorough Darwin was being in his current research. Darwin tested the response of the worms to every kind of situation, confronting them with all sorts of experience: different kinds of light, heat, smells, vibrations and music, including the bassoon and the grand piano:

> What struck him most about the worms was their mentality. They seemed to 'enjoy the pleasures of eating' judging by their eagerness for certain kinds of food, and their sexual passion was strong enough to 'overcome . . . their dread of light'. He even found 'a trace of social feeling'. He observed how they dragged leaves into their burrows. The habit was instinctive, but what of the technique? Digging the objects out of the burrows, he discovered that the great majority had been pulled in the easiest way, by their narrower end or apex. Worms had somehow acquired a notion, however rude, of the shape of an object.[7]

Moreover, by investigating these things, he made the revolutionary discovery that earthworms, which had till then been considered either insignificant or pestilential, in fact played a central part in recycling vegetation and turning it into usable soil. Without them, this process would be far too slow for other life forms to profit by it.

Today, the kind of work that Darwin did here is of course respected; it may sometimes even get grants. But it is still seen as one of the humbler and more everyday parts of science. It does not get exalted with the kind of ecstatic, semi-religious fervour that Weinberg shows in celebrating astro-physics.

Similarly, people like Aveling expected from Darwin something very different from his direct scientific interest in creatures for their own sakes. Aveling was one of many people who, both then and now, welcomed Darwin's doctrines mainly as weapons in a war that they were already waging about human affairs, in his case a war between Man (sic) and God. Aveling was a humanist, which for him meant a campaigning atheist. In fact, he was visiting Darwin just then in the hope of involving him in the campaign to allow the atheist Bradlaugh to take his seat in Parliament.

Darwin refused to be dragged into this war. He had a reason for refusing to do so that was entirely beyond Aveling's comprehension. He wanted

to distance himself from both combatants. The point was not only that –
on the question of God – he was an agnostic rather than an atheist. Much
more deeply, it was that he had no wish at all to be a 'humanist', in the
sense of a fighter on behalf of Man. In his view, the learned had concentrated far too much of their attention already on the self-important species
called *Homo sapiens*. It was now time for them to turn their attention to
the other species that populated the rich earth around it.

20

SCIENCE LOOKS BOTH WAYS

———◦•◦———

THE LURE OF SIMPLICITY

Both Darwin and Aristotle tried to correct an earth-avoiding bias that has always slanted our scientific tradition. This bias did not, of course, dictate a total neglect of phenomena outside human life. But it did dictate a strangely selective way of attending to them, a much greater willingness to notice things in the heavens than things on the earth. Scholars looked for system and significance in the stars much more readily than in terrestrial things.

We have seen that one reason for this preference lay in the natural symbolism of height and light. But another reason, particularly powerful with the learned, was the apparent clarity of heavenly patterns. The special appeal of astronomy to mathematically-minded thinkers like Plato and Pythagoras centred on the simplicity of the order that they found there. Greek reasoners could see at once how they might hope to apply their mathematical methods to the sky. Applying them to the more complicated things on the earth looked much more difficult, and for a long time it remained so. That is why, until the Renaissance, earthly things usually continued to be treated as genuinely messy and incomprehensible, a surd, chaotic mass that could often only be dealt with by rule of thumb based on experience. Aristotle protested against this, but he was not widely followed.

Thus, when scientific efforts to understand the physical world began once more at the Renaissance, they again began with astronomy. Distant things were studied long before near ones, even when those near ones were of urgent practical importance. Galileo did indeed pay attention to the flight of cannonballs, since this was something that particularly interested his princely patrons. But apart from a few such selected issues, he preferred to concentrate his enquiries on the motion of stars and planets. So did Copernicus. And what they chiefly looked for was again simplicity. The traditional pattern of circles supplemented by epicycles had turned out not to give simplicity, so they tried to find it by altering their starting-point.

This brings up a matter of the greatest importance about the nature of science itself. *Science always oscillates between two magnets, two equally important ideals.* On the one hand it aims to represent the hugely complex facts of the world. On the other, it aims at clarity, and for that it needs formal simplicity. When mathematicians are in charge, the second ideal always tends to predominate over the first. And, for a long time, mathematics provided the only model of intelligibility that physical scientists saw how to work with. Within mathematics, too, they looked for the simplest and most regular forms.

This is why the ideal of using circles exercised such great power. Thus, when Kepler and his colleagues were trying to calculate the orbits of the planets, they found it quite impossible for a long time to admit that these paths might possibly be elliptical. They spent many years trying to avoid this conclusion and only accepted it in the end with the greatest reluctance. Like Plato, they had assumed firmly that orbits must be circular, because that was self-evidently the perfect shape for them.

THE EARTH FAILS TO BE ROUND

This same longing for perfect circles also impinged on questions about the shape of the earth. Here, our planet's original mean position was compounded by involvement in the Fall of Man. Mediaeval and Renaissance writers speculating about the earth commonly deplored its rough and disorderly state, its infestation by mountains and holes which stopped it from being the perfect sphere that God must surely have meant to create. They concluded that this imperfection must surely be due to corruption caused by human sin.

As scientific speculation advanced, various ingenious theories were proposed to explain just how this had happened. In the 1680s Thomas Burnet insisted that its present shape could not possibly be the original one. As he said,

> There appearing nothing of any order or regular design in its parts, it seems reasonable to believe that it was not the work of nature, according to her first intention, or according to the first model that was drawn in measure and proportion, by the line and by the plummet, but a secondary work and the best that could be made of broken materials.[1]

He called it 'a hideous ruin', 'a broken and confused heap of bodies', 'a dirty little planet'. He explained that its original smooth form must have been shattered by Noah's flood, which had let loose the waters under the earth. These waters had originally formed a continuous layer beneath the

surface. But when human sin became too flagrant, God made them break
out and cover the globe. This shattered the earth's crust, which has remained
in pieces to the present day.

Since that time, the only process that had been at work was the gradual
erosion of the mountains by rain. The present-day earth was thus a decaying
ruin, a constant reminder of the disastrous effect of human wickedness.
Like degenerate descendants of an ancient house, we were camping out in
the damaged kitchens of the ancestral castle, the rest of it having been
destroyed by the vice and folly of our ancestors.

WHAT SHAPES ARE REASONABLE?

Speculations like this may well strike us as naive, and we may certainly be
surprised that they were thought necessary. But the conviction that there was
something *wrong*, that the planet really ought to be a perfect sphere, was
not just a religious one. It struck scientists of that day as a demand of reason. And indeed, when God is seen as the guarantee of order, the distinction between religious and scientific thinking on such questions hardly arises.

We need to understand this inability of genuine enquirers to see any less
simple shape than a circle as rational. It is the kind of imaginative difficulty
that recurs whenever we need to change and expand the language of thought
– whenever we come (as they say), to a paradigm shift. It is the kind of
difficulty that we are facing today about the concept of Gaia. I think it is
perhaps somewhat like the trouble that we often have in responding to an
unfamiliar kind of music or architecture. At first the patterns presented seem
meaningless, indeed, they don't seem to be patterns at all. Then, rather mysteriously, given time and good will, their order begins to make sense to us.
Just so, geographers found the idea of an earth that failed to be spherical
not just blasphemous but irrational, an unintelligible suggestion.

That objection arose as naturally in direct thoughts about nature as it
did in religious thoughts of a divine creating mind. The ideal of intelligibility was the same in both contexts, and of course it centred on a
simplification of mathematics itself. Classical geometry was essentially the
study of regular shapes. Nobody had yet proposed fractal geometry as an
alternative way of detecting order.

GEOLOGY TO THE RESCUE

The effect was that the earth's moral and spiritual reputation could not
improve until it could somehow be seen as being more intelligible – that
is, until somebody found a more suitable way of trying to understand it.
Finding one was the achievement of eighteenth-century geologists, notably

of James Hutton.[2] These geologists' first success was in discovering a repair mechanism that could balance the process of erosion: a way in which the earth might be rebuilding itself so as to constitute a lasting system. They did this by showing how the weight of accumulated sediments crushes and eventually melts the lowest layers of rock, causing them to erupt through volcanoes and so to rebuild the mountains.

This meant that the motions of the earth could be seen as a continuous cycle, an effective ongoing process of maintenance, no longer a one-way path to decay. The geologists' second achievement, which followed from this, was to show that the process was not a recent expedient but had apparently been going on for countless ages. It was a vast, steady, regular, reliable machine that showed, in Hutton's memorable words, 'no vestige of a beginning – no prospect of an end'.[3] It might even be something comparable to the eternal system which Newton had proposed for the heavens.

This was the point where the earth began, once more, to appear as something understandable and therefore potentially respectable. As Hutton's friend Playfair wrote after seeing a rock-formation that illustrated this vast process,

> On us who saw these phenomena for the first time, the impression made will not easily be forgotten . . . We often said to ourselves, What clearer evidence could we have had of the different formation of these rocks, and of the long interval which separated their formation, had we actually seen them emerging from the bosom of the deep? . . . Revolutions still more remote appeared in the distance of this extraordinary perspective. The mind seemed to grow giddy by looking so far into the abyss of time.[4]

Hutton's explanation of these upheavals had at last made sense of the jagged contours of the earth's surface. The special music of those contours began at last to be heard. Unevenness which could not be understood in terms of space now became clear and reasonable when the dimension of time was added. And the sheer vastness of the time involved shifted the process away from the painful drama of human sin. Earth's behaviour could now take its place on something more like the Newtonian pattern that was accepted for the celestial bodies.

MUST TIME ONLY GO ONE WAY?

This was great progress. Yet, beyond it, still another painful change was going to be needed, one that brought in the perspective of history. Hutton's notion of rationality required that the rhythm of the earth's movements should be – over a long time – as unchanging as that of the planets. There could be oscillations, but there could be no continuous cumulative change. And after Hutton, Charles Lyell formulated this same demand in terms of Uniformitarianism. Lyell, like Hutton was a deist. This made both of them eager to get rid of the biblical story of creation at a particular moment in time, which they saw as arbitrary and irrational – why should one time be more suitable for the beginning than another? The worry was the same as that which many people feel today about the timing of the Big Bang. From one point of view, unchangingness seems to be a demand of reason. Yet later enquiry has not supported this impression. We now live, officially, in a model of continuous, cumulative, irreversible cosmic evolution.

The issue here is surely one of what you will accept as an explanation – what you are prepared to consider as rational. To Lyell and Hutton, serious, lasting, irreversible change seemed simply contrary to reason. They found this form of music discordant and meaningless. According to Newton, change of this kind did not occur in the heavens and it ought not to do so on earth. These geologists, having found processes that could reverse many supposedly permanent changes, understandably ruled that all change was reversible – as, indeed, it was assumed to be in physics until the discovery of thermodynamics, which occurred about the same time. The music of history, which constantly deals in unique events and irreversible changes, was then still unfamiliar. Thinkers such as Vico, Hegel and the inventors of thermodynamics were beginning to make it heard. But it still awaited its Beethoven in Charles Darwin.

THE BEASTLINESS OF BEASTS

Much of the shock that attended Darwin's work was due to his treating the development of life as a continuous, directional change in this way. But the most disturbing point about it was, of course, that it brought human minds once more in relation to the earth by tracing their descent from other animals. The scandal was not really due to an attack on God. (As Charles Kingsley said, God could just as well have created the world in one way as in another.) Darwin's real offence was to the dignity of MAN. He openly proposed to break down the fence that shut off our own species from other creatures. Being a true natural historian, he was deeply aware of kinship with the life around him. He thought this division was arbitrary and misleading.

Most of his contemporaries, however, still saw that division as an indispensable defence against chaos. Though the geologists had managed to bring the earth within the confines of science, they had by no means tamed its symbolism to the point where it could cease to be frightening. People might now be willing to speculate about the vast and distant processes that formed its history. But it was quite a different matter to be asked to acknowledge kinship with its non-human inhabitants. Those inhabitants – worm, rat, wolf, wasp, raven, serpent, ape – seemed to them chiefly embodiments of the vices. Here, once more, the earth seemed to link them horribly with human sin. Once more, they shied away from it in alarm.

MAKING SENSE OF THE EARTH AT LAST

That symbolism, with its attendant horror, still persists today. It underlies, not just American creationism but a wide range of confused objections to the idea of evolution. During the twentieth century, however, two things weakened its grip considerably. One is the serious study of animal behaviour. The other is the discovery of continental drift.

On the one hand, ethologists have observed earth's living inhabitants carefully and have testified at last that they are not, in fact, simply embodiments of the vices. On the other, geologists – once they had accepted the alarming discovery that the continents move – have been able to add a further dimension of intelligibility to the state of the earth's surface by plotting these movements. In both these ways the earth has gradually come to look less alien and more intelligible. And a third, more comprehensive, way of coming to terms with it has now been added to them.

It is not an accident that the acceptance of these two advances has been followed by the rise of James Lovelock's Gaia theory: the idea of an inclusive, self-maintaining system that involves both the earth and its living inhabitants. This concept finally bridges the dualistic gaps which have fragmented our understanding of the earth. It shows it, at last, as an intelligible working system rather than as a jumbled, meaningless background to human life.

SPIN-OFF FROM SPACE

To see the earth in this comprehensive way is surely a tremendous leap in our understanding of the whole universe. It is one that requires a notable willingness to stand back from the jumble of detailed reactions to the earth that pervades our experience. It involves the leaping of barriers between academic disciplines, something which our age of academic specialisation finds very hard. In this case, however, the leap was, rather surprisingly, helped by the twentieth century's experiments with space. Astronauts who were trying to move away from our planet could no longer think of it simply as a background, a boring, dark, indefinite stuff that was always under their feet. Instead, they were forced to visualise it as a whole, as a planet moving through the sky – in effect, as one of the heavenly bodies.

They reported that seeing the earth from a distance in this way is a quite astonishing experience, and the photos they took of it have to some extent

SCIENCE LOOKS BOTH WAYS

conveyed that experience to the rest of us. They have deeply changed our response to the planet. Quite simply, they show it in its place in the heavens, as a body plainly entitled to whatever kind of honour and glory we associate with the sun and stars. They finally expel the secret flat-earther who, till now, has apparently been lurking at the back of all our minds. They debunk the symbolism of height. Besides this, however – as has been pointed out – they show this earth as having a distinctive honour of its own among the heavenly bodies in being visibly alive. It has a shimmering, multi-coloured surface quite different from that of the moon and the other planets. It is a planet of which we need neither be afraid nor ashamed, and we ought now to find it easier to understand it.

Thus the planet as a whole has acquired a higher symbolic value than it used to have. As happens on these occasions, we think better of it today than we used to and we begin to wonder why we did not do so earlier. But its rising reputation does not necessarily extend to cover all its inhabitants. The status of the animals that live on it is still a considerable problem to us. We will have a look at this in the next chapter.

21

ARE YOU AN ANIMAL?

———·◆·———

'He who understands baboon would do more towards metaphysics than Locke.'

Charles Darwin's notebooks

THE QUESTION

We have noticed that one main reason for the alarm that greeted Darwin's
revolution was the way in which his views linked humanity with other
animals, and through them with the morally threatening earth. The complex
of symbols which surged up here deserves our attention.

What is an animal? If anthropologists from a strange planet came here
to study our intellectual habits and customs, they might notice something
rather odd about the way in which we classify the living things around us.
They would find us using a single word – animal – to describe an immense
range of creatures, including ourselves, from blue whales to tiny micro-
organisms that are quite hard to distinguish from plants. On the other
hand, they would note also that the commonest use of this word 'animal'
is that in which we use it to contrast all these other organisms with our
own single species, speaking of *animals* as distinct from humans. It might
strike them that in virtually every respect gorillas are much more like
ourselves than they are like (say) skin parasites, or even worms and molluscs.
This use of the word is therefore rather obscure.

Those two distinct ways of thinking are our topic now. Both are used readily in everyday life. If a small child asks what an animal is, we are likely to
choose the first meaning, and our answer will probably be wide, untroubled
and hospitable, especially if we are scientifically oriented people. We shall
explain that the word can include you and me and the dog and the birds
outside, the flies and worms in the garden and the whales and elephants and
the polar bears and Blake's tiger. In other contexts, however, we may find

ourselves using the word very differently, drawing a hard, dramatic black line across this continuum. 'You have behaved like animals!' says the judge to defendants found guilty of highly sophisticated human social offences, such as driving a stolen car while under the influence of drink.

What is the judge doing here? He is, it seems, excluding the offender from the moral community. His meaning, as widely understood, is something like this: 'You have offended against deep standards and ideals which are not mere local rules of convenience. You have crashed through the barriers of culture, barriers which alone preserve us from a sea of hideous motivations. The horror of your act does not lie only in the harm that you have done to your victims, but also, more deeply, in the degradation into which you have plunged yourselves, a degradation that may infect us all.'

This seems a fair interpretation of such common remarks, an interpretation that covers their main points, though of course in such an emotive and disturbing matter more is probably involved. This notion of an 'animal' clearly takes us into somewhat mysterious areas of our ill-understood habits of symbolism. The ambiguity is not a casual one that could be remedied by updating the dictionary. By the nature of the case it touches on matters that it will frighten us to think about.

In its second use – the one that excludes humanity – the word 'animal' stands for the inhuman, the anti-human. It represents the forces that we fear in our own nature, forces that we are unwilling to regard as a true part of it. By treating those forces as non-human, it connects them with others that we fear in the world about us – with fire, floods, wind, earthquakes and volcanoes. It thus dramatises their power, but it also enables us to disown them. It implies that they are alien to us and are therefore incomprehensible.

We insist, then, that we are not responsible for these motives. But the peculiar kind of horror that they produce suggests that there is a lot of bad faith in this insistence, that we are not altogether convinced of their externality. We see these alarming forces, not just as outside dangers like earthquakes but also as dangers within us, seeds that lie hidden in our own nature and that may at any time develop if outside offenders are allowed to encourage them by their example.

That, I am suggesting, is the traditional attitude, both in our own culture and to some extent in many others, to what an 'animal' is. The second part of it is not often spelt out these days, but then it does not need to be because it is a powerful, ancient imaginative background that works by being taken for granted. Clearly, any concept riven by an ambivalence as deep as this is not going to yield us a single clear meaning, but a thicket of instructive confusions.

Thus, the word 'animal', though used as a perfectly good term of science, does most of its work in areas that are not in the least detached or scientific. This makes it a very illuminating example of the way in which our scientific and our everyday thinking interrelate. Its two usages play, I believe, a very important part in our thinking, notably in forming our communal self-image – our notion of the kind of being that we ourselves are. In trying to define ourselves, we contrast ourselves with something outside us. Accordingly, whatever propaganda humans in a particular age want to put about concerning themselves demands and gets corresponding alterations in the typical notions entertained about non-human animals.

OUTER DARKNESS

These conflicting ideas about the meaning of the human/animal frontier are very old, but their clash is sharpened today by the notion we now hold of ourselves as thoroughly scientific beings, individuals too clear-headed and well-organised to use blurred or ambivalent concepts. The concepts that we need to use for everyday life are, however, often in some ways blurred or ambivalent because life itself is too complex for simple descriptions. For instance, notions such as love, care, trust and consent are incredibly complicated. The concept of a friend is not a simple one, and people who insist on oversimplifying it cannot keep their friends, nor indeed be friends themselves, because they do not properly understand what a friend is. The same difficulty constantly arises about many concepts in biology, for instance selection, evolution, adaptation and indeed life itself. Oversimple definitions of terms like these have again and again distorted science. The standards of clarity that we manage to impose in our well-lit scientific workplaces are designed to suit the preselected problems that we take in there with us, not the larger tangles from which those problems were abstracted.

The ambivalence just noticed in our attitude to the species-barrier is one of those large tangles, and needs to be taken seriously. Our twofold use of words like 'beast' or 'animal' is not just a chance ambiguity that we can set right by policing usage. We cannot, for instance, rule that only the first usage (the inclusive one) is scientific, on the grounds that it accords with current taxonomy and the theory of evolution, and therefore say that it alone has a right to survive. For one thing, some objectors might at once say that the second meaning is really the scientific one, because non-human animals must be used as subjects for scientific experiments. After all, it is people who actually do science, so the apparatus that they use must be classed separately from them so as to point out that it has no rights that might prevent this. Here 'scientific' would mean something like 'involved in the practice of science'. More subtly, however, others would say that, in the interests of truth itself, the scientific approach demands that the difference between humans and other animals should be treated as paramount because these creatures are in fact beings of a different kind, much more like machines than they are like people.

This approach arose in the first place out of Descartes's naive mechanistic belief that animals were actually unconscious. Later, it was immensely encouraged by crude behaviourist psychology. During the twentieth century, it was radically undermined by the advance of ethology, which has supplied for the first time solid, incontrovertible evidence that the lives of many other social animals resemble human life far more closely than had been believed, and cannot be properly described without using many concepts suited for describing the behaviour of humans. No serious and well-qualified reader can dismiss the accounts given by Jane Goodall, Arthur Schaller, Dian Fossey and their many colleagues as merely sentimental or 'anthropomorphic' wish-fulfilment. Plainly, these people are scientists.

On the other hand, the speculative excesses of early, metaphysical behaviourism under Watson have not worn well and, as we have seen, its central doctrines do not now seem 'scientific' at all. More generally, too, mechanism itself has been losing ground since machine models have proved less and less useful in physics, which was the field where they originally gained their prestige. But these changes are slow. The set of ideas that ruled at the beginning of the twentieth century still has great influence. Many people do still habitually think that mechanistic explanations are always more scientific than ones that use concepts appropriate to a human context, even in situations where they demonstrably fail to do any useful explaining.

It would not, then, be easy to arbitrate between the two uses of the word 'animal' merely by deciding which was the more scientific. But even if that decision could be made, usage could not be forced to conform with it, because people are in any case not always talking science. Both usages are common because both are emotive. To think of ourselves seriously as animals is to regard the other animals as our kin; it inevitably leads us in some degree to welcome them, to identify with them, to see their cause as our own. That, indeed, is just what people find both attractive and frightening about this way of thinking.

THE VALUE ASPECT

In general, value concepts are not actually tidily separated from factual or descriptive ones, however much it might simplify our arguments if they were. There are nearly always conceptual links, and indeed this question about the species barrier is a good example of such an irremovable connection. How we regard this barrier cannot be a neutral matter for us. To some extent and in some ways, an idea of this barrier that recognises its complexity is bound to suggest to us that we belong in a wider sphere. Yet it is also natural to use this barrier to indicate the frontier of value, so that 'human' becomes an important term of praise.

138

This last thought is as unavoidable as the other. Since humans have to live a human social life, which they often find hard, especially in childhood, the notion of the great, dark, non-human area outside is bound to strike us in some ways, right from our earliest days, as something forbidden, alien and probably frightening. This area includes, in uncertain relation, the unacceptable parts of our own nature and the entire natures of the other animals around us. That is why an obvious and familiar kind of horror attends situations in which human beings are treated, as we say 'like animals' – for instance, where they are herded into cattle-trucks or left to starve or, most particularly, are eaten without scruple. Similar horror is conveyed by the thought of their 'behaving like animals', and this, as we have noticed, may simply mean 'not how human beings are supposed to behave in our culture', with a special emphasis on the kind of motives involved. As we have seen, the idea of mixed, partly human monsters such as the Minotaur symbolises this special kind of fear and disgust.

I have begun by stressing the hostile, exclusive half of our divided attitude, because I think we often do not realise how much it influences us. The sense of drama that attends controversy about human origins, and the way in which new speculations about the source of human uniqueness spring up full-grown on the heels of even the slightest archaeological discovery, show clearly how nervous people still are about the idea of a 'missing link' that might bestride the species barrier. People are afraid, not just of finding that they have discreditable ancestors, but of something that those ancestors might reveal about human nature today.

We know we do not fully understand our own nature. Of course, we have certain working notions about it, but continually we find difficult cases cropping up in which these notions fail us, precipitating us into theoretical and (still more obviously) into practical disaster. If we think seriously about it today, we are surely likely to find ourselves still in agreement with the view of humanity that Alexander Pope expressed in his *Essay on Man*:

> Perched on the isthmus of a middle state,
> A being darkly wise and rudely great . . .
> He hangs between, in doubt to act or rest,
> In doubt to deem himself a god or beast . . .
> Sole judge of truth, in endless error hurled,
> The glory, jest and riddle of the world.[1]

But this is a disturbing picture. That is why, during the Enlightenment, thinkers made great efforts to simplify and domesticate it by treating the darker, more mysterious, aspects of human life as mere historical accidents, effects of unnecessary moral and political failures, 'artefacts of the system'. If they had succeeded in establishing this view – that is, if they had managed to abolish these blots by altering educational methods – then perhaps we might today be able to look at other animals more dispassionately, as beings quite separate from ourselves, which we were not called upon to judge as either good or bad. But, in spite of many important minor gains, of course they could not produce that total revolution. Human conduct did not dramatically improve, nor were the dark places of the soul found to vanish. At the same time, however, the advance of science connected human beings more firmly than ever with the other animals through the theory of evolution.

THE FEAR OF CONTINUITY

Darwin himself responded positively to this change. It seemed to him obvious that the new ideas implied a strong and significant continuity between human nature and the nature of other creatures. Scientific method therefore now called for the end of all prejudice against a serious, dispassionate comparison between their psychologies. The best prospect for understanding human motivation lay in assimilating the conceptual schemes used for these two studies, and in developing both through the systematic comparison between them. For this purpose, Darwin was prepared to raid the full range of psychological concepts that have been developed for describing human feeling and behaviour: a range so rich and varied that, if intelligently handled, it can be expected to provide suitable ways of describing the traits that we share with other animals, as well as those that are peculiar to ourselves. Darwin used this method effectively himself in *The Expression of Emotions in Man and Animals*,[2] and it was later taken up and developed for the founding of modern ethology by Niko Tinbergen and Konrad Lorenz.

After Darwin's death, however, the tide turned against all such thinking. Behaviourist psychology did indeed officially treat humans and other animals as similar, but it did it in exactly the opposite way from Darwin, by treating both as insensate machines. Early, dogmatic, metaphysical behaviourism ruled that everything equally was a mere object; there was no such thing as a thinking subject, and the whole idea of 'consciousness' was merely a superstition. The fearful confusions that resulted from this idea led John Watson's heirs to abandon it, but unluckily they did not openly think through and set straight the wider metaphysical notions that had first produced it, but merely cursed metaphysics and withdrew to slightly safer ground. For the study of humans, academic psychologists have continued to use mechanical models alongside nominal admissions that subjectivity was present, without any real attempt to resolve the clashes that these two discrepant ways of thinking constantly produced. But for animal psychology, pure mechanism still largely ruled, because it was still held up as 'scientific'. (For a full and balanced account of this fascinating story, see Robert Boakes's book *From Darwin to Behaviourism: Psychology and the Mind of*

Animals.[3]) Sociologists and anthropologists, however, continued meanwhile to treat human beings as unique, usually denying flatly that comparisons from any other species could possibly be relevant to them.

Thus from the time of Darwin's death until the development of ethology in the mid-twentieth century, most of the scholars whose studies neighboured the species barrier viewed the gap as unbridgeably wide, and the behaviourists who thought otherwise did so because they assimilated both parties to machines. Moreover, behaviourists and sociologists alike largely denied the presence of inborn behavioural tendencies in humans. Many things contributed to produce this change from Darwin's position, but among the intellectual factors involved, probably the foremost was the increasing specialisation that went with the professionalisation of science. Social and physical scientists increasingly treated each other as alien tribes, and were not surprised to find that they were thinking on different lines.

I do not think that we can fully understand this change without also noticing wider social and emotional factors as well as professional ones. The notion of an animal is, as I have suggested, a deeply and incurably emotional one, about which we cannot be emotionally neutral. If we do not respond to it with a positive sense of kinship, as Darwin did, we are almost certain to do so with the hygienic, rejective horror already mentioned. Darwin was exceptional, not just in his scientific ability, but in his awareness of the symbolic forces that cluster round such topics, and in the bold and generous spirit that often enabled him to make good choices among them. Once his approach was written off as amateurish, scientists who supposed themselves to be thoroughly detached and impartial often responded very confusedly to these symbolic cues.

That, I think, is why chronic, endemic exaggeration of the differences between our own species and others became for a time widespread. (I have discussed its distorting effects elsewhere.[4]) This exaggeration was especially dogmatic in the social sciences, but biologists too seem often to have accepted it without much question as part of a scientific attitude, and have been willing to agree that reasonings belonging to their own discipline could not possibly apply to the human race – until the ethologists began to suggest otherwise.

22

PROBLEMS ABOUT
PARSIMONY

———•◆•———

EXTRAVAGANCE AND MISERLINESS
IN EXPLANATION

This problem of making room for consciousness tended to be seen as one of *parsimony* – that is, of how to avoid adding anything to the notion of an animal as simply a machine – as if its mechanicalness were a given literal fact. Given that initial starting-point, the addition of consciousness was viewed as a piece of extravagance, and any further attribution of subjective attitudes such as purpose or emotion appeared more extravagant still. Behaviourism had originally taken the same supposedly austere line about human beings, and in principle it continued to do so, but this method worked so badly over most of the field of social science that it never became dominant there. It was fairly quickly realised that the machine model is just one possible way of thinking, with no special authority to prevail where it does not give useful results. On the non-human scene, however, mechanism was not seriously questioned because scientists had not yet seen its general disadvantages, nor had they paid sufficient attention to animal behaviour to see that it worked just as badly there.

Thus there was a remarkable discrepancy between what was treated as a parsimonious explanation for a piece of human behaviour, and what could count as such when the behaviour was that of some other animal. The practice was that, in the human case, the normal, indeed practically the only, licensed form of explanation was in terms either of culture or of free, deliberate choice, or both. Anyone who suggested that an inborn tendency might be even a contributing factor in human choices tended to be denounced as a fascist. The burden of proof was accordingly laid entirely on this suggestion, and was made impossibly heavy. To put it another way, any explanation that invoked culture, however vague, abstract, far-fetched, infertile and implausible, tended to be readily accepted, while any explanation in terms of innate tendencies, however careful, rigorous, well-documented, limited and specific, tended to be ignored. In animal psychology, however, the opposite situation reigned. Here, what was taboo was the range of concepts that describes the conscious, cognitive side of experience. The preferred, safe kind of explanation here derived from ideas of innate programming and mechanical conditioning. If anything cognitive was mentioned, standards of rigour at once soared into a stratosphere where few arguments could hope to follow.

The tide in both areas has certainly turned, and I do not think the tradition can last much longer. Nicholas Humphrey was one of the first to float the convincing suggestion that consciousness and intelligence in social creatures must have evolved largely to deal with social problems rather than merely practical ones – a suggestion which makes the continuity with human life so glaring that ignoring it any longer is scarcely possible.[1]

On the issue of parsimony, Donald Griffin effectively shifted the burden of proof, pointing out how odd it was to suppose it *more* parsimonious to account for highly complex and flexible behaviour by positing a program so elaborate that it can provide for every contingency, than to make the much more economical assumption that the creature had enough brain to have some idea of what it was doing. As he points out, the attempt to make pre-programming account for everything has only been made to look plausible by constant misdescription: by abstract, highly simplified accounts of what creatures actually do, accounts that have repeatedly been shown up as inadequate when observers take the trouble to record more carefully what happens.

Highly complicated performances by relatively simple animals can indeed be accounted for to some extent by positing that they possess inborn 'neural templates', which they use as patterns. But considering the skill and versatility with which they adapt these patterns to suit varying conditions and materials, it makes little sense to suggest that the templates reign alone and can, so to speak, work themselves:

> Explaining instinctive behaviour in terms of conscious efforts to match neural templates may be *more parsimonious* than postulating a complete set of specifications for motor actions that will produce the characteristic structure under all probable conditions. Conscious efforts to match a template may be more economical and efficient. ... *It is always dangerous for biologists to assume that only one of two or more types of explanation must apply universally.*

He cites the well-known case of birds which lead predators away from their broods by distraction behaviour, acting as if they could not fly properly until they have moved the threat well away from the nest, and then flying back in a normal manner. Scientists have gone to great lengths to account for this well-established practice without invoking conscious intention, by positing conflicts of inborn drives such as fear and parental concern. These conflicts are supposed to produce hesitant and contradictory behaviour, which then happens, by an incredibly lucky chance, to be regularly misinterpreted by predators as inability to fly. Griffin comments:

> The thoughts I am ascribing to the birds under these conditions are quite simple ones, but *it is often taken for granted that purely mechanical, reflex-like behaviour would be a more parsimonious explanation* than even crude subjective feelings or conscious thoughts. But to account for predator-distraction by plovers, we must dream up *complex tortuous chains of mechanical reflexes.* Simple thoughts could guide a great deal of appropriate behaviour without nearly such complex mental gymnastics on the part of the ethologist or the animal.[2]

In this case the traditional explanation is particularly feeble, because plainly parents in very many species must actually engage in conflict behaviour on these occasions; but only with these particular species of birds does it take this form and so strangely mislead the predators. For these species, however, the mistake is regularly made by a wide variety of predators, although it is the business of all predators to understand well the typical behaviour patterns of their proposed prey. Moreover, the point at which the conflict behaviour unaccountably stops and the bird flies home just happens to be one where the predator has been led far enough off from the nest not to go back. This is surely an explanation that no one would put forward except to save a dogma that is no longer worth saving. The dogma is that non-human animals cannot plan, and in particular cannot deceive. But there is by now plenty of evidence that they sometimes can, and there is no need for fantastic solutions of this kind to be devised for such problems.

WHICH COSTS MORE?

The question Griffin raises here is central. Why is it supposed to be more economical to account for the behaviour of animals *without* treating them as conscious? Why is consciousness regarded with suspicion as a sinister extra entity, instead of as the normal function of a developed nervous system? How could it be economical to *remove* such an obvious function from the brain when that brain already exists? What – more generally – does scientific parsimony usually require of us? Parsimony plainly does not have the purely negative aim of just leaving things out, of making explanations as simple as possible, for if it did the best explanation would always be the shortest. On these principles, the biblical account of creation would excel all others, since it names only a single cause – God – and abstains from complicating matters by adding any details about his modes of working. We are, of course, sometimes forced to accept accounts as simple and general as this, where our ignorance is very deep, but such honest admissions of ignorance are not explanations.

Neither – again – can parsimony mean just refusing to use more than one pattern of explanation, economising on our basic methods of thought. That was indeed the idea that led the early dogmatic behaviourists to exclude all reference to subjective motives from their accounts of both animal and human behaviour. Their approach has been found unsatisfactory for human cases, because it involves ignoring a mass of relevant and useful evidence. Indeed it has proved scarcely possible even to describe the 'objective' evidence about human beings on its own, without constantly referring to the subjective aspect that forms an inseparable part of it – namely, motivation.

Behaviourist psychological methods did, however, impress many people for a time as scientific because they used terms that were familiar in the physical sciences, and avoided ways of thinking unique to human psychology. Griffin rightly calls attention to the misleading effect of this deliberate imitation of another science, and the dangerous false reassurance that can be derived from thinking that this mere surface imitation makes one's methods scientific, when in fact one's distinctive subject-matter demands a method of its own. The mere negative effect of removing subjective elements from a given explanation has no special value. What parsimony calls for is that we remove *irrelevant* elements. And it is not clear why subjective elements should be supposed to be irrelevant to behaviour.

Why is concern with subjective states thought to be unscientific? One thing that seems to give some people this impression is a fairly simple confusion about the status of subjectivity itself, an impression that to study subjective phenomena is the same thing as 'being subjective', that is, being tossed about by one's own moods and feelings. This seems to be the same mistake as supposing that the study of folly must be a foolish study, or the study of evil conduct an evil one, or in general (as Dr Johnson put it) that 'who drives fat oxen should himself be fat'.

Behind this simple error there lies the rather more solid point that there is a difficulty in seeing how we can know anything about the subjective states of others. It is true and important that our knowledge of these states is limited. But if we really had no such knowledge our world would be very different from what it is, and we should not possess any concepts for describing or understanding our own subjective states either.

If we say that we never know at all whether anybody else is angry or afraid, or in pain, or aware of something, or expecting something of us, our actions will immediately give us the lie, and we know very well that to pretend to suspend judgement on such matters would in fact be mere humbug. If, for instance, a torturer were to excuse his activities by claiming not to know that his victims suffered pain, he would not convince any human audience. And an audience of scientists need not aim at providing any exception to this rule.

23

DENYING ANIMAL CONSCIOUSNESS

———•◆•———

DILEMMAS ABOUT PRIMATES

If we accept Griffin's contentions as at least evening up the score on the issue of parsimony, are there any other considerations that ought to convince us that animals do *not*, in fact, think and feel as their conduct and the size of their brains makes it natural to suppose that they do? Or that their thoughts and feelings in particular situations are *not* roughly of the kind that we would expect them to be, when our expectations are based on human experience gathered over the ages, experience both of our own species and of those around it? Is there, for instance, any good reason to suppose that a baby rhesus monkey, when removed from its mother at birth and placed in a stainless steel well, does *not* feel something like the same kind of misery and fear that a human baby might be expected to feel in the same situation?

It is interesting to notice that language does not really seem to make much difference here. Most of us would not doubt that a human baby would feel these things, even though it could never tell us so. And in general, in dealing with babies, we never let their speechlessness make us doubt that they do have thoughts and feelings, because it is only possible to deal with them successfully if we do treat them as conscious in the same kind of way as ourselves. Babies, as much as human adults, insist on being treated as people, not as things. Scepticism that required a different method could lead only to disaster.

The same thing is true of baby apes and monkeys, and those who deal with them have constantly to act accordingly. This case is interesting, too, because of a dilemma that arises out of the justifications that have been given for such experiments. These justifications have centred on the claim that they threw light on the origins and nature of depression and other mental troubles in human beings. States such as depression are, however, ones in which subjective elements are of the first importance, and this is normally assumed to be true also of the history that leads to it. If the rhesus infants were really to be regarded as mere robots, crying only in a mechanical manner like unoiled machinery creaking (as Descartes's followers put it[1]), could any useful parallel be drawn between their reactions and those of a human being? Even if they have sensibilities, but ones much simpler and less intense than those of humans, can the parallel be of any value?

Because of the obscurities surrounding this point, it is not surprising that the long series of experiments of this kind seems in fact to have had virtually no consequences of value for the treatment of human mental illness.[2] The ill-effects of maternal deprivation were known before it started, and the further damage done by environments such as steel wells have little relevance since these things do not happen to humans. In recent years, increasing numbers of scientists have begun to be worried by this disturbing dilemma about primates, and to reason that if they are sufficiently like us to be really comparable, they may be too like us to be used freely as experimental subjects.

Ought we, then, to promote all primates – or at least the great apes – to the position of honorary humans, crediting them with human-like subjective states and according them human-like rights, while leaving the rest of the animal kingdom still outside in the darkness? This has been proposed, but a moment's thought shows that it cannot be the answer. There is too much continuity between primates and the rest. No single sacred mark picks the primate order out from all the others, as the possession of an immortal soul has been held to pick out the human race. If we think that rhesus monkeys are capable of having thoughts and feelings that deserve our consideration, then we must think the same of other mammals and birds and quite likely very many other creatures too, such as octopi. Though the nature of their subjective states will doubtless vary vastly and often be obscure to us, their mere existence puts us in a relation with these creatures that cannot be the same as our relation with a stone or a tin tray. How close then are they to us?

DIVIDED FEELINGS

I have discussed our ambivalence about this question rather fully because I think it is a very important factor, though a negative one, affecting all the positive conceptions that we form of other species. In so far as it obstructs our free thinking on these subjects, it is something of which we need to be aware. How far it actually does obstruct it is a matter of opinion, and the influence certainly varies a lot in different areas. Jane Goodall single-handedly has, I think, done a great deal to transform our view of the great apes, simply by showing what a high degree of scientific rigour can be combined with an entirely personal approach to the individuals studied, and how much the personal approach then helps the rigour in furthering our understanding, not just of these particular apes, but of animal and human nature altogether. She is, however, part of a much wider etho-logical tradition which has been working in this way across the board, and has profoundly altered our attitudes. About the primates in particular, this new approach has, as I mentioned earlier, begun to raise doubts affecting the ethics of experimentation, and is already beginning to change scien-tific practice. This change, however, has not yet got very far, and the most striking thing about the present situation is its extraordinary unevenness.

Quite often we are moved by a strong Darwinian or Franciscan sense of kinship with other creatures, which can be just as influential as the distancing and revulsion that replace it at other times. What is really worrying at present is the impression many people have that the revulsion is somehow more scientific than the affection and respect. This idea rests on two very strange suppositions: first, that science ought not to be inspired by any emotion, and secondly, that disgust and contempt are not emotions, whereas love and admiration are. It would seem to follow that all enquirers who have worked out of pure admiration for their subject-matter, from the Greek astronomers gazing at the stars to field naturalists who love their birds and beetles, would be anti-scientific, and ought if possible to be replaced by others who are indifferent to these things, or who actively dislike them.

This is an attitude that nobody is likely to endorse once it is openly spelt out. In general, most people now admit that it is wrong to ill-treat animals unnecessarily. But reformers who want to draw attention to ways in which we seem to be ill-treating them have to use our existing moral language, which is of course largely adapted to describing relations between humans. When, therefore, it is suggested that we ought to be concerned also about the suffering of other animals, this idea can have the disturbing effect that I mentioned earlier – it can sound monstrous. This happens particularly easily when the creature in question is a familiar one, but is not integrated into human life as a companion or servant. People hearing protests on behalf of such creatures often take refuge from their scandalised reaction in laughter: 'Are you really making all this fuss about guinea-pigs – or pigs – or (still stranger) rats?'

SELECTIVE DESENSITISATION

All these cases have some features of interest. Rats are in fact lively, intel-ligent and sociable creatures, an opportunist species that naturally explores its environment, so they are capable of being bored when that exploration is frustrated. They are also able to respond well to human beings, as those who keep them as pets know. But their public image has of course been largely formed by their long history not as pets but as pests, that is, first as sharp competitors with us, from the dawn of agriculture, for access to stores of grain, and then as carriers of disease. Their tactless failure to grow fur on their tails also gets them a bad name by reminding many people of snakes, which are another symbolic focus for fear and hatred.

All this has made it easy for modern people to see rats as some kind of undeserving monster. The projected fear that goes into describing a bad human being as 'a rat' serves to dramatise this notion yet further. Mice, being smaller, convey a slightly less vicious impression, but do not do much better out of it because what is smaller seems less considerable anyway. Moreover, a strange new twist was given to the rodent image in the heyday of behaviourist psychology, when rats and mice were so extensively used as standard experimental subjects that one researcher actually dedicated his book 'to Rattus Norvegicus, without whose help it could never have been written'.

This mass of 'rattomorphic' psychological theory supposedly applicable to humans is not now thought to have been very useful, but it did manage to do one thing. It fixed the notion of the rat itself as simply a standard object, a piece of laboratory equipment with the function of being used to test hypotheses, a kind of purpose-made flesh-and-blood robot. And it served to condition scientists to this view of the animal. This conditioning is partly visual, because anyone who frequently sees a stack of standard small metal cages, each containing one bored white rodent which is never seen otherwise occupied, will be liable to absorb this impression. It is, however, also verbal. In scientific articles, experimental animals never moan, scream, cry, growl, whimper, howl, snarl or whine; they just discreetly vocalise. Similarly, they seldom do anything so vulgar as getting killed; to the contrary, they are politely sacrificed – a term that combines a sense of devout awe at the importance of the project with an urbane sense of the scientist's reluctance to proceed to such gross courses.[3]

Many other desensitising cues serve to inculcate the same attitudes in a way somewhat like the kind of hardening that medical students necessarily undergo: a conscious suppression of normal sensibilities. There are, however, interesting differences. For medical students, it is well understood that the hardening must be only against superficial disgust about the appearance of blood, slime, etc.; it must not produce callousness towards the patient. Over experimental animals, it is by no means so clear that this is true. Again, the medical students' training is supposed to produce attitudes that apply to the whole of the human race; any human patient is expected to receive the same respectful and compassionate treatment. But in dealing with other species, striking anomalies appear. A few selected individuals get similar consideration, while others are treated with little or none, being so far as possible approximated to things.

The visiting scientists from another planet whom I mentioned at the beginning might be surprised at this, and might ask what determines

the difference. Does it (they would wonder) depend on ethological obser-
vations about the nature of the beasts themselves, on their varying capacities
for various kinds of enjoyment and suffering? The answer would be, 'Well
no, actually it just depends on whether we happen to have chosen these
particular animals as friends or not.' This decision is purely social and
emotional, and a lot of it is mere chance. It seems also to be very ancient,
and the custom of choosing and cherishing some such animal friends is
found in a great range of human societies, as James Serpell has fascinat-
ingly shown.[4] Scientists, like other people, usually keep the two categories
sharply distinct. Not many of them would even want to imitate the great
physiologist Claude Bernard, who fistulated his wife's domestic dog without
warning, any more than they would calmly take their children's rabbits to
cook for supper. And it is interesting to note that laboratory technicians
sometimes pick out a particular mouse or mice to keep as pets, viewing
them quite differently from the mass of their relations in the main stack
of metal cages. The same distinction is most interestingly shown in the
horror expressed in the biblical story of the rich man who took away and
cooked the poor man's one ewe lamb.[5]

There is, too, a whole group of scientists – vets – whose work normally
involves taking the personal, considerate approach to non-human creatures,
because their clients are already doing so. But the two approaches cannot
really be kept distinct without mutual interference, any more than they
could in the well-known case of human slavery. Many situations bring them
sharply into practical conflict, notably those that affect the vets themselves
in relation to modern industrial methods of stock-keeping, and also about
experimental animals. Vets have therefore begun to be active in the current
movement to study and reform conditions in these areas, notably in
shaping the Animals (Scientific Procedures) Act of 1986 in Britain. These
vets are among those who are beginning to find that they can no longer
combine two such diverse systems as their normal humane attitude and
the perverse behaviourist approach that regards animals – or even certain
selected animals – purely as things, excluded by arbitrary fiat from the
moral community.

ON BEING A GUINEA-PIG

This old approach is well illustrated by what has happened to the guinea-
pig. The experimental use of these South American cavies has been so
common that their very name has come to denote it. We speak with horror
of a person being used 'as a guinea-pig' for some experimental purpose
such as testing radiation effects, without even remembering that there are
actual guinea-pigs, capable of living lives of their own, who are treated in
this way as a matter of course. If, on some distant planet, human beings

who had arrived there were found to be a specially convenient experimental animal and were bred for that purpose, the word for 'human being' might well, after a time, come to have the same meaning. And of course, if the human beings complained, the scientists there might well make the same excuse that is likely to be made here in the case of the terrestrial cavies – namely, that these were not, by local standards, very large animals, nor indeed particularly intelligent ones.

Pigs are interesting too. They are lively and intelligent creatures. People who have tamed feral pigs in New Zealand have found them about as bright as dogs, and quite as active. Pigs made the mistake, however, of being the sacred animal of Baal, which gave the Hebrews a bad opinion of them, and has done them a lot of harm ever since. In this country, too, they acquired the servile and somewhat disreputable image that results from close confinement on a farm. Having nothing to do but eat, and happening to do it noisily, they were deemed to be greedy; having no room to be clean, they were considered to be dirty. Recently they have become still more closely confined in industrial units, which is likely to intensify these traits. In these circumstances, nobody is likely to notice their behaviour patterns except in so far as they cause practical inconvenience. The image merely becomes more and more stereotyped. Though they are not yet specially prominent as experimental animals, pigs are of interest because, like rats, they are another glaring case of an animal that is treated without consideration because it is thought of as an embodied vice – an attitude which, whatever else may be said of it, is certainly not scientific.

Is there, however – as the customs of our culture still make us wonder – something foolish and monstrous about the whole suggestion that we ought to treat rats and guinea-pigs with some consideration? There may be cultures where such a suggestion could not be understood at all, especially when the animal is urgently needed for food. But ours is not really one of them. Humane values are central to our official morality. In general, we do not think it is a quite trivial matter whether we are inflicting suffering. So at times we see the creatures' objection to such treatment quite plainly, and if (for instance) our children were to start cutting them up for fun, we would interfere. Similarly, if other intelligent beings were to start cutting us up, we should probably think that, apart from merely disliking it, we had a serious grievance against them, which we would try to state. We do not really put this issue right outside morality, we simply find it confusing, and therefore deal with it (as we do with other doubtful cases) by avoiding thinking about it as much as possible. Scientific use of animals is now held to need justification, which is provided partly on grounds of human benefit and partly by stressing the value of knowledge. These, however, are not all-purpose defences. If either the use or the knowledge is trivial, the justification vanishes.

CHANGING VISIONS

This is not an easy topic. Nevertheless, it is possible to think about it. Traditional ideas about it have been confused, and supposedly scientific replacements for tradition have often been no better, sometimes worse. The moral community to which we take ourselves to belong is not a clear, fixed one; it has shifting and shadowy boundaries. The differences between our species and those around us are not simple and definite but complex and obscure. We are not the only unique species. Elephants, as much as ourselves, are in many ways unique; so are albatrosses, so are giant pandas. All serious study of the peculiarities of any species ought to send us back to the drawing-board.

In recent times, we have been becoming aware of this need. Simple world-pictures that display our species on a pedestal, isolated from the physical realms around it, make us increasingly uneasy. But, as we have seen, such myths are not loose cargo. They cannot be jettisoned promptly and replaced by new ones. Habits of thought that express them are deeply woven into our lives.

What we usually do in such cases is gradually to weaken the effect of the unsatisfactory vision by contemplating others, already available, that suggest different attitudes, and to pick up material from them. We oscillate between these different ways of thinking, generating much confusion and inconsistency. Our conflicting ideas produce tensions, which we sometimes allow to burn away uselessly in irritation and cognitive dissonance. Sometimes, however, those tensions prove creative and allow better visions to emerge.

A dialectic of this kind may now be developing over our ideas about animals. In the last few decades, our wish to find more realistic ways of relating to the rest of the natural world has led us to sketch out a number of possible ways of thinking that can help us there. One of these approaches is the ecological way of thinking. The notion of an *ecosystem* – of a wide context involving many interdependent species, in which we, as well as other organisms, may find a place – has now become hugely important in our thought. This is quite a recent development; my copy of the OED, which dates from 1971, does not give an entry for the word. By emphasising our dependence on the rest of life, this idea has influenced our attitude to other animals, bringing them, as well as plants, within our moral horizon.

That attitude, however, has also been coloured by ideas arising from a quite different context, namely from the political controversy about moral rights. People who are uneasy about our treatment of animals have begun to bring that issue into the context of political obligation. They ask: If all human individuals have certain rights, do not other animals have them too? This concern for individual animals can sometimes call for different policies from the ecological perspective, which deals in whole populations, and result in practical conflict. It raises a debate which we will visit in the next chapter.

24

BEASTS VERSUS THE BIOSPHERE?

——·◆·——

THE ISSUE

Is there a necessary clash between concern for animals and concern for the environment as a whole?

Some thirty years back, when both these causes first became prominent in our lives, they were often seen as clashing. Extreme 'deep ecologists' tended then to emphasise the value of the whole so exclusively as to reject all concern for the interest of its parts, and especially for the interests of individuals.[1] This went for individual animals as well as humans. On the other side, extreme 'animal liberationists', for their part, were busy extending the very demanding current conception of individual human rights to cover individual animals.[2] That did seem to mean that animal claims – indeed, the claim of any single animal – must always prevail over every other claim, however strong, including claims from the environment. Each party tended to see only its own central ideal, and to look on the other's concern as a perverse distraction from it. This is a typical case where a particular myth, expressing a particular vision, impresses some people so deeply as to fill the whole moral scene.

RECONCILING FACTORS

Since that time there has been considerable reconciliation, which has partly flowed from mere practical common sense. People have begun to notice how much, in practice, the two causes converge. Animals and the organisms around them always need each other. The whole environment cannot be served except through its parts, and animals form an essential part of every ecosystem. The huge majority of animals still live in the wild, where their chance of surviving at all depends on the plants, bacteria, rivers, etc. around them. (Only a few species, such as rats and herring gulls, can do well by exploiting resources provided by humans.) Equally, plants and rivers commonly need many of their accustomed animals. Obvious examples are pollinating insects and birds, beavers to maintain swamps, scavengers to recycle waste, and insectivorous creatures, from anteaters to frogs, to keep insect populations from overeating the vegetation. The bad effects of removing such animals have been repeatedly seen. Even with captive animals, too, large-scale ill-treatment inevitably does have bad environmental effects. It is not just an accident that factory farming produces appalling pollution. It is bound to do so, because proper treatment of waste would cost too much to allow the cheapness which is its main aim.

Thus the two causes do overlap widely. Naturally, however, both have also parts which still remain separate. Concern for the whole environment gives no direct motive to oppose bullfighting, nor does humane concern for bulls directly forbid the proliferation of cars. These are distinct campaigns. Even if they seem closely connected and are often pursued by the same people, they differ widely in emphasis. But that kind of difference does not make all-out conflict necessary.

It is not surprising that there was real disappointment among the early crusaders at finding that those whom they had welcomed as allies were not complete soulmates, only helpers for some of their aims. In all serious campaigning, once general talk needs to be cashed in action, this kind of bond-breaking disillusionment crops up and makes real difficulties. The sense of unity with one's allies is a powerful support in the hard work of politicking, and when differences appear, they always seem to threaten that support. If, however, we want to keep the legitimate element in that support, we must clear our minds about what kind of unity we need and can expect. Learning to do this is a central mark that a campaign has become serious.

There are, of course, also some exceptions to this general convergence of the two causes, some cases of real conflict. They are important, and we must look at them carefully in a moment. But in general, at the pragmatic level, there really is convergence, and in spite of the endemic tendency to pick quarrels where possible, the rivalry has come to look much less fierce than it did. The gradual perception of this convergence has paralleled the still more necessary shift by which people are, at last, also beginning to realise that human welfare, too, converges very considerably both with the interests of the biosphere and with those of other animals. The public, if not yet its governments, is coming to realise that the biosphere is not a luxury, a theme park to be visited on Saturday afternoons, but something necessary for human survival. However hesitantly, that public is starting to understand that no environment means no people, and that a dismal, distorted environment means dismal, distorted people.

The public is also coming to suspect, far more sharply than it used to, that brutal and uncontrolled exploitation of animals cannot be compatible with true human welfare. People are growing more critical than their forebears were about some of the human purposes for which animals are exploited, purposes such as cruel sports, or wearing fur coats, or enlarged drug use, or constantly eating meat. They are more ready now to think that these things are less essential to human welfare than they used to suppose, and that having a clear conscience about cruelty may be more essential to it.

I do not mean that this new sensibility is yet translated into effective action. It is not. By a grim historical accident, the huge new technologies by which industries now exploit animals were established before this sensibility arose, and are now protected by solid vested interests. There is, however, a real moral shift towards disapproval of them, a shift that has made it harder for these vested interests to defend their habits directly, forcing them to rely much more on secrecy or straightforward lying.

The idea that the aims of life must somehow embrace the welfare of all life, not that of humans only, is gaining ground. The special qualities that make humanity worth preserving are now seen, much more than they used to be, as involving care for the rest of the planet, not only for ourselves. Vague though this sense may be, it does supply a context within which the claims of the animate and inanimate creation can in principle be brought into some kind of relation, instead of being perceived as locked in a meaningless, incurable clash. This idea still needs much clearer expression, but it is plainly growing.

THE TROUBLE WITH FANATICISM

At the pragmatic level, then, the competition looks noticeably less fierce than it did. But of course we want more than that. We need to think out the principles involved. We would need to do that anyway, in order to clear our own thoughts, even if the rough convergence we have did not leave plenty of specific conflicts outstanding. But we need it all the more as things are, because, in the initial stage of unbridled conflict, both sides seemed to be suggesting that there really was no moral problem involved at all. Each party was inclined to see its own moral principle as unquestionably supreme. Each found the other's stand an irrelevance, a perverse trivialisation, a distraction from what was obviously the only point morally relevant.

This is fanaticism. Fanatics are not just stern moralists, they are obsessive ones who forget all but one part of the moral scene. They see no need to respect ideals that seem to conflict with their chosen ones, or to work out a reconciliation between them. This frame of mind is not, of course, peculiar to full-time fanatics. It is easy to fall into it whenever one is, for the moment, completely absorbed in some good cause, and good causes often do seem to demand that kind of absorption.

Nobody, however, can afford to stay with this way of thinking. Moral principles have to be seen as part of a larger whole, within which, when they conflict, they can in principle somehow be related. The impression that a simple, one-sided morality is in itself nobler than a complex one is a mistake, as the issue that we are now considering shows. Any sane and workable approach to life has to contain *both* an attitude to individuals *and* an attitude to larger wholes.[3] Neither of them is reducible to the other. It is always possible for the two to conflict, but it is always necessary to try to bring them into harmony.

THE PARADOX OF MORAL PLURALISM

Attempts by moral philosophers in the last few decades to find some single 'moral theory' such as Utilitarianism, which can organise the whole moral scene, have been misguided. They ignore the complexity of life. Of course we do need to relate our different moral insights as well as possible, and to work continually at bringing them into harmony. But our aims are complex. We are not machines designed for a single purpose, we are many-sided creatures with a full life to live. The ambition of finding a single underlying rationale for all our aims is vacuous. (Maybe God can see one, but certainly we cannot.) Yet we do indeed need to integrate our aims as far as possible. This difficult two-sided enterprise is now being further obscured by one more irrelevant distortion from academics pugnaciously attacking or defending 'pluralism'. We ought to be through with this kind of thing. We should be asking 'what is pluralism?' or 'what kinds of it are necessary?', not wasting energy on yet one more polarised squabble.

The reductive, unifying ambition has, however, haunted many great philosophers from Plato's time on, and it was particularly strong in the founders of Utilitarianism, especially in Jeremy Bentham. As a controversial weapon, the idea that all valid morality can be reduced to one's own favoured principle, so that anything not so reducible can be discredited, has enormous appeal. But its crudity has repeatedly become obvious. Utilitarianism, like other moral insights, was a light cast on a certain range of problems – centrally on punishment – not a final, comprehensive revelation for all choices. Accordingly, recent attempts to reduce moral philosophy to a tribal battle between Utilitarians and 'Kantians' or 'rights theorists' is a shallow and futile evasion of its real problems, a point that both Kant and Mill in their better moments already saw clearly, though Bentham perhaps did not.

What great philosophers do for us is not to hand out such an all-purpose system. It is to light up and clarify some special aspect of life, to supply conceptual tools which will do a certain necessary kind of work. Wide though that area of work may be, it is never the whole, and all ideas lose their proper power when they are used out of their appropriate context.

That is why one great philosopher does not necessarily displace another, why there is room for all of them and a great many more whom we do not have yet.

Because our aims are not simple, we are forced somehow to reconcile many complementary principles and duties. This reconciliation, hard enough in our own lives, is doubly hard in public work, where people devoted to different ideals have to cooperate. This calls on them, not just to tolerate each other's attitudes, but to respect and understand them. Fanatical refusal to do this is not just a practical nuisance; it is a sin. But it is so tempting that it is endemic in all campaigning, and we are not likely ever to get rid of it.

It was not, then, surprising that, in the 1970s, both deep ecologists and animal liberationists should have been slow to see this need. Both causes were indeed of the first importance, and both had previously been disgracefully neglected. In this situation, tunnel vision and mutual incomprehension are normal reactions. Since that time, however, as we have grown more familiar with both causes, there has been increasing realisation that they can and must in principle somehow be brought together. Concern for the whole and concern for individuals are simply not alternatives. They are complementary, indeed inseparable aspects of a decent approach to moral problems.

Neither integrity nor logical consistency forces us to choose between general ideals of this kind. When they clash on particular issues, they do so in the same way as other moral considerations that we already know we have to reconcile somehow. We are familiar with such clashes between other important ideals: between justice and mercy for example, or between all our duties to others and the duties of our own development. There is no clear, reductive way of settling who wins this kind of contest. We know that in these cases we can face a real choice of evils, and we then have to find some way of deciding which of these evils is, in this particular case, the worse.

25

SOME PRACTICAL DILEMMAS

——•◆•——

CULLING PROBLEMS

As far as general principles go, then, the issue between animals and the rest of the biosphere has grown easier to handle in the last twenty years. Cooperation has become more natural to us, friction less habitual, and that is an undoubted gain for campaigning purposes. But of course it is not the end of our troubles. There is still a great deal of detailed work to be done on genuine, specific clashes of interest. Some of these occur within one of the two causes – between two rival ways of protecting ecosystems, or between the interests of two kinds of animals. But naturally, some also occur at the border, between ecosystems and animals. Indeed there are plenty of these, and we are not likely to get rid of them.

Consider a very common and pressing kind of example. What should happen when a population of herbivores – deer, elephants, rabbits, monkeys, feral goats, New Zealand possums or whatever – begins to damage its habitat seriously by overgrazing? Very often, of course, this trouble has been caused by earlier human actions. People have encroached on the habitat, or have removed predators, or have introduced the herbivores in the first place. But knowing that they shouldn't have done this does not necessarily help us, because these past actions often cannot be undone. We probably cannot now take the rabbits out of Australia. We need to think what to do next. In cases where, after considering all alternatives, culling seems to be the only practicable means of saving the habitat, is it legitimate? Or ought we to ban all killing?

It is essential not to treat a problem like this as an arbitrary dilemma, a blank, unintelligible clash between unrelated moral principles, each espoused by a different tribe, an issue to be settled by tribal combat between exploiters and humanitarians. Both the values involved here are recognisable to all of us. There is a real choice of evils. To leave a habitat to degenerate is to injure all its animals, including the species concerned. It may be to destroy them all. To cull is indeed in itself an evil, and it risks setting the example for other and much less justifiable slaughter. It is perfectly true that the choice of individual animals to cull has nothing to do with justice to individuals. As often happens in human affairs when (for instance) it is necessary to allot food or transport hurriedly to one valley rather than another, culling would ignore individual desert for the sake of the common good. In human affairs, we think this legitimate if the danger to the common good is severe enough. Does that make it legitimate here?

The trouble is that some sort of compromise does have to be reached. The point centrally important here is a general one, not just about culling. It is that we have to do justice to the complexity of the problem. There really are two evils. In such hard cases – as also in ones where either of these interests conflicts with those of humans – we have to proceed by careful study of the local factors, not by any sweeping fiat from general principles.

Moreover, we cannot dismiss a particular method wholesale simply because the *pretence* of it has previously been used as a screen to excuse disreputable practices. Culling is indeed a practice whose name has been misused very grossly. (Almost all hunting has now become culling, justified by 'wise management'.) Yet the repeated misuse of a name cannot damn a practice. There is, after all, scarcely a good practice in existence whose name has not been borrowed at times to gild something disreputable. Hypocrisy is indeed the tribute that vice pays to virtue. But the question in each particular case is, what actually – here – is the lesser evil? It is surely of the first importance to confront such questions realistically, and not to discredit one's cause by refusing to admit that any clash exists.

BENIGN BY-PASSING

If anyone can find a way round that clash by inventive thinking, that is of course an excellent solution, or partial solution. Conservationists have recently found many such ways, and are deeply engaged in working out their details. Tourism, intelligently managed, can sometimes be used to finance protection of habitat. Though there are many practical difficulties about doing this effectively, and also some objections of principle to relying heavily on it, yet it certainly has made much conservation possible. Again, careful education of the local people to value and respect their creatures can do much to protect reserves and keep down the conflict. Jane Goodall has managed, in this way, to prevent poaching of chimpanzees in the Gombe.

But then, these chimps are not an expanding population, in fact, they are scarcely maintaining their existing numbers. The real trouble arises over populations that do expand, or that are already too big for their habitat. If they are confined to this habitat, they will wreck it; if (as usually happens) they escape, they will wreck the surrounding fields and become 'crop pests'. They may well do both. The problem is immediate; what is to be done?

Contraception is sometimes suggested as an answer. Contraception, however, requires careful and accurate dosing; we have already seen the bad effects of its slapdash use for humans. Using it properly for wild creatures would, on the face of things, mean more or less domesticating them. It is possible indeed to imagine a small population of large and easily recognised creatures – say elephants – being so treated. They would presumably need to be regularly called in, examined and dosed. But there would then be unpredictable behavioural effects from the different age-balance of herds and the absence of calves, effects which would need careful watching. Indeed the entire behaviour would have to be carefully monitored, inevitably increasing the interference with the animals' lives.

For such creatures, the thing is probably not impossible, but – apart from expense – would it satisfy the demands expressed in claims for animal rights? It would certainly be a major, unchosen, lasting interference with the creatures' existence. And it is one that cannot possibly be supported by those who are in principle opposed to experimentation on animals, since a large, ongoing programme of such experiments would clearly be needed to make it possible.

When, however, we turn from elephants to large populations of small crop-eating creatures such as birds, mice and rabbits, imagination boggles and the whole scheme begins to look hopeless. Does anyone see a way of dosing them? Even at the middle level things are not much better. Processing a whole population of deer or baboons in the way suggested for elephants would be a desperate business, and again it would have quite unpredictable effects on behaviour. However carefully it were done, too, some would be pretty certain to slip through the net, producing unplanned descendants to mess up the project.

CONCLUSION

I find no pleasure at all in raising these difficulties. If contraception could be made to work, it would have great merits, and if anyone actually does find a way to make it work, good luck to them. As I have just said, inventive, unexpected ideas of this kind are badly needed. But ideas that are not worked out at the practicable level remain as mere fantasies, dreams that only console us and enable us to make speeches. They do real harm by discrediting the central cause and distracting us from fresh thought about the real problem.

That problem mainly arises, of course, from steadily growing human numbers and human bad practice. In meeting it, we are certainly going to have to take many measures that are in one way or another objectionable.

For instance, we will need to restrict human freedom to do many things that would be harmless in themselves but that have become ecologically damaging. Circumstances will force us to keep making unwelcome changes in what we permit and forbid. Morally, that is going to call for great honesty and scrupulous discrimination between changes that are actually needed and ones that are not.

But there will also be unavoidable dilemmas concerning the outside world. There too, we shall have to choose between ways of acting that are both objectionable. The matter at issue here – the conflicts between the interests of particular animals and those of the wider environment – is only one of these cases. Where it is possible to find ways of keeping the bio-sphere going without killing or injuring any members of other species – or indeed of our own species – it is surely our business to use those ways, and we ought to make great efforts to find them. Where we cannot find such harmless devices, we ought to keep down the destruction to what is actually unavoidable. But when the only other choice is serious, large-scale damage – for instance by letting a forest turn into a desert – it is hard to see any justification for a continued veto on killing.

We are not, in any case, beings that can exist without doing any sort of harm. We are not pure minds but dependent animals who cannot, any more than other organisms, live at all without destroying other living things, animals as well as plants. Whatever our wishes, we are unavoidably a part of the great mass of predatory and destructive creatures that produce most deaths in the wild. And among such deaths, those of the violent kind are often easier than deaths from starvation.

Of course this is not an excuse for wanton killing. But it is relevant when the question becomes 'which deaths and when?' We are already in the unlucky position where we are bound to do some sort of harm, a position where our decision about which kinds of harm to do can affect almost every other living thing on the planet. This, however, means that, by accepting and using this responsibility, we can also do much good. We have somehow to direct things so as to minimise large-scale damage. It seems plausible that this responsibility should sometimes override the objections to culling.

About insects, most people already accept this position. (Objections to insecticides on grounds of pollution are of course another matter.) And even about slightly larger 'crop pests' – mice, rabbits, small birds – humane people's attitude is, in practice, usually much the same. Even vegans, after all, would not get their grain and vegetables if crops were not protected, both in field and granary, by killing great numbers of these small poten-tial competitors.

As we go 'up' the scale of life, our acceptance of culling becomes more hesitant. This is reasonable, because individuality does become more impor-tant in the lives of more social and intelligent beings. It means that we should be less willing to cull deer than rabbits, and elephants than deer. It also calls for special care about the choice of individuals for culling, if we do cull. But to veto all culling, however bad the alternative, seems to be an unrealistic oversimplification.

'RIGHTS?'

Proposing this kind of compromise does not mean that we have abandoned the idea of rights, after approving its use in the concept of human rights in our earlier discussion. Even on the human scene, that idea is a somewhat crude tool. Because it is essentially competitive, it is much more appropriate for certain large-scale political situations than for subtler transactions between individuals. (For instance, my right to free speech does not necessarily prevail over your right not to be insulted.) But if we think that the essence of human rights centres on the concept of human wrongs – on the idea that there are some things that should not be done to anybody, anywhere – I am inclined to think that this does indeed extend to other species. One might instance such experiences as being deliberately boiled alive, which happens to lobsters, or being placed, as an infant, in complete isolation in a steel well and left there, as happened to the young rhesus monkeys in psychological experiments on social isolation.

By contrast, if one conceives the idea of human rights as centring on the notion that each individual is completely autonomous and should have entire control over its own fate, this seems to me unrealistic even for human beings, and far too one-sided to be used as a central tool of morality. The language of rights is only one part of the wide repertoire of moral language that we have at our disposal. Nothing compels us to use it in places where it clashes with other insights that seem more important.

About animals, the language of rights has been widely used because it struck campaigners as a powerful tool that could be used to win their case in a single move. Sometimes, indeed, it does work in this way, persuading people at once that profound change is necessary. At other times, however, it simply discredits the whole project because it seems too unrealistic to be taken seriously. This two-edged effect of extreme language is a very common feature of moral debates, one that constantly presents dilemmas to intending reformers. It is one more instance of the conflicts we have been looking at throughout this book between different imaginative visions: different world-pictures, different myths by which we try to make our choices intelligible. In the next chapter, we will look at some further interesting conflicts between the various ways in which we envision the animals that live around us.

26

PROBLEMS OF LIVING
WITH OTHERNESS

———— •◆• ————

SHOULD WOLVES COME BACK?

At present there are various schemes afoot for reintroducing wolves and other large mammals – lynxes, beavers, wild boars – to parts of the United States, and indeed to parts of Europe. One such proposal, which at present is raising a lively discussion, is to bring back wolves to forests in the Adirondacks, in northern New York State. It seems interesting to consider the symbolism connected with such projects. I shall not try here to say anything about the practical issues involved because these must, of course, be left to people who have studied the facts. It is clear that there is much to be said on both sides.[1] But I do want to say something at the outset about the interesting question of priorities.

How does this project rank in comparison with other possible ways of saving the environment? Is it more or less urgent than, for instance, finding a way of cutting down pollution or saving fossil fuel? What about the general need to save habitat? Ought we perhaps always to concentrate on stopping current ways of doing damage before we try to reverse the injuries that we have done earlier?

This question about priorities surely is a real one, something which we ought always to consider when we are choosing which causes to promote. But the answer to it is not, I think, quite as simple as it may seem. In the first place there must always be some division of labour between different sides of a change. We cannot all agree to place them objectively in rank order and then all converge in supporting the one that comes out top. There are always many good causes with more or less equal importance. And, in the second, these various causes often work to help each other. In particular, environmental projects that are psychologically gripping can serve to bring home the importance of wider issues to people who other-wise would not take them in. Thus, when Rachel Carson's book *Silent Spring* made clear to a wide audience that insecticides were destroying songbirds, the extent of the general danger reached them more sharply than it would have done if they had merely been told generally that the soil and atmosphere were being degraded. Even though that general degradation included a practical threat to their own welfare, they would not have seen that threat so clearly without the dramatic and unexpected reference to the birds. In this way the need to save songbirds pointed up ideals that supplied motivation for other, less exciting projects. Drama, in fact, is not necessarily a distraction from practicality but can sometimes help it.

AMBIVALENCE ABOUT THE WILD

I think this may be particularly true in the case of wolves because it is one on which our motivation has been exceptionally confused, not by the absence of drama but by a pre-existing drama which is almost entirely misleading. We need the new drama to correct the old one. In general, we human beings have always been ambivalent about the natural world that we live in, and particularly about its other large inhabitants. On the one hand, we know that we are part of that natural world, that we owe our lives to it and that it continually pours out treasures that delight us. On the other hand, it is also a potent source of death and danger.

Our ancestors, being physically weak, had good reason to be alarmed about many of the creatures around them. But, beyond this practical threat, wild creatures have always been seen as powerful symbols, vessels filled with disturbing meaning. The strongest of them, those that are most often depicted in cave paintings, obviously had a particular grip on the human imagination. But even smaller and less alarming creatures could be seen as a psychic threat simply because they represent a kind of life so different from our own. They are mysterious, and mystery can always mean danger.

In very early times people seem often to have dealt with this threat, as surviving hunter-gatherers still do, on the principle that if you can't beat 'em you should join 'em. They identified with these potent and mysterious creatures, propitiating them through suitable rituals and trying to tap their peculiar force by means of sympathetic magic. Thus they hoped to domesticate the alien power, to make it less alarmingly alien and external. Totemism is a systematic attempt to defuse the psychic dangers presented by otherness in this way. Later on, however, as people developed their peculiarly human skills and set up larger communities, this kind of identification seems to have grown harder. People whose way of life has become quite different from a porcupine's eventually find it hard to think of the porcupine as a close relation.

At this point the stark fact of otherness emerges more clearly. The human way of life begins to be seen as different in principle from that of other creatures. That change probably becomes really marked when people start keeping flocks and herds – still more so (of course) with agriculture. When you are dependent on the produce of your domesticated animals you cannot any longer afford to identify with them, nor with other creatures who might threaten your flocks by attacking them or by competing for their fodder. And if you have sown crops you want above all to stop those crops being eaten by someone else.

This seems to be the point where the clash of interests between humans and other creatures became too sharp to be smoothed over by mythical identification. Of course that clash of interests itself goes back much further. It arose already for hunters and they have often devised very interesting rituals to deal with it. For instance, native American peoples who hunted buffalo and depended on buffalo products often maintained elaborate rituals which showed the buffalo accepting their fate in return for spiritual trans-actions that honoured them and celebrated their relation with their human friends. Whether or not the buffalo would actually have signed up for these deals, it is clear that such ceremonies served an important purpose for the hunters themselves. Similarly, trees are often thanked, honoured and placated before being cut down.

This kind of symbolism does have some practical importance in controlling human greed. But it also has a deeper psychological importance which I think has been less noticed. It shows that even people who regularly consume trees or buffalo or the like quite as a matter of course, are already feeling some guilt, some uneasiness about their systematic exploitation of these impres-sive beings. They sense that they do not fully understand them, that there is something sacred about them, and that there may be some danger, whether practical or spiritual, in simply subjugating them to our needs and wishes. These people regularly take life, but they are not wholly happy about taking it. There are myths everywhere about disasters following such exploitation. Shooting the sacred stag of Diana is likely to turn out badly, and it is no good pleading that one didn't know that this particular stag was hers.

NATURE RED IN TOOTH AND CLAW,
WITHOUT AND WITHIN

Now this kind of guilt and uneasiness is well known. The interesting ques-tion is: *What happens to it after people turn to pastoralism and agriculture?* Does guilt of this kind just evaporate or does it take other forms? It is worth while to look for these other forms because strong motives like this do not usually vanish without trace. And there surely is such a residue to be found in the tendency of more settled people to downgrade morally the creatures that they are now more freely exploiting.

With domesticated animals, this downgrading chiefly takes the form of contempt, a contempt that is sometimes mild and kindly but can easily

165

become brutal. This contempt is expressed when one human being calls another a dog, a cow, a pig, a goat or a sheep. But over wild animals things can be far more serious. If these animals impinge on human life at all, they tend to be viewed, not just as a practical nuisance but as embodying human vices. To speak of somebody as a wolf, a rat, a viper, a shark or a vulture is not just to say that they are contemptible or troublesome. It is to accuse them directly of vice. And among these vicious animals the most vicious of all in our tradition has usually been the wolf, as one can check by looking up the entries under 'wolf' in any dictionary of quotations.

There are indeed some interesting exceptions to this equation of wildness with evil. A few wild animals are given a favourable meaning. They show up an interesting ambivalence, which we will look at presently. But the general equation of nondomestic animals with evil is so strong that it really deserves attention. This projection clears us from any guilt for killing them or for persecuting them when they are alive, since they deserve it for their wickedness. That attitude still persists in ordinary discourse, for instance in the sexual use of the term 'wolf'. Wolves are blamed, not only for predation but for being sly and underhand because they do not shout a warning to their prey before they pounce on it. Similarly, rats are hated for being dirty, as if they had deliberately dirtied themselves out of malice before creeping in to infect the houses of their victims. In general, the animals are pictured as if they were human beings who had deliberately acted in such an antisocial way that they deserve to be killed. Up to a point, of course, this kind of justification is also used for killing humans who belong to an alien culture – 'savages'. But its most central use is in dealing with other species. The most serious charge that can be laid against savages, the one that finally justifies annihilating them, is that they have behaved like animals.

This projection of human vices seems to serve the purpose of making people in settled society feel justified in killing these creatures for their own convenience. But it surely also serves another, even more interesting psychological purpose. *It provides settled people with a personification for those persistent vices in themselves which constantly make settled life so difficult.* The killing of the personification makes them feel they have actually killed the vice. They are symbolically destroying their own wildness.

PROJECTION AND SELF-RIGHTEOUSNESS

The idea of wildness sums up, then, all those anti-social tendencies that frighten us so much in ourselves, tendencies which are, of course, a constant threat to civilised life. This is surely why civilised people, even urban people, continue to be so keen on hunting, especially on hunting predators. In such hunting, ritual and conventionalised forms surround the actual killing, disinfecting it from the dangerous social consequences that might otherwise follow on from violence. It allows people to act out some of their own savage wishes and at the same time to feel that they are destroying savagery in the outside world. The old photographs of big-game hunters in Africa standing triumphantly with one foot up on various deceased creatures surely express this sense of having conquered something seriously noxious. Trophy-heads on the hunters' walls convey the same impression – a fact that various cartoonists have at times happily exploited.

Just to show that I am not making this up, here is an example which shows this rather curious kind of self-righteousness. It comes from a journalist's account of a crocodile-hunter called Craig, who has been harrying his crocodile for many hours. He has fired several harpoons into it, driving it to the bottom of the river, and is now waiting for it to come up for breath and be finally killed. Meanwhile he soliloquises about it:

> 'He's got the morality of a laser-beam', said Craig as we sat there
> ... 'The croc emerging from the egg will snap at anything that
> moves, no matter if it's a leech or a human leg.' As he spoke he
> was tugging on a harpoon line, trying to coax the beast below to
> move. 'He's a dedicated killing machine, the killer of any fish,
> animal or bird.'[2]

This rather odd kind of moral judgement is not, of course, confined to hunters. As civilisation has expanded, as more and more land has been settled, the conquest of the wild has been widely celebrated as symbolising the victory of good over bad, order over chaos, virtue over vice. Thus in Tennyson's poem 'Northern Farmer, Old Style', the old man, who is meditating on his deathbed about his life's achievements, finds only one that really satisfies him. This is that he has 'stubbed up Thurnaby Waste'. Skipping most of the dialect, here is his reflection on it:

> Do but look at the waste, there weren't not feed for a cow
> Nowt at all but bracken and fuzz, an' look at it now –
> Warn't worth nowt a hacre, an' now there's lots of feed
> Fourscore yows upon it, an' some on it down to seed

He did not just see wildness as unprofitable. He was not a mercenary man; indeed the point of the poem is to contrast him with his mercenary son. His mind was not on profit. He saw wildness as essentially alien and dangerous, and here Tennyson clearly applauds him. In this he was not alone. In the early twentieth century highly respected sages were still expressing this view – still busily grubbing up Thurnaby Waste – still speaking of our need to wage a general 'war against nature'. Thus Freud wrote that the proper human ideal is that of 'combining with the rest of the human community and *taking up the attack on nature*, thus forcing it to obey human will, under the guidance of science'.[3] Marx had taken a similar line, and William James had made the same proposal in his famous essay 'The Moral Equivalent of War', where he said that the cure for human militarism was simply to redirect our aggression – into the war against nature.

Of course both James and Freud had a serious reason for making this suggestion. They both wanted to provide an outlet for human aggression other than fighting other humans, and they both saw how fearfully hard it was to do this. But providing a war against nature as a substitute takes it for granted that 'nature' is something sufficiently like a human opponent to make this psychological shift workable. The drama is assumed to be the same in a way that can only work if the wildness in nature is assimilated pretty closely to the wildness of a human enemy. This involves making natural beings personify human vices. These prophets aren't talking only about working off aggression by throwing one's energies into physical labour. That idea would not call for the mention of war. They are talking about redirecting it into a different kind of hostility.

Now Thurnaby Waste itself cannot really be seen as a suitable mark for personal hostility. It seems to me that the sinister enemy envisaged in the War against Nature must actually be the enemy within, the savage motives in all of us that cause us constant alarm by blocking our efforts to lead a civilised life. That, I suggest, is the kind of nature red in tooth and claw that really frightens us. When we find ourselves demonising some group in the outside world in order to provide ourselves with an external enemy, that is really the direction in which we need to be looking.

27

CHANGING IDEAS
OF WILDNESS

————— ·◆· —————

THE OTHER SIDE – NATURE BENIGN

There is of course, another set of symbols, a countervailing tendency to
honour and celebrate certain creatures as symbols of human glories and
virtues. Some very strong animals have had a remarkably good press even
though they were actually dangerous, as images of human virtues. Lions
are the prime example, constantly cited as showing noble and kingly virtues
such as magnanimity. Thus Chaucer:

> For lo! the gentle kind [nature] of the lion!
> For when a fly offendeth him or biteth
> He with his tail away the fly smiteth
> All easily, for, of his genterie
> Him deigneth not to wreak him on a fly
> As doth a cur, or else another beast.[1]

This kingly lion was often taken to stand for Christ, an idea of which
C. S. Lewis's Aslan is a recent example, standing for a special kind of
wildness which is so grand as to be acceptable ('He's not a tame lion, you
know'). Eagles, elephants and (among fish) the whale were also seen as
symbols of kingship and thus as examples of kingly virtues. In the *scala
naturae*, the natural hierarchy, these impressive chosen species were held
to reign as kings over their own particular grouping (or as we still say,
their natural 'kingdom'). Thus they represented order – not the disorder
that was associated with other wild creatures. Bees too got credit for their
social virtues, being seen as civilised rather than wild. Doves, swans and
some other attractive birds were praised as examples of faithful monogamy.
Horses and dogs were sometimes also praised for their faithfulness, a kind
of praise that was, of course, quite different from the language of symbolism
because it was realistic. But it did not inhibit the far commoner rhetoric

of contempt. Thus Falstaff: 'I tell thee what, Hal, if I tell thee a lie, spit in my face, call me horse.'[2]

WHY SYMBOLS MATTER

By bringing out these symbols, I am trying to show how unreal, how fantasy-laden our inherited traditional ideas about the wild animals of our planet have been until very lately and indeed often still are. Throughout most of modern history, people in the West have divided these animals into a few simple groups. First there were the small creatures that make themselves more or less of a nuisance to civilised life, handily classed as vermin and calling for no detailed attention. Then there were certain grand and distant species who existed mainly as symbols but might occasionally be seen in the menageries of powerful humans, where they gained an extra symbolic meaning as indications of their owners' power. Neither of these groups seemed to raise any particular moral problems.

Then there were animals that were hunted, notably bears, wolves and other predators, wild boar, deer, and the exotic big game that was typically found in Africa. These creatures were often seen as deserving some kind of respect, because the hunter derived his honour from conquering them. Beyond this, hunters who took the trouble to study them were often impressed by their courage, intelligence and other good qualities. Yet they were still so wild that they could properly be killed. This sometimes led these hunters into a kind of ambivalence in which, without giving up hunting, they genuinely honoured their game-animals and took trouble to preserve their habitat, not just so as to do more hunting but for the sake of the creatures themselves. Theodore Roosevelt was a notable player of this dual role but there have been plenty of other effective hunter-conservationists – a fact which conservationists who hate hunting need to remember.

Among these creatures, however, wolves retained a peculiarly sinister symbolism. Except for some Norse myths, sympathetic representations of them in literature and mythology are very rare in our tradition. The contrast with the lion is striking and is probably due largely to the simple difference in their posture. Lions live and hunt on open plains, so they rely largely on their sight and often need to gaze attentively into the distance. This gives them that dignified, highbrow appearance that so much impresses human observers. Wolves, by contrast, are mainly woodland creatures, hunting largely by smell, so they work under cover much more than lions and do not have much occasion to raise their heads. Hence the appearance of slinking which humans have found creepy. On top of this, Europe in the Middle Ages was largely lion-free, whereas wolves survived and attacked flocks in some places until the nineteenth century. Though they rarely attacked humans, this caused them still to be feared and it determined their special symbolic value. They stood for nature in so far as nature was opposed to civilisation. And for a long time nobody seriously questioned that civilisation was essentially a good thing.

DOGMATIC SLUMBERS OF
ANTHROPOCENTRISM

This world-picture was not really shaken in the western tradition until our own time, even though protests against it have been rumbling for the last three centuries. It is impossible to exaggerate the enormous moral confidence with which Europeans invaded non-European countries, profoundly certain of their civilising mission. Wordsworth and other Romantic poets did indeed protest (following Rousseau) that modern civilised life was diverging too far from nature, but they were widely seen as a dissident, impractical minority. But during the nineteenth century a rather wider range of people did begin saying unkind things about civilisation.

Thus, Carlyle spoke sardonically of 'the three great elements of modern civilisation – gunpowder, printing and the Protestant religion'.[3] Such comments have continued and sharpened in our own century. Will Rogers observed 'You can't say civilisation don't advance, however, for in every war they kill you in a new way.'[4] And a journalist once asked Gandhi, 'Mr Gandhi, what do you think of modern civilisation?' Gandhi replied, 'That would be a good idea'.[5] But the received opinion among most people in positions of power was still the favourable one expressed by Calvin Coolidge: 'Civilisation and profits go hand in hand.'[6]

Only very lately has it begun to look as if this might not always be so. Only lately has it begun to seem that modern people might actually in some monstrous sense win their bizarre war, that they might 'defeat nature', thus cutting off the branch that they have been sitting on, and thus upsetting, not only the poets, but the profit-margin as well. To grasp this change calls for an unparalleled upheaval in our moral consciousness. Even those of us who campaign to promote this realisation do not really take it in completely.

Since the mid-twentieth century, starting from the first atomic explosions, a number of physical facts have gradually brought the change home to public consciousness. Most people who follow current events at all do now grasp, in theory, that there is a danger and they want to do something about it. But *we don't have the concepts ready to express this need*. The change that is called for in our attitude to nature is extraordinarily large – larger, probably, than any such moral change since the rise of agriculture. And our current ideas on that subject happen to be ones that have been deliberately narrowed, during the last four centuries, so as to make that change particularly hard. Especially in political thinking, these ideas have been carefully framed to fix our attention solely on relations between humans within society.

As we have seen, Enlightenment thought largely broke with the idea that political obligation took its force from above, from our duty to God, deriving that obligation instead from the social contract. In human political life this was surely a huge gain. But it left out the rest of Nature, which does not sign the contract; nor do its constituent parts. Thus Enlightenment political language makes it almost impossible to say that we can have any duties to them. Yet every sane person who looks at our current situation can see that we need to do something about them. The question is, in what terms are we to express that need?

This is the gap in our current moral thinking that leaves us floundering over problems like the one we have here. To some extent we can bridge it by talk of self-interest, by thinking of these needs as matters of prudence rather than of duty. But this bridge is too thin to carry the heavy traffic that we need. It is perfectly true that we are all in danger of disaster if we do not attack pollution, clean up the seas and try to mend the ozone hole. But this looming disaster still seems to most people somewhat distant and diffused compared with (say) the danger of losing one's job, or of doing without a car, or of becoming poorer by making a protest. There is a natural tendency to balance the personal risks and to hope that the world will last our time.

It is possible to enrich contract thinking somewhat so as to widen our notion of prudence a little. For instance we can say that we are all parts of a society which includes posterity, so that our own interest includes that of our descendants. The idea of signing an agreement with possible future people is not a very clear one, yet perhaps the contract often is conceived in that more generous way. But if that is indeed the intention, then we are no longer talking in terms of hard-nosed self-interest. This kind of contract thinking has already become a good deal less reductive, less crude, less distinct from morals than it sometimes tries to appear.

In that more idealistic spirit, people have sometimes enlarged it still further so as to include talk of a universal contract with nature, a basic agreement that we all make by accepting the gift of life. But at this point the myth of contract becomes thin and visibly mythical. It is important in any case to remember that this talk of contract always *is* just a myth, and it does not seem to be quite the myth that we really need here. Its language is not direct enough for the duty that we feel. When we see the need to save the whales, or the redwoods, or the Great Lakes, it is *these things* that we have to try and save. We are not trying to fulfil a contract with a remote and abstract nature. The claim on us is felt as specific and immediate.

THE RELIGIOUS BACKGROUND

Most cultures other than ours have indeed acknowledged such claims and have dealt with them under the heading of religion – or at least something in the wide category that anthropologists call religion. Their beliefs about them do not, however, necessarily commit any of the distortions that made many Enlightenment thinkers so hostile to religion. They don't necessarily even involve reference to any personal deities. Buddhist and Japanese reverence for nature is not theistic at all, it is direct. (I think that this is one reason why many western people are now so impressed with Buddhism.) And in cultures where deities are involved, they are often expressions of the natural human tendency to personify rather than damaging forms of superstition.

Our own tradition does, of course, include quite a powerful strand of respect for nature as God's creation, a strand which is strong in Judaism and Islam and is now being re-emphasised by Christian theologians. But in the early days of Christianity the Church Fathers pushed this notion into the background because they were so anxious to destroy any trace of nature worship. In spite of St Francis, it largely remained there during the Middle Ages. And since the Renaissance, humanism has largely dictated that Christian as well as atheistic thought should confine moral consideration entirely to human beings. In our own time Christians are extending it to non-human animals, but they get little help from their own tradition in doing so.

Repeatedly, thinkers in our culture have tried to break out of this straitjacket. I have already mentioned the campaign for direct reverence for nature that stems from Rousseau. That campaign had a special resonance in the United States because people who came to America were often already in protest against many aspects of civilisation in their native countries. The idea of civilisation as such did not have for them quite the same kind of sacredness that it tended to have in Europe. Moreover, in early times they necessarily lived a less protected, urban life than they had done at home, and some of them came because they were positively attracted by the thought of this simpler existence. Thus many agreed with Thoreau and the founders of the great National Parks in celebrating the wilderness.

On the other hand, however, many of them had come deliberately in order to conquer wildness, not to accept it, and they devoted their huge energies to urbanising things as fast as possible. Yet they still retained a kind of awe of the forces that they were fighting. The commonest compromise between these two sentiments is, of course, that which is expressed by shooting large animals.

Another such compromise is the excitement felt at the idea of a wild frontier with wild inhabitants behind it, a frontier which is always there but is always being pushed further back. This idea is both a romantic celebration of wild nature and at the same time a declaration of war on it. The power of this double dream can be seen in the remarkable shift by which it has now managed to survive the taming of the actual western frontier and has been transferred to outer space, to the Restaurant at the

End of the Universe. There, it is probably safe from any kind of inter-
ruption by reality and can continue to go round in gratifying circles
indefinitely. But down here we need a more realistic response.

WHAT THEN MUST WE DO?

That is why we are having to develop new ways of thinking and why we get
so desperately muddled when we have to apply them in detail. In the last
few decades we have learnt a lot of new words: 'ecology', 'ecosystem', 'biosphere', 'symbiosis', 'Gaia', 'sustainable development' and the rest. These
are words that are framed to express a cooperative rather than a competitive
relation with other life forms, a relation that is crucial in the workings both
of our own nature and of the nature around us, but which our culture has,
since the Enlightenment, refused to take seriously. Moreover, this cooperative approach clashes strikingly with the competitive individualism that has
lately been so prominent in our social and political life.

Two such different outlooks cannot be reconciled quickly. They cannot
quickly educate each other. It is hard to see how we can combine them
in a way that uses the best insights of both. Yet we can see that they do
actually need each other because it has become clear that neither alone is
adequate. Competitive individualism is already in grave trouble because it
has become so extreme as to be quite impractical, as is plain from spasms
of lethal lurching in the money-markets. It has appealed to a one-sided
romantic exaltation of individual freedom which badly distorts public life
and it is proving not to deliver private happiness either – a point which
Robert Bellah made in his impressive book *Habits of the Heart*.[7] And
ecological thinking, for its part, has to grapple with the realities of a compet-
itively organised human society if it is to put its saving projects into practice.

Muddles about ideals are thus piled on top of practical difficulties. This
is, of course, what makes controversy about particular environmental
projects, such as that about re-introducing wolves, so irredeemably messy.
They necessarily involve larger ongoing changes in thought and feeling.
These projects each have their own special importance. But the wider
changes of attitude that they involve are no less important than the details
of what happens on the ground.

What is crucial about the change of attitudes is the negative side. We profoundly need to get *rid* of something. We need to get rid of the notion that
all natural things are valueless in themselves, merely pretty extras, expendable, either secondary to human purposes or actually pernicious. That notion
is so fearfully misleading that we must ditch it somehow, even though we
don't yet have a perfectly clear map of the ideals that we shall need to put
in its place. We have partial and scrappy notions of those ideals on which we
shall need to work further, as always happens when people make a necessary

shift of priority. We can only make this move if we unmistakably jettison the exploitative attitude that has governed us so far. It is a habit of mind that our society desperately needs to reverse, and it has, of course, been an extremely deep one, as the symbolism that I mentioned earlier on testifies. It is an attitude expressed in countless customs in our lives.

In order to dig out something so deep in our psyches we do indeed need to reverse it explicitly in practice. The painful words WE WERE WRONG must not only be spoken but spelt out in action, and this needs to be action with a strong symbolism that bears on the offences that have been central to our crimes. That is why it is right that the Pope apologises to the Jews for the Church's anti-Semitism, even though that apology may seem absurdly inadequate and disproportionate to the offence. Similarly, it is right that people who are proved to have been wrongly convicted of offences are rehabilitated after their death, even though this can no longer help the victims themselves.

Moves like these are not just futile hand-wringing over the past. They are ways of *committing us to changing direction* for the present and the future. Similarly, when today's hyper-civilised people first save an existing habitat and then go beyond this by calling back its previous inhabitants, that seems to be what they mean to do. They don't necessarily do it as an isolated and somewhat artificial move confined to the wilderness, but as an earnest of a far wider campaign that will need to involve huge changes in human life. They are changing the myth in order to commit themselves to changing the wider reality, and that is the way in which serious changes are eventually brought about.

NOTES

—·•·—

1 HOW MYTHS WORK

1 C. H. Waddington, *The Scientific Attitude* (Harmondsworth: Penguin, 1941), p. 170, emphases mine.
2 Jacques Monod, *Chance and Necessity*, trans. Austryn Wainhouse (Glasgow: Collins, 1972), pp. 160–4, author's emphases.
3 René Descartes, *Discourse on Method*, part 2, opening section.

2 OUR PLACE IN THE WORLD

1 For a drastic questioning of this claim, see Ken Booth, 'Human Rights and International Relations', *International Affairs*, 71 (1995), pp. 103–26.
2 For further discussion of this useful concept see *Human Rights in Global Politics*, ed. Timothy Dunne and Nicholas Wheeler (Cambridge: Cambridge University Press, 1998).
3 I have discussed the kind of relativism that would make this agreement seem impossible in *Can't We Make Moral Judgements?* (Bristol: The Bristol Press, 1991) and, more briefly, in 'On Trying Out One's New Sword', ch. 5 in *Heart and Mind* (London: Methuen, 1981).
4 See his book *Biophilia: The Human Bond with Other Species* (Cambridge, Mass.: Harvard University Press, 1984).
5 See James Lovelock, *Gaia: The Practical Science of Planetary Medicine* (London: Gaia Books, 1991).

3 PROGRESS, SCIENCE AND MODERNITY

1 Rudolf Carnap, *The Logical Structure of the World*, trans. R. George (Berkeley: University of California Press, 1967), p. 290, emphasis Carnap's. For a fuller discussion of such claims, see Tom Sorell, *Scientism: Philosophy and the Infatuation with Science* (London: Routledge, 1994) ch. 1.
2 See his article 'The Limitless Power of Science', in *Nature's Imagination: The Frontiers of Scientific Vision*, ed. John Cornwell (Oxford: Oxford University Press, 1995), pp. 122–33.

3   *Proceedings of the National Institute of Science of India*, vol. 27 (1960), p. 564, emphasis mine.

4   See John B. Watson, *Psychological Care of Infant and Child* (New York: W. W. Norton, 1928), pp. 5–6, 9–10 and 82–3, and a good discussion of such passages by Barbara Ehrenreich and Deirdre English in *For Her Own Good: 150 Years of the Experts' Advice To Women* (London: Pluto Press, 1979), pp. 183–5. On Skinner, see the child-rearing arrangements in his early Utopia, *Walden Two* (1948).

5   See Bernard Doran's fascinating book *From Taylorism to Fordism: A Rational Madness*, trans. David Macey (London: Free Association Books, 1988).

6   Paul Davies, 'Seven Wonders', *New Scientist*, 21 September 2002, p. 28.

7   Ibid., p. 33, emphasis mine.

4 THOUGHT HAS MANY FORMS

1   See two excellent books, Brian Goodwin, *How the Leopard Changed its Spots* (London: Weidenfeld and Nicolson, 1994) and Steven Rose, *Lifelines: Biology, Freedom and Determinism* (London: Allen Lane, Penguin Press, 1997).

2   In Lynn Margulis and Dorion Sagan, *What Is Life?* (London: Weidenfeld and Nicolson, 1995), p. 1.

3   Thomas Nagel, *The View from Nowhere* (Oxford: Oxford University Press, 1986), p. 5, emphasis mine.

4   A clear, typically confident statement of this orthodox view may be found in E. O. Wilson, *On Human Nature* (Cambridge, Mass.: Harvard University Press, 1978), pp. 7–10.

5   Descartes, *Philosophical Writings*, trans. and ed. G. E. M. Anscombe and P. T. Geach (London: Nelson, 1970), pp. 28, 66.

6   See my *Science and Poetry* (London: Routledge, 2001), ch. 7, pp. 81–3.

5 THE AIMS OF REDUCTION

1   Friedrich Nietzsche, *The Will to Power*, para. 1067 and *Beyond Good and Evil*, para. 269. See also *Beyond Good and Evil*, para. 36. *Beyond Good and Evil*, trans. Marianne Cowan (Chicago: Gateway, 1955).

2   Richard Dawkins, *The Selfish Gene* (Oxford: Oxford University Press, 1976), pp. 2–3.

3   J. D. Bernal, *The World, the Flesh and the Devil* (London: Jonathan Cape, 1929), pp. 35–6.

4   Francis Crick, *What Mad Pursuit?* (Harmondsworth: Penguin, 1989), p. 139.

5   Thomas Hobbes, *Leviathan*, Part 1, ch. 6, emphasis mine.

6   *Correspondence, Albert Einstein–Michèle Besso, 1903–1955* (Paris: Herman, 1972). Quoted by Ilya Prigogine and Isabelle Stengers in *Order out of Chaos: Man's New Dialogue with Nature* (London: Collins, Fontana, 1985), p. 294, emphasis mine.

7   Stephen Hawking, *A Brief History of Time* (London and New York: Bantam Press, 1988), p. 139.

8   'Will Science Ever Fail?', *New Scientist*, 8 August 1992 (emphasis mine), answering an article of mine, oddly titled by the editor 'Can Science save its Soul?', *New Scientist*, 1 August 1992.

6 DUALISTIC DILEMMAS

1   David Hume, *Enquiry Concerning the Principles of Morals*, Sec. III, part ii, para. 163.
2   David Hume, *Treatise of Human Nature*, Book II, part 1, sec. 4.
3   See *Psychiatric Polarities, Methodology, and Practice*, ed. P. R. Slavney and P. R. McHugh (Baltimore: Johns Hopkins University Press, 1987).
4   B. F. Skinner, *Beyond Freedom and Dignity* (Harmondsworth: Penguin, 1973), pp. 20–1.
5   Thomas Nagel, *The View from Nowhere* (Oxford: Oxford University Press, 1986), p. 4, emphasis mine.
6   Bernard Williams, *Morality: An Introduction to Ethics* (Harmondsworth: Penguin, 1972), p. 94.

7 MOTIVES, MATERIALISM AND MEGALOMANIA

1   Thomas Hobbes, *Leviathan*, Part 1, ch. 15.
2   Sigmund Freud, 'On Narcissism' (1914–16), in Vol. XIV, *Collected Works*, translated under the editorship of James Strachey (London: Hogarth Press), p. 91.
3   David Barash, *Sociobiology, the Whisperings Within* (London: Souvenir Press, 1980), p. 3.
4   Edward O. Wilson, *On Human Nature* (Cambridge, Mass.: Harvard University Press, 1978), p. 167.
5   Ibid., pp. 154–5.
6   Edward O. Wilson, *Sociobiology*, pp. 4 and 575.
7   For instance by John D. Barrow and Frank R. Tipler in their remarkable tome *The Anthropic Cosmological Principle* (Oxford: Oxford University Press, 1986), pp. 618–19.
8   J. D. Bernal, *The World, the Flesh and the Devil* (London: Jonathan Cape, 1929, pp. 41–2. Reprinted Bloomington, Ind.: Indiana University Press, 1989). For Haldane's contribution see his *Possible Worlds* (London: Chatto and Windus, 1927), p. 287.

8 WHAT ACTION IS

1   Colin Blakemore, *The Mind Machine* (London: BBC Books, 1988), pp. 269–71, emphasis mine.

9 TIDYING THE INNER SCENE: WHY MEMES?

1   Richard Dawkins, *The Selfish Gene* (Oxford: Oxford University Press, 1976), ch. 11, pp. 203–15.
2   John Lyons (ed.), *New Horizons in Linguistics* (Harmondsworth: Penguin, 1970). Editor's abstract introducing ch. 4, 'Phonology', by E. C. Fudge, p. 76.
3   See a good discussion of tropisms in Robert Boakes, *From Darwin to Behaviourism* (Cambridge: Cambridge University Press, 1984), pp. 138–40.
4   C. B. A. Behrens, *The Ancien Régime* (London: Thames and Hudson, 1967), pp. 123–4.
5   Especially in *Darwin's Dangerous Idea* (Harmondsworth: Penguin, 1996).

NOTES

10 THE SLEEP OF REASON PRODUCES MONSTERS

1 Daniel Dennett, *Darwin's Dangerous Idea* (Harmondsworth: Penguin, 1996), p. 63.
2 Ibid., pp. 82 and 144.
3 Edward Clodd, Spencer's follower and interpreter, thus triumphantly described his achievement. See A. C. Armstrong, *Transitional Eras in Thought, with Special Reference to the Present Age* (New York: Macmillan, 1904), p. 48.
4 *The Autobiography of Charles Darwin, 1809–1882, with Original Omissions Restored*, ed. Nora Barlow (New York: Harcourt, Brace and World, 1958), p. 109, emphasis mine.
5 Ibid., 6th edn, 1872, p. 395.
6 Edward O. Wilson, *Consilience: The Unity of Knowledge* (New York: Alfred A. Knopf, 1998), p. 50.
7 Ibid., p. 134.
8 Ibid., p. 135.
9 Richard Dawkins, *The Selfish Gene* (Oxford: Oxford University Press, 1976), pp. 206–10.
10 Ibid., p. 210, emphasis mine.
11 Dennett, *Darwin's Dangerous Idea*, p. 344.
12 Ibid., emphasis mine.
13 Ibid., pp. 354–5, author's emphases.
14 Ibid., p. 347.

11 GETTING RID OF THE EGO

1 Richard Dawkins, *The Blind Watchmaker* (Harlow: Longman, 1986), p. 196.
2 Daniel Dennett, *Darwin's Dangerous Idea* (Harmondsworth: Penguin, 1996), p. 368.
3 Ibid., p. 346.
4 Susan Blackmore, 'Meme, Myself, I', in *New Scientist*, 2177, 13 March 1999, pp. 40–4. See also her book *The Meme Machine* (Oxford: Oxford University Press, 1999).
5 Richard Dawkins, *The Selfish Gene* (Oxford: Oxford University Press, 1976), p. 207, emphases mine.
6 Dennett, *Darwin's Dangerous Idea*, p. 340.
7 Ibid., p. 362, author's emphasis.
8 Ibid., p. 349.
9 Ibid.
10 In *Dennett and His Critics: Demystifying Mind*, ed. Bo Dahlen (Cambridge, Mass.: Blackwell, 1993).
11 Karen Green and John Bigelow, 'Does Science Persecute Women? The Case of the 16th–17th Century Witch-Hunts', in *Philosophy*, 73, no. 284, April 1998, p. 199.

12 CULTURAL EVOLUTION?

1 Robert Boyle, *Works*, ed. T. Birch, vol. 1 (London, 1744), p. 20.
2 For a most interesting analysis of that mix see Margaret Wertheim, *Pythagoras' Trousers: God, Physics and the Gender Wars* (London: Fourth Estate, 1997), chs 5 and 6.

3 Herbert Spencer, *A System of Synthetic Philosophy* (London: Williams and Norgate, 1862–96), 5th edn, vol. 1 (1884), p. 396.
4 Herbert Spencer, *Autobiography*, vol. 2 (London: Williams and Norgate, 1904), p. 11.
5 Herbert Spencer, *Social-Statics* (New York: D. Appleton, 1864).
6 James R. Moore, *The Post-Darwinian Controversies* (Cambridge: Cambridge University Press, 1979), p. 168.

13 SELECTING THE SELECTORS

1 John Ziman (ed.), *Technological Innovation as an Evolutionary Process* (Cambridge: Cambridge University Press, 2000), pp. 3 and 313, emphases mine.
2 Gerry Martin, 'Stasis in Complex Artefacts', in Ziman, *Technological Innovation*, p. 92.
3 Charles Lyell, *Principles of Geology* (London: John Murray, 1830), vol. 2, ch. 11, emphasis mine.
4 Alexis de Tocqueville, *Democracy in America*, 1835–40, Part 2, Book 2, ch. 27.

14 IS REASON SEX-LINKED?

1 Steven Pinker, *The Blank Slate: The Modern Denial of Human Nature* (London: Allen Lane, 2002), p. 31.
2 For a brief but highly revealing account of *different* Enlightenment visions of the 'man of reason', see G. Lloyd, *The Man of Reason in Western Philosophy* (Minneapolis: University of Minnesota Press, 1984).
3 See S. Möller Okin, *Women in Western Political Thought* (London: Virago, 1980).
4 Jean-Jacques Rousseau, *Émile, or On Education*, trans. Barbara Foxley (London and New York: Dent and Dutton, 1966), Book V, p. 332.
5 Ibid., p. 359.
6 In 'On Not Being Afraid of Natural Sex Differences', in *Feminist Perspectives in Philosophy*, ed. M. Griffiths and M. Whitford (London: Macmillan, 1988), pp. 29–41.

15 THE JOURNEY FROM FREEDOM TO DESOLATION

1 See Brian Easlea, *Science and Sexual Oppression* (London: Weidenfeld and Nicolson, 1981).
2 However, for a brilliant recent exposé of the dangers to feminism of an over-hasty alliance with 'Nietzschean' post-modernism, see Sabrina Lovibond, 'Feminism and Postmodernism', *New Left Review*, 178 (1989), pp. 5–28.
3 Friedrich Nietzsche, *Twilight of the Idols and The AntiChrist*, trans. R. J. Hollingdale (Harmondsworth: Penguin, 1969), sec. 11, p. 121.
4 London: Routledge, 1984, ch. 2.
5 J. P. Sartre, *Existentialism and Humanism*, trans. Philip Mairet (London: Methuen, 1948), p. 54.
6 Philippa Foot, 'When is a Principle a Moral Principle?', in *Aristotelian Society Supplementary Volume XXVIII, Belief and Will* (London: Harrison 1954), pp. 95–110.

7 J. S. Mill, *The Subjection of Women* (London and Cambridge, Mass.: MIT Press, 1970), p. 21.
8 For a clear discussion of the brands of feminism that have succeeded its initial (individualistic and 'liberal') form, see Alison Jaggar, *Feminist Politics and Human Nature* (Brighton: Harvester Press, 1983).
9 J. P. Sartre, *Being and Nothingness*, trans. Hazel E. Barnes (New York: Washington Square Press, 1966), pp. 776–7, 782.
10 See his *The Language of Morals* (Oxford: Clarendon Press, 1952) and *Freedom and Reason* (Oxford: Oxford University Press, 1963).
11 I have discussed it in *Science as Salvation: A Modern Myth and its Meaning* (London: Routledge, 1992).
12 Freeman Dyson, 'Time Without End: Physics and Biology in an Open Universe', *Reviews of Modern Physics* 51, 1979, pp. 447–60.
13 J. D. Bernal, *The World, the Flesh and the Devil* (London: Kegan Paul, 1929), pp. 56–7, my emphasis.
14 Useful compendia of views on the matter of personal identity are: *Personal Identity*, ed. J. Perry (Berkeley: University of California Press, 1985) and *The Identities of Persons*, ed. R. Rorty (Berkeley: University of California Press, 1976).
15 This is evident from the selection of essays in *The Mind–Body Problem*, ed. R. Warner and T. Szubka (Oxford: Blackwell, 1994), despite the care taken to include a full range of opinions.

16 BIOTECHNOLOGY AND THE YUK FACTOR (NO NOTES)

17 THE NEW ALCHEMY

1 J. B. Elshtain, 'To Clone Or Not To Clone', in *Clones and Clones, Facts and Fantasies about Human Cloning*, ed. M. K. Nussbaum and C. R. Sunstein (New York: W. W. Norton, 1998), p. 184.
2 J. Lederberg, 'Experimental Genetics and Human Evolution', *Bulletin of the Atomic Scientists*, October 1996, p. 6.
3 T. Burckhardt, *Alchemy, Science of the Cosmos, Science of the Soul*, trans. W. Stoddart (London: Stuart and Watkins, 1967), p. 25.
4 R. Sinsheimer, 'The Prospect of Designed Genetic Change', *Engineering and Science*, April 1969, pp. 8–13, emphases mine.
5 Gregory Stock, *Redesigning Humans* (London: Profile Books, 2002).
6 Ibid., pp. 1, 13, 20–1, 124–5.
7 Ibid., p. 173, emphasis mine.
8 Ibid., p. 158.
9 'Chemical Ecology and Genetic Engineering: The Prospects for Plant Protection and the Need for Plant Habitat Conservation', Symposium on Tropical Biology and Agriculture, Monsanto Company, St Louis, Mo., 15 July 1985.

18 THE SUPERNATURAL ENGINEER

1 K. Devlin, *Goodbye Descartes* (New York: John Wiley, 1997); G. Ryle, *The Concept of Mind* (London: Hutchinson, 1951), ch. 1.
2 J. Addison, 'Ode', *Spectator*, no. 465.

3   A. Pope, 'Epitaph Intended for Sir Isaac Newton'.
4   R. Sinsheimer, 'The Prospect of Designed Genetic Change', *Engineering and Science*, April 1969, pp. 8–13.
5   Or perhaps, as some authorities claim, Hilaire Belloc.
6   J. H. Barrow and F. W. Tipler, *The Anthropic Cosmological Principle* (Oxford: Oxford University Press, 1986), p. 659, emphases mine.
7   J. Rifkin, *The Biotech Century* (London: Gollancz, 1998), pp. 197–8, emphases mine.

19 HEAVEN AND EARTH, AN AWKWARD HISTORY

1   Paragraphs 44–6.
2   See John D. Barrow and Frank R. Tipler, *The Anthropic Cosmological Principle* (Oxford: Oxford University Press, 1988). I have discussed this doctrine in *Science as Salvation* (London: Routledge, 1992), ch. 17.
3   Paragraphs 38–40.
4   See Steven Weinberg, *The First Three Minutes* (London: André Deutsch, 1977), p. 155.
5   *De partibus animalium*, trans. W. Ogle, Book 1, ch. 5, 645a, in *Aristotle's Works in Translation*, vol. 5 (Oxford: Oxford University Press, 1912).
6   James Lovelock, *The Practical Science of Planetary Medicine* (London: Gaia Books, 1991), p. 9.
7   Adrian Desmond and James Moore, *Darwin* (London: Michael Joseph, 1991), p. 650.

20 SCIENCE LOOKS BOTH WAYS

1   Thomas Burnet, *The Sacred Theory of the Earth*, with an introduction by B. Willey (Carbondale: Southern Illinois University Press, 1965), p. 102. See a thorough discussion by Stephen Jay Gould in *Time's Arrow, Time's Cycle* (Cambridge, Mass.: Harvard University Press, 1987).
2   Hutton (1726–97) is sometime called the father of geology but should really share that title with a number of European sages. See Rachel Laudan, *From Mineralogy to Geology: The Foundations of a Science* (Chicago: University of Chicago Press, 1987).
3   *Theory of the Earth, Transactions of the Royal Society of Edinburgh* 1788, pp. 1209–305.
4   Cited by Gould in *Time's Arrow, Time's Cycle*, p. 62, from J. Playfair, *Illustrations of the Huttonian Theory of the Earth* (Edinburgh: William Creech, 1802).

21 ARE YOU AN ANIMAL?

1   Alexander Pope, *Essay on Man*, Epistle 2, lines 11–15.
2   London: John Murray, 1872.
3   Cambridge: Cambridge University Press, 1984.
4   In *Beast and Man* (New York: Cornell University Press, 1978); *Heart and Mind* (Brighton: Harvester Press, 1981); and *Animals and Why They Matter* (Athens, Ga.: University of Georgia Press, 1983).

NOTES

22 PROBLEMS ABOUT PARSIMONY

1 See his article 'Nature's Psychologists', *New Scientist*, 78 (1978), pp. 900–3.
2 Donald Griffin, *Animal Thinking* (Cambridge, Mass.: Harvard University Press, 1984), pp. 116 and 94, emphases mine.

23 DENYING ANIMAL CONSCIOUSNESS

1 See N. A. Rupke, *Vivisection in Historical Perspective* (London: Croom Helm, 1987), p. 27.
2 See *Maternal Deprivation – Experiments in Psychology: A Critique of Animas Models*, a report of the American Anti-Vivisection Society, 1986.
3 See Gill Langley's essay 'Plea for a Sensitive Science', in *Animal Experimentation: The Consensus Changes*, ed. Gill Langley (London: Macmillan, 1989).
4 See his *In the Company of Animals: A Study of Human–Animal Relationships* (Oxford: Blackwell, 1986).
5 See the Second Book of Samuel, 12: 3.

24 BEASTS VERSUS THE BIOSPHERE?

1 The first trumpet here seems to have been Aldo Leopold's *Sand County Almanac* (New York: Oxford University Press, 1949). Leopold's alarming pronouncements, along with others from later prophets, are well discussed by John Passmore in *Man's Responsibility for Nature* (London: Duckworth, 1974), ch. 1 and throughout.
2 The main architect of this position has been Tom Regan, in his books *The Case for Animal Rights* (London: Routledge, 1983), *All That Dwell Therein* (London and Berkeley: University of California Press, 1982) and many other writings.
3 I have discussed the need to consider both, and the difficulty of bringing them together, in *Animals and Why They Matter* (Athens, Ga.: University of Georgia Press, 1983).

25 SOME PRACTICAL DILEMMAS (NO NOTES)

26 PROBLEMS OF LIVING WITH OTHERNESS

1 For the Adirondacks project the practical issues can be studied in *Wolves and Human Communities, Biology, Politics and Ethics*, ed. Virginia A. Sharpe, Bryan Norton and Strachan Donnelley (Washington, DC: Island Press, 2001).
2 London *Observer*, colour supplement, 15 February 1976.
3 Sigmund Freud, *Civilization and its Discontents* (Vienna, 1930), section 11.

27 CHANGING IDEAS OF WILDNESS

1 Geoffrey Chaucer, *Legend of Good Women*, Prologue, line 377.
2 Henry IV Part 1, Act 2, scene 4, line 195.
3 Thomas Carlyle, *Critical and Miscellaneous Essays*, vol. 1, essay on 'The State of German Literature'.

4   *New York Times*, 23 December 1929.

5   E. F. Schumacher, *Good Work* (London: Jonathan Cape, 1979), ch. 2.

6   Speech in New York, 27 November 1920, in *New York Times*, 28 November 1920, p. 20.

7   *Habits of the Heart: Middle America Observed* (Berkeley: University of California Press, 1985).

INDEX

———•◆•———

influence of 77, 116
and Marxism 65, 76, 78–9, 86
on nature 168
Marxism
fatalism 76
illusion of impartiality 78–9
as scientific ideology 6, 17, 78–9
and social injustice 81
materialism 23, 36, 40, 45–6, 76
mathematics 128, 129, 130
Mead, Margaret 75
medicine 18, 38, 60
megalomania 45
memetics 56–8, 59, 63–7, 68–71, 72
metaphysics 36, 38
Mill, John Stuart 77, 98, 156
the mind 20, 33, 88–9
mind/body dualism
alienation 114–15
epiphenomenalism 38–9
gender and 91, 98–9, 101
idealist reduction 36–7, 88, 89
inner conflict 89–90 (*see also* will)
intellect 99–101
ostensible rejection of 101
residual dualism 21, 38, 58–60
Minsky, Marvin 17
misogyny 91–2, 94, 95
Monod, Jacques 3
monsters 109, 139
Montaigne, Michel Eyquem de 107
Moore, James 80, 126 (n7)
morality
acts and consequences 102–5
common good 159
communal background 94, 96
as contract 8
fanaticism 155–6, 157
invented values 95–6
pluralism 156–7
privatisation of 94–5, 96–7
reduction and 39–41
role of feeling 105–6, 107
subjectivity *vs.* objectivity 39–41
'unnatural' 106–7, 108
Utilitarianism 156
see also animal rights; human rights
Moravec, Hans 111
Morris, Dick 19
motivation 37, 43–4, 71–2, 87
myths 1–2, 4–5, 6, 19, 109
see also symbolism

Nagel, Thomas 24, 39
natural selection
abstractions 85
artefacts 84–5
biological concept 62
as 'designer' 118
social change and 82–4
units of selection 83–4
nature
attitudes towards 174–5
civilisation and 171, 173
reverence for 10–11, 128, 172–4
see also wildness
Nehru, Pandit 14–15, 16
neuroscience 52, 54, 64
New Scientist 34–5
Newton, Isaac
and Eckhart 110
the Enlightenment and 58, 59, 77
eternal system 131, 132
and mechanism 117
on utility 37
Nietzsche, Friedrich
on change 4
misogyny 94, 95
on morality 94–5, 97
on power 29, 31
religion 40

objectivity
degrees of 24–6
morality 39–41
scientific 2, 3, 17–19, 78–9, 145
Occam, William of 70
Odyssey 65
omnicompetence 6, 7, 13–15, 22–3, 35
otherness 164–8

Paine, Tom 78
parental love 43, 44
parsimony 30–1, 142–5
Paul, St 89
perception 26
phonemes 57–8
physics
causation 49
and chemistry 26, 32–3
mechanism 5, 19, 117–18, 138
objectivity 17, 25
omnicompetence 35
primacy of 33–5, 77
theory of everything 19–20, 23
thermodynamics 132